CHARLES II

CHARLES II
From the Cradle to the Crown

Claire Hobson

PEN & SWORD
HISTORY

AN IMPRINT OF PEN & SWORD BOOKS LTD.
YORKSHIRE - PHILADELPHIA

First published in Great Britain in 2025 by
PEN AND SWORD HISTORY
An imprint of
Pen & Sword Books Ltd
Yorkshire – Philadelphia

Copyright © Claire Hobson, 2025

ISBN 978 1 39906 451 4

The right of Claire Hobson to be identified as Author of this work has been asserted by her in accordance with the Copyright, Designs and Patents Act 1988.

A CIP catalogue record for this book is available from the British Library.

All rights reserved. No part of this book may be reproduced, transmitted, downloaded, decompiled or reverse engineered in any form or by any means, electronic or mechanical including photocopying, recording or by any information storage and retrieval system, without permission from the Publisher in writing. NO AI TRAINING: Without in any way limiting the Author's and Publisher's exclusive rights under copyright, any use of this publication to "train" generative artificial intelligence (AI) technologies to generate text is expressly prohibited. The Author and Publisher reserve all rights to license uses of this work for generative AI training and development of machine learning language models.

Typeset in Times New Roman 11/14 by
SJmagic DESIGN SERVICES, India.
Printed and bound in the UK by CPI Group (UK) Ltd.

The Publisher's authorised representative in the EU for product safety is Authorised Rep Compliance Ltd., Ground Floor, 71 Lower Baggot Street, Dublin D02 P593, Ireland.
www.arccompliance.com

For a complete list of Pen & Sword titles please contact
PEN & SWORD BOOKS LIMITED
George House, Units 12 & 13, Beevor Street, Off Pontefract Road, Barnsley, South Yorkshire, S71 1HN, England
E-mail: enquiries@pen-and-sword.co.uk
Website: www.pen-and-sword.co.uk

or

PEN AND SWORD BOOKS
1950 Lawrence Rd, Havertown, PA 19083, USA
E-mail: uspen-and-sword@casematepublishers.com
Website: www.penandswordbooks.com

Acknowledgements vii
Author's Note viii
Introduction ix
Prologue xiii

Chapter 1 1
Chapter 2 8
Chapter 3 15
Chapter 4 22
Chapter 5 30
Chapter 6 37
Chapter 7 45
Chapter 8 54
Chapter 9 62
Chapter 10 71
Chapter 11 79
Chapter 12 87
Chapter 13 95
Chapter 14 104
Chapter 15 113

Chapter 16	122
Chapter 17	130
Chapter 18	140
Chapter 19	149
Chapter 20	159
Chapter 21	169
Notes	180
Selected Bibliography	201
Index	210

Acknowledgements

Writing this book has been one of the best experiences of my life, and my foremost thanks for this go to my parents Lauretta and Paul. Their skills with language helped draw me towards a writer's career, their feedback on the manuscript has made a world of difference and their encouragement spurs me on daily. In addition, it's hard to imagine where I'd be without the support, love and patience of Phillip Barlow, particularly as he's given immense advice on referencing.

I nevertheless owe most direct thanks to Sarah-Beth Watkins at Pen & Sword. From the start, she has been a wonderful guide about the publishing process and always put me at ease with her understanding at difficult times. Claire Hopkins was similarly brilliant. I also appreciate kind communications from Lucy May and from Laura Hirst, and copyeditor Chris Cocks did a superb job, working with amazing speed while paying great attention to detail.

In research, some of my biggest gratitude goes to British History Online editor David Levin as well as my friend Jenny Stowar and most of all novelist and biographer Mark Turnbull. Mark has been supportive in several areas, including reading drafts of a couple of my chapters and pointing me in super-helpful directions. What's more, his passion for Stuart history helped drive my own passion, as did historian Andrea Zuvich. Both online and through her books, Andrea is such an inspiration. Being in touch with author Stephen M. Carter has also been wonderful, and I reserve a special mention for researcher and writer Susan Margaret Cooper. Her belief in my ability to tackle biography means a lot to me.

Author's Note

In the seventeenth century, England used the Julian calendar while the date in mainland Europe was ten days ahead, adhering to the Gregorian calendar. However, to ensure consistency, all dates in this book are based on the Julian calendar. For instance, 8 June in the Netherlands is 29 May in this book, as it was in England. The book also treats every year as beginning on 1 January.

Despite the question over Charles II's biological father, I do not think Charles II was illegitimate, and mentions of Charles II's father are of Charles I.

Introduction

At the age of 9 in 1640, the heir to the English throne feared the throne would be lost before he could inherit it. He was one of the most perceptive royals who ever lived.

His perception failed occasionally. For instance, in 1648 he was enchanted by a seductress who later proved murderous. In 1651 his insistence on marching into his homeland ended in catastrophe, and in 1655 he had no idea the secrets he was sharing with a certain pair of ears were consequently travelling to his enemies. However, throughout these years that helped his perception grow, he had what he termed a difficult game to play. He never quit the game, because of who he was.

Rumour stated he was an illegitimate product of adultery, but he initially lived as an eminent Stuart prince in the lap of luxury. Adding to his numerous titles, civil war then made him a 14-year-old general handling hot-tempered officers. From there, he became an exile in Europe, where broken financial promises rendered him a pauper, and in essence he was a nomad. He encountered squalor, even though a stadtholder and a cardinal were just two of the grand powers who sheltered him in splendour, but only for so long would they dare link themselves to his name.

Royalists called him King Charles II from 1649. Not till 1660 did he rule England and Ireland though, and his 1650s rule of Scotland was a short-lived ordeal. Aged 20, he cunningly wormed his way into Scottish power after suffering daily oppression at the hands of Covenanters over the previous months, but really, he could expect little better. Royalist disputes with Covenanters lay in the origins of the troubles that were ongoing, and these troubles had precipitated regicide on his beloved father, with Westminster MPs taking control of England and voting to abolish its monarchy in 1649.

Attempting to restore this monarchy was the difficult game Charles played with fervour. In the process, he risked life and limb through combat and conspiracy. He also dreamed of shaking everything up via a scheme to marry a daughter of his nemesis, and most ironically Charles betrayed his own cause, by sacrificing episcopal principles. None of this worked though. He therefore receives little credit for the fact the Stuart monarchy was restored in 1660, yet he was democratically invited to restore it.

In a flash, he then let women into the theatrical profession, established historic penal laws on paper, while opposing these laws in practice, and encouraged scientists to further our knowledge of the world. During his youth, however, Charles acquired his own knowledge of the world. He used this knowledge to calculate how to rule England.

And his methods largely worked, against the odds. Governing in ardently Protestant England, Charles showed 'a very good understanding' of the nation but, according to eyewitness Bishop Gilbert Burnet, *deliberately* 'seemed to have no sense of religion'.[1] The king also refused to alter the succession. Thwarting Parliament here, he risked repeating disastrous history.

When offered the opportunity to write this book on the first three decades of Charles's life, I knew I had a very special project to tackle. Essentially, I was to shed light on the formative years of an influential enigma.

His childhood therefore deserved deep exploration. Around the time he started walking, Charles was fascinating to watch. He hugged a piece of wood night and day, and his mother noted he applied seriousness to everything he did. Before long though, 'the prettiest innocent mirth' was coming from 3-year-old Charles, by which time his 'sweet' temperament had begun shining through.[2] Naughty friends saw this clearly, as did attendants, some of whom were greatly loved. In fact, Charles harboured such fondness for his favourite wet nurse that he had an erotic relationship with her in his fifteenth year, and the governor assigned to him in 1638 was a major role model, one who allegedly doubted the existence of God. With this governor, the prince delighted in swishing about with fencing swords and excelled at equestrian pursuits, but he struggled learning to write. All the while, between happy family bonding sessions, he was taught about divine right of kings and attended stately ceremonies, in constant preparation for his role as supreme ruler. However, before even the first year of war against Parliament ended, 12-year-old Charles was scared of ascending the throne.[3]

He wasn't scared of fighting for it though. Wielding a pistol at the Battle of Edgehill, he demonstrated this when Roundhead cavalrymen were charging, and during adolescence afterwards he worked diligently to oversee pivotal Cavalier manoeuvres as everything collapsed around him. Jersey showered him with monarchism in 1646, but he was safer in France. He just resented being there. Although he enjoyed glitzy entertainments at King Louis XIV's court, a potential for naval warfare enthused Charles more and put him proud on deck in direct line of fire in 1648. Hopeful of victory this way, he decided against sailing a rescue party to his imprisoned father.

The bereaved Charles turned increasingly to politics after this. In his early twenties he hurled propositions at Holland when the Dutch fought republican England, and he ignored maternal advice as he riskily dabbled in talks to end French rebellion. Later, in Germany, he incensed the Pope, who would not be conned into funding an uprising for the Royalists, but Charles incensed family too. He did wonderfully well to secure alliance with Spain in 1656, then found his mother and his eldest siblings scorn him for it. Meanwhile he swore at valued father figure Edward Hyde, who continued to scold him for laziness.

And 'laziness' here translates as 'lasciviousness' too. Letters show Charles respectful of various women, often irrespective of class, but one woman may have born him three babies within three years in the late 1650s and a little-known baby George Swan seems proof that Charles simultaneously cheated on this woman. He also cheated on the seductress Lucy Walter, whom some say he wedded before she gave birth to his son in 1649.[4] However, in assessing Charles, Lucy's own promiscuity should be remembered. At first, did revenge lead Charles into philandering? Either way, although he had 'a thousand irresistible Charms' and pandered to adoring mistresses,[5] he allegedly employed prostitutes from around 1652, and this poses new questions, especially if he concealed his identity when in brothels.

He certainly had the capability. On New Year's Day 1651 he was honing skills in the art of deception, at his first coronation. Then of course, that autumn, he engaged in major masquerading. Trounced as a 'traitor' in ferocious battle at Worcester, he fled, and so came the story of how he donned disguises, blended in with peasants and hid up an oak tree, from which he nearly fell onto Roundhead soldiers thirsty for his blood. Parts of this are famous, but is that simply because the story is so exciting? No. It first found fame because Charles never shut up about it, proud of his own savvy and touched by the people who risked execution to spare him execution. Irony seems present here though. 'I began to think of the best way of saving myself', Charles said when setting the scene for yet another retelling.[6] Before, during and after the battle, however, he communicated words that appear quite to the contrary, and his actions could speak louder than words.

Having researched Charles's early life, I feel I understand why his legendary escape meant so much to him. Thanks to a lewd poem,[7] we dub him the Merry Monarch, but evidence from his youth reveals much more of Charles deep down, at dark depths. Keeping track of his emotions and behaviour has been fascinating for me, and I hope readers will be interested to see a little beneath the surface.

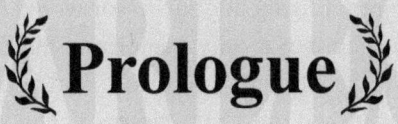

Prologue

The Restoration stood 100 years into the future when the Reformation ushered Scotland into a new age. Rebellion, by contrast, was just around the corner.

In the biting February snow south of Edinburgh, an extraordinary double murder struck in 1567. The tall victim known as Lord Darnley was none other than Scotland's king consort Henry Stuart, and the first man hanged for killing him was Captain William Blackadder, the first found at the scene.[1] Most notable on the list of suspects, however, sat the consort's Catholic widow Mary, Queen of Scots.[2] The couple's eighteen-month marriage had been a hotbed of jealousies and tensions. It had nevertheless produced an heir, and opposition to his mother intensified in May when she married the 'vainglorious'[3] James Hepburn, Earl of Bothwell. Therefore having surrendered to a confederate army the following month, the queen received an ultimatum. She could either vacate her throne or have her throat slit.[4]

Mary's resultant abdication was how her son James Stuart began his Scottish reign. James's son Charles would not be so easy to shift, but that is partly due to James. In fact, king since 13 months of age, James left his mark on much that shaped those 100 years preceding the Restoration.

Mary's son was passionately Protestant by the time he waved farewell to regents, and he believed himself bound by God to govern his nation. Via 1584's Black Acts, he thus took control of the Church of Scotland, the Calvinist national Kirk founded in 1560. By doing so, teenaged James defied its 1578 Second Book of Discipline, which Scots widely embraced as it asserted that Kirk rules were to be agreed by elected elders known as presbyters. Notably, James would partially concede in 1592, but until then he had the power he wanted for appointing bishops to dictate Kirk rules, in much the same way Mary's cousin Elizabeth I appointed bishops for the Anglican Church. Elizabeth's successor would too. Like successors to come, he was to inherit not only her crown but also her position of Supreme Governor of the Church of England. And after initial uncertainty, Elizabeth's successor turned out to be James. Therefore, when the Virgin Queen died on 24 March 1603, James VI of Scotland also became James I of England and Ireland, with his territory including Wales – part of the English kingdom.

So what did this mean for Scotland? Within two weeks, James abandoned his Scottish home. The more industrious England was where he'd live forevermore, and his wife and children settled in with him, as did the handsome young men by his side. Releasing prisoners[5] and distributing £14,000 in gifts[6] had helped the king earn a welcome, some citizens so enthusiastic to see him they 'hazarded ... death' jostling for a glimpse,[7] but of course such enthusiasm wasn't exactly unanimous.

In an undercroft beneath Westminster's House of Lords lay a cubic ton of gunpowder on 5 November 1605. Had Yorkshireman Guy Fawkes not been caught there, with slow matches, he'd probably have triggered an explosion audible over five miles away, and the whole country soon heard he'd tried to do so at the State Opening of Parliament. They also heard he was acting in the name of Catholicism. Remembered as the Gunpowder Plot, this attempt at regicide and mass murder was a design to seize state control and abolish popular English laws forbidding Church of Rome practices. Annual bonfires immediately began celebrating the conspiracy's thwarting. Meanwhile sermons fiercely decried what was termed 'papism'. One ran: 'there is never a corner in all Europe, which these Idolaters have not washed with streams of the blood of Martyrs',[8] and Europe included England, where 1550s Catholic queen Mary I had earned her sobriquet Bloody Mary.

If Fawkes and his co-conspirators had met their aims, another Catholic queen would have been reigning from 1605. Heir Henry would have died in the earth-shattering explosion, and their plan had further involved kidnapping James's daughter Elizabeth, installing her as a puppet monarch, converting her to their own religion and marrying her to a Catholic. In actuality, Henry died on 6 November 1612, and Elizabeth not only remained Protestant but, in February 1613, also married Elector Palatine Frederick V, a Calvinist.

The death of Henry nonetheless shook hearts and minds. Aged 18, his athletic body[9] had been spirited away with symptoms of typhoid fever.

Prologue

James and queen consort Anna of Denmark were thus struggling as bereaved parents when newlywed Elizabeth moved to Heidelberg, and her only surviving sibling was the new heir Charles. He was 'very dear' to family,[10] but he also resembled the runt of a litter. Born on 19 November 1600, Charles had been unable to walk before his fourth year, and he suffered a stutter throughout life. His 'placid'[11] temperament seemed to accompany unease inside him. James now had to prepare him to rule.

The basis of his preparation can be seen in *Basilikon Doron*, an epic letter serving as a manual on kingship. Penned by James and printed in three volumes in the 1590s, it was addressed to Henry but passed to Charles, and it portrayed monarchs as servants of God who were chosen by God, and as possessors of divine rights. The text also highlighted a monarch's duty to serve the people, but James believed this sometimes entailed maintaining the status quo. In the second volume, he advised: 'hold no Parliaments but for necessitie of new lawes, which would be but seldome'. A few pages on furthermore, he warned against rebellion and described a 'just war' as preferable to 'disaduantageous peace'.[12] However, as he demonstrated in practice, peace was a fundamental goal.

There was someone who could persuade James to embark on war, though. In fact he could persuade James to do almost anything under the sun.

In 1614, this someone was a Leicestershire commoner by the name George Villiers who benefitted from aristocratic connections through his stepfather Sir Thomas Compton. Villiers perfected skills in courtly etiquette, helping to ensure 'every Bending of his Body was admirable'[13] whether in dancing or in fencing, but nature contributed to the beauty he oozed. Having set eyes on him in the summer, James would call him Steenie, likening him to the reputedly angel-faced Saint Stephen. It only took till the following April before the king granted the 22-year-old a knighthood and the esteemed role of gentleman of the bedchamber, and the bed itself became integral. By August 1615, James and Villiers were together between the sheets. Sex was probably in the equation.[14] Either way, the king would soon be displaying 'extraordinary affection' in patting the head-turner on the face at a masque[15] and declaring love for him at a Privy Council meeting. From February 1617, Steenie was even part of this council, the main body of regal advisers, and the following year Charles, now Prince of Wales, held a feast to celebrate forming his own friendship with Steenie, now Marquis of

Buckingham. Envious of the new courtier at first, Charles had taken such actions as drenching him with water.[16] Steenie had grown so cocksure as to raise his hand to the prince in front of 'an infinite concourse'.[17] However, by 1623, they were glad to accompany each other on a secret mission to Madrid, for months, during which Charles happily watched Steenie rise to the hilt and become Duke of Buckingham. The favourite had carte blanche, and he used it to further trade monopolisation. He was also now heavily involved in foreign policy.

In Europe, the Thirty Years' War raged, and part of this conflict pitted Frederick and Elizabeth against the Catholic Habsburgs of the Spanish Empire. James's daughter and son-in-law were losing, defeat at 1620's Battle of White Mountain stripping them of the titles King and Queen of Bohemia, but James needed help to help. To make use of Habsburg hostilities with the French royal House of Bourbon, Buckingham therefore led negotiations for English union with France. There, he'd pay too much attention to France's queen consort Anne of Austria, but his plan centred on joining two other individuals.

James never saw it come to fruition. With ill health worsened after administration of medicines, the peace-loving absolutist died on 27 March 1625. As the plan nevertheless went ahead, this meant a grieving 24-year-old Charles sat on the Stuart thrones that spring when, though devoutly Anglican, he married 15-year-old Henrietta Maria, devoutly Catholic daughter of Henri IV of France and his Florentine widow Maria de' Medici.

The marriage suffered a rocky start. His first night with the bride left Charles uncharacteristically jocular, but she denied him conjugal rights on a whole list of days on the Catholic liturgical calendar.[18] Meanwhile physical contact took the form of restraint from the king when he evicted most of his wife's French retinue in the summer of 1626, hoping 'the devil go with them', and Henrietta Maria turned hysterical, the struggle leading to smashed windows at St James's Palace.[19] At first, as the queen deprecated English culture and contradicted the king in public,[20] arguing seemed to be all the childless couple did together.

Not even politically was their union succeeding. By mid-1627, France had less quarrel with Spain, and an Anglo-French War was in progress. As Charles's best friend, Buckingham in effect still ran the Stuart kingdoms, but not particularly well. His handling of military affairs saw the loss of

Prologue

far more than half the troops sent to invade the Isle of Ré[21] off the Atlantic French coast.

Of course this affected the survivors too. Sullen English lieutenant John Felton was tortured by nightmares having witnessed horrors at Ré. He was also impoverished and sought a captain's rank. Without promotion, he couldn't live, he'd told Buckingham, but the duke's answer was a contemptuous suggestion of hanging. Felton ensured this fate for himself. On 23 August 1628, he was again in Buckingham's presence, at Portsmouth inn The Greyhound. Standing behind Colonel Thomas Fryer, he gripped a dagger, and when Fryer bowed, Felton lunged forward and drove it into Buckingham's chest.[22]

Upon news of the duke's instant death, the king cried his eyes out. Buckingham meant so much to him that in June 1626 he'd dissolved Parliament to save the duke from impeachment. A similar scenario had also occurred ten months earlier, Steenie under attack by MPs at the time of the king's decision to dissolve the 'Useless Parliament'. Another major issue, however, was tonnage and poundage, Crown-funding taxes. These had been granted for life to every monarch of England since Henry VII's reign[23] in the fifteenth century, but Parliament refused to honour this tradition for Charles. He consequently took it upon himself to collect the taxes. When his third parliament objected, he dissolved that too, on 10 March 1629, and this time proclaimed he'd never fill Westminster again until people 'see more clearly into his Intents and Actions'.[24] One intent of his father was assured through this; because Parliament held the key to the financing of war, Anglo-French peace came in April. On the downside, hopes of Stuart assistance for Frederick and Elizabeth shattered, but Charles was quite content to be beginning his Personal Rule.

His personal life also now made him content. By this time, Henrietta Maria was somewhat acclimatised to the English court, and her caustic tongue balanced against her fun-loving penchant for glitzy masques, both attracting brash courtiers into her circle. Yet while conversely 'very grave and polite',[25] her husband was becoming her biggest admirer. In April 1627, in fact, he'd felt enough affection to give her a supersize diamond, a gesture she appreciated as a French envoy noted.[26] It was then Henrietta Maria whom the king sought during bereavement, and her flames of rage faded into a warm glow of sympathy. Now, in 1629, she was pregnant.

The joy of this was not to last. On 12 May, she entered a perilously early labour, an estimated quarter of pregnancy left to go. A local midwife was procured with haste, but she fainted in the magnificence of Greenwich Palace, leaving surgeon Chamberlaine as a 'man-midwife'. Not before the next century would this role be well established though; Chamberlaine didn't usually deliver babies, and here he faced a breech delivery. His skills hence seem admirable as the tiny weak baby was born alive, at 3 am the following morning, but little could be done for him beyond an urgent baptism. Christened Charles James that same day, the new prince died an hour after his admission into the Anglican Church.[27]

Devastating though the loss was, it brought the king and queen even closer, their love growing into a hardy thriving plant rooted at the helm of the Stuart kingdoms as Henrietta Maria let Charles kiss her a reported 100 times in the passing of sixty minutes,[28] but there was distinct chance she had childbearing problems.

Off she set for Tunbridge Wells, to drink waters that purportedly worked wonders for women hopeful of motherhood. She was accompanied by her gentleman usher Henry Jermyn, a favourite of hers, and he stayed beside her as she moved on to Oatlands Palace[29] on 5 August. Her husband was travelling to Oatlands too. The queen 'could not bear the King's Absence',[30] and the king could not keep away, now 'very fond of his wife' as the great artist Peter Paul Rubens noted in person.[31] The royal couple then proceeded to bask in their mutual love; there at Oatlands, they tried again for a Charles II.

Chapter 1

Queen Henrietta Maria was suffering 'some inconvenience' in January 1630,[1] but she wanted it to last another four months. Not till May were her waters due to break, and round her neck she wore a heart-shaped charm to ward off miscarriage. She would tremble if parted from this.[2] As her husband, England's ruler King Charles I felt immense pride. Gone were the days of the couple's slanging matches in French, and not just because Henrietta Maria was mastering English. According to the king, only one dispute now existed between him and his consort. It centred on which of them would 'vanquish the other by affection', and he assured Henrietta Maria's mother, who had sent the precious charm, that his wife was 'so careful' in her current pregnancy that he needed 'exert no other authority than that of love'.[3]

Medical authority nevertheless helped. In the role of first physician to the king and queen sat Sir Theodore de Mayerne, a Swiss-born doctor renowned for innovative use of chemistry. For three decades he had been making inroads in medicine this way, but while he claimed his treatments aligned with the teachings of revered Greek physician Galen, his experimentation was decried on the Continent, despite the lives he saved. From 1613 Mayerne resided with greater acceptance on St Martin's Lane near Westminster Abbey, following royal appointment, and he continued to gain experience. His meticulous note-keeping demonstrates the breadth of ailments he saw in anyone wealthy enough to pay his astronomical fees. For instance, on 19 September 1628, he was consulted by a 29-year-old man who endured unrelenting pain in his left side, stomach cramps three hours after eating and apparent skin dehydration. Mayerne also recorded him as *'valde melancholicus'* (very melancholy). This patient had the name Oliver Cromwell. His surname would have been Williams, but he was descended from Katherine Cromwell, sister of one of the

English Reformation's most influential proponents Thomas Cromwell, and Katherine's original surname was passed down the generations while her husband's was shunned.[4] Oliver Cromwell had served as MP for Huntingdon till the 1629 dissolution of Parliament. Other than that, however, he seemed of little consequence. He was no top priority for Mayerne. Henrietta Maria occupied that spot. The king ensured it. During the queen's premature labour in 1629, Charles I had stated his heir emerging from the womb must die if the mother would thereby be saved.[5] The chances were he'd say the same in 1630.

However, if the delivery went well, thanks would go not just to Mayerne but also to the country in which he'd been educated, France. The French were trailblazers in childbirth techniques adopted as standard in later years, and Henrietta Maria was to have support from French nurse Frances Mounbadiac while grandmother-to-be Maria de' Medici dispatched her own midwife Madame Peronne from France too.

Unfortunately, Peronne experienced a frightening delay. An English vessel picked her up with two months to spare, but while progressing north across the Channel it was captured by privateers, specifically 'Dunkirkers'[6] who operated for the Spanish Empire during the anti-Habsburg Dutch Revolt. They often seized English boats with Holland-bound supplies. Now they had Peronne. As Henrietta Maria cried tears of distress, 'it was necessary to send a courier to Brussels',[7] the capital of the Spanish Netherlands, but Spanish Netherlands governor Isabel Clara Eugenia ordered release in a heartbeat. To the relief of the court, Peronne was therefore by Henrietta Maria's side in April, ready for when the time came, and it didn't come too quickly on this occasion. Halfway into May, the birthing chair still awaited, upholstered with red velvet.

Meanwhile, at a cost of £675, a new resplendent bed with green satin hangings was to be among the first sights to greet the infant,[8] and a bed rail belonging to Henrietta Maria, ornately decorated with a floral design and crosses, was gilded in 1630 by gilder Philip Bromfield.

If installed for the birth, this could be found at St James's Palace, a site conveniently close to London but surrounded by rural tranquillity with deer roaming in the vista. Here, just after dawn on Saturday, 29 May 1630, a screen was pulled across the birthing chamber, the queen and attendants on one side and the king on the other with a host of officials listening intently.[9] They hoped to hear Henrietta Maria's cries replaced with joyous exclamations and the yells of a newborn. And around noon, their wish was granted. After all the anguish, both mother and baby had made it successfully through an agonising labour.

Then came the big question, of course. The answer? It was a boy. In fact, it was a huge, emphatically strong boy, an heir apparent who would surely live to inherit rule over England, Scotland and Ireland, and he was named Charles as envisaged.

He didn't look as envisaged, though. The future Charles II was denied the blond, fair or flaxen hair thought most desirable in early Stuart England. Instead, his face would be framed with a bold, striking ebony, and even his Caucasian complexion was tinted with shadowy darkness, a feature considered less attractive still. Among his countrymen, his hair and skin were unusual to say the least, but as the animated suckling writhed in blissful ignorance of his life ahead, something far less common was also observed. Instead of curling his fingers in and forming little fists (the natural palmar grasp reflex seen in almost all young babies), he held his hands open. This prompted predictions that he'd grow into 'a prince of great liberality'.[10]

Other signs were perceived too. Also around noon that day, what was labelled a silver star appeared with brightness above the London sky. Some said it was Venus, others believed it a comet and recent evidence implies it could have been supernova Cassiopeia A.[11] Correctly identified or not, it was no pure coincidence, Charles's contemporaries claimed, and it attracted their intrigue like a magnet. In an age when Christianity dominated the thoughts of so many, the likeness to the Star of Bethlehem and the Nativity story did not pass them by. However, this brilliant phenomenon would be followed two days later by a near-total eclipse of the sun,[12] a seemingly contradictory omen.

Public reaction to the birth was also mixed. After all, the prince had a Catholic mother. And before his arrival, the succession had been routed down the solidly Protestant Palatine path via Charles I's sister Elizabeth and her Calvinist son Charles Louis. To Puritans, for instance, Charles Louis had spelled a decent future for England. Now along came Charles, healthy and hearty, and nobody could replace him in the line of succession. Puritans showed 'sorrow'.[13] 'God had already better provided for us', were the words of one.[14] Puritans nevertheless wielded limited influence, for the time being, and the queen was expected to defer to her Anglican husband. Therefore, happy jigs were danced while the monarch rode in state to

St Paul's, paying immediate thanks to higher powers. He did not, however, display excitement. To do so was unbecoming in the eyes of Charles I. Having offered him congratulations, Venetian ambassador Giovanni Soranzo described England's king as a royal 'of few words, and even on this great and extraordinary occasion he was as reserved as usual'.[15]

News then travelled across Europe to stately reception. While Henrietta Maria's native France rejoiced over adding the Stuart prince to the Bourbon family tree, bonfires flickered in celebration at Habsburg palaces and honour was paid to the English ambassador at a public bullfight in Madrid.[16] The Spanish capital was also where a horoscope drew some attention a few weeks after the birth of Charles. It predicted he'd grow up 'handsome' and have a 'thin beard, shrill voice' and 'mincing gait'. Looking at this horoscope even gave high hopes of seeing him live to the age of 108, and anyone convinced of its forecasts expected Charles to prosper from war, prove 'very fortunate' and possess 'every good quality'. He would develop great fondness for 'mathematicians, sailors, merchants, learned men, painters, and sculptors', it further announced.[17]

Charles I's expanding collection of fine art implied some of this was likely, and portraiture of the boy would soon find pride of place on canvases hanging in the royal palaces, but one of the earliest depictions of the future Charles II can be seen on a rare gold medal struck to mark his safe delivery. On the obverse of this medal, his father features in profile wearing a luxurious ruff, while the reverse shows the infant 'in a superb chair, with Mars and Mercury holding a wreath over him'.[18]

The most important item on the postnatal agenda, however, was Charles's christening, the admission of the next supreme governor of the Anglican Church into the Anglican Church. Ideally, the Archbishop of Canterbury would handle this, but Charles I critic George Abbot occupied the see of Canterbury at the time and, conveniently for the king, was 67 and too infirm for such duties. An imperfect air thus hung over the baptism as William Laud, Bishop of London was delegated to officiate. This hardly surprised people though. As a member of the Privy Council from 1627, Laud had a hold on the reins of power, and he was an old confidant of Steenie, the 1st Duke of Buckingham, whose murder still traumatised the king. Charles I seemed to lap up Laud's every word, unaware of the damage this favouritism was doing. He had few qualms about the prelate's oppression of Puritans. He also admired Laud for advancing ceremonial practices in religious service, making Anglican worship more akin to Catholic worship.

Chapter 1

The monarch was nevertheless desperate to limit any presence of the Church of Rome at his heir's baptism. Fortunately, Catholic godparents Maria de' Medici and her son Louis XIII of France remained on the other side of the Channel, and orders drafted by Secretary Dorchester set out that the font must be placed on a specially erected stage[19] allowing full witness of the Anglican rite. Taking place at the king's chapel of St James's Palace on 27 June 1630, the ceremony would end to the sound of artillery fired in jubilation two and a half miles away at the Tower of London, while white satin and crimson silk were worn and Dorchester's instructions further outlined that the aldermen sport their scarlet gowns and the mayor his velvet. In addition, tapestries were to adorn the chapel and the procession route from the nursery.[20] Of course most of this escaped the notice of the gurgling centrepiece, although a choir accompanied by an organ filled his little ears with beautifully arranged hymns, and he found himself passed from aristocrat to aristocrat, making an afternoon nap tricky. Then, come the sacrament, he probably detected a juddering of his body; as the big moment arrived, Laud was literally shaking.[21] So historic was the occasion that it called for another medal to be commissioned,[22] and the Lord Mayor of London presented the king with a gold cup 'of a yard in length, or thereabouts' and valued at £1,200 by goldsmiths.[23] Meanwhile the Duchess of Richmond gave exquisite gifts to some of the carers closest to the baby. For the baby himself, she also gave a jewel worth approximately £7,500.[24]

Little expense was spared day to day either. The retinue established for Charles was a tightly managed system allocated £5,000 per annum and run by governess Mary Sackville, Countess of Dorset. Within it, servants had servants of their own, and sources such as state papers show it included maids, cradle rockers,[25] nurses, kitchen staff, a laundress (to wash little Charles), a gentleman usher, a physician,[26] an apothecary and even an attorney general for the prince.[27] Restrictions were nevertheless placed on who could show their face at Charles's home, the finely furnished nursery of St James's Palace. Attached to a list of the baby's attendants came instructions: 'No one is to presume to lodge or diet there but only such as belong to the Lady Dorset, and no other persons, [such] as husbands, friends, or servants of those who are here specified, are to come on visits until the King's pleasure be known'.[28] What's more, just a select few individuals had direct contact with Charles, and the majority of those few were female, as was customary. Naturally only women could satisfy the infant's hunger through wet-nursing, but this function meant more than just breastfeeding. Because Charles was to become Prince of Wales, a Welsh-speaking wet nurse seemed a must in the hopes she'd render his first word a Welsh one.[29]

Luckily for all his nurses, the baby proved no great challenge to look after, so placid that he rarely cried. 'He thrives well', doctor James Chambers had noted on 15 August. Twelve days later the physician also documented how Charles's 'likelihood, strength, mirth, and night's rest' increased constantly, though health concerns had surrounded both the governess and nurse Mrs Skipwith.[30] Chambers was responsible for keeping the king updated on the prince's health. Inaccurate reports could therefore land Chambers in serious trouble, yet his 15 August report to Secretary Dorchester perhaps stretched the truth when it stated that the complexion of the infant altered daily. Spurred on by wishful thinking, people expected Charles's features to lighten. In September, his mother decided to hold back his portrait, promising to send one to her old friend and servant Madame St George when Charles was 'a little fairer'. Henrietta Maria certainly wasn't waiting for him to change in other areas though. She also told Madame St George: 'he is so fat and so tall, that he is taken for a year old, and he is only four months: his teeth are already beginning to come'.[31]

Although the rapidly developing Charles lived apart from his parents, both played more active a parental role than expected, and one example of their input revolved around his clothes. English babies of the time were usually swaddled, constricted all around the body, but this was not the norm among French nobility.[32] In light of this, Henrietta Maria had her son dressed in loose frocks, though caps fitted his head snugly and were often tied under the chin. Meanwhile infants' tendencies to stain everything within their reach was ignored, the traditional white being the colour of choice, and satin and linen were dominant in the materials woven.[33] These were woven quite excessively; Charles's frocks measured considerably more than him.

Thanks to a work of art attributed to Leiden-born painter Justus van Egmont, Charles can still be seen modelling these garments. In this portrait, the prince is 4½ months if its French inscription is correct, and he sits on a cushion of shimmering white to match his attire. The picture reveals more of his earliest experiences, too. His left hand grips a teething whistle attached to a long chain round his neck, and protruding from the whistle is a stick of pink coral to bite on. This was something that drew Charles's gaze due to its brightness. On the canvas, however, little detracts from the sitter's plump rounded cheeks and big chocolatey eyes. The Mona Lisa effect comes through here, an arguable smile lurking under a somewhat pensive countenance while Charles stares ahead as though summing up the character of Van Egmont at his easel, and the artist did a wonderful job. A vague resemblance to Charles's adult self is detectable, especially around the eyes. Added to this, the infant appears nicely content with a spaniel on his lap. Clearly elements of the Merry Monarch were evident from the start.

Given his passing of the 1660 Indemnity and Oblivion Act, it also appears fitting that further honouring of his birth entailed a 'general pardon', convicts rescued from execution. His father was petitioned to continue this clemency for months afterwards, though only crimes committed before the prince's arrival were applicable, and they included manslaughter 'by a blow on the head with a fire-pan' and thefts of two mares and three cows. Many of the reprieved languished 'in prison in great misery, suffering hunger, thirst' and the biting cold while five in Newgate Prison pleaded for transportation to Venice.[34] Their lives were nonetheless saved, by the mere existence of Charles.

What's more, thanks to the Countess of Dorset's careful choice of staff, the baby was about to acquire a new wet nurse whose mothering skills were so good that nine of her own ultimately ten children would reach maturity.[35] Christabella Wyndham was her name, and in she stepped in 1631. Later results are interesting, especially from a Freudian perspective.

Her beauty was widely acknowledged. Irrespective of that, however, Christabella was a daughter of the Somerset gentry's Hugh Pyne, whose performance as a barrister had earned him a place as junior counsel to Anna of Demark until 1619. His opposition to the government in the 1620s had nevertheless been quite dramatic, seeing him accused of casting aspersions on Charles I's mental capacity to rule, but he'd forced his way out of trumped-up charges of treason. Pyne's family therefore retained decent enough standing to serve royalty, and young Charles would be most pleased about this. He took to Christabella like a duck to water, forming a close trusting bond with her as she became the most significant woman of his infancy. Incredibly, her personality did little to put him off.

Chapter 2

Anyone meeting the royal suckling for the first time was still in for a shock. With his chubby little face peeping out from his caps, there was no hiding Charles's Mediterranean characteristics, and the fact they were there to stay became obvious. Resignedly, his mother sent his portrait to Maria de' Medici and followed it up with another letter to Madame St George: 'He is so ugly, that I am ashamed of him', Henrietta Maria's words of 1631 read. However, she went on to describe her observations from watching him. Referring to her infant as 'the gentleman', she noted: 'he is so serious in all that he does, that I cannot help fancying him far wiser than myself'. She also let on: 'I think I am on the increase again'.[1]

Indeed, from 4 November 1631, Charles would have a sister, a princess Mary he'd be expected to befriend, but he was more interested in his best friend. Unlike Mary, this companion never shrieked the palace down or tugged people's hair, and for one very simple reason; the prince's best friend was nothing more than a piece of wood.

Having stumbled upon this mundane object about the time he took his first steps, Charles used to toddle round with it in his arms, and the pair became inseparable as he refused to go to bed without it. Not even his dolls were acceptable substitutes, neither those in miniature horseman costumes nor those made of sugar and gum. The latter were delicious when stuffed into the mouth.[2] But while the king believed himself chosen by God to rule the Stuart realms, the prince seemed to believe this little wooden offcut was God's gift to the world. Little did he realise what this allegedly said about him. Some ascertained that 'oppressors and blockheads would be his greatest favourites', that he would rather 'command his people with a club, than rule them with a sword' or that he'd end up 'like Jupiter's log, for everybody to deride'.[3]

Christabella clearly had a formidable rival in this piece of wood, but her days were far from numbered. As an attendant Charles adored, she

Chapter 2

transitioned from wet nurse to assistant governess after weaning, so stayed by his side through his most formative years. Christabella was so often the one who picked Charles up if he toppled over and the one he ran to when she hadn't been there. Her success with the tot went before her. Three and a half decades later, in-the-know diarist Samuel Pepys would hear of Charles I 'putting mighty weight and trust upon her',[4] and Christabella did not let her recognition go to waste; it was no coincidence that a door at court opened to her husband Edmund Wyndham. Like his father-in-law Pyne, Wyndham had been educated in law at Lincoln's Inn and become an MP, his election as representative for the Somerset borough of Minehead occurring in 1628. Of course, the king's Personal Rule from 1629 meant the parliamentary job was now a thing of the past, but thanks to the star nurse he was married to, Wyndham served as a gentleman of the privy chamber from at least 1632. Despite this, he found little chance to hold his head especially high. By 1633, his wife was known to possess the toxic combination of prettiness and peremptoriness, with gossip maintaining he lived under her thumb.

So aged 2, Charles was drawn to a woman of an overbearing nature. In Christabella, he found comfort and security, and rarely did she struggle to pacify him. Mid-May 1633, however, there would be no pacifying him at all, because along came one of the most distressing episodes of his childhood.

The king was preparing for his Scottish coronation. After eight years on the throne, he'd delayed this so long that Scots felt insulted, but although major consequences of such feelings seemed unlikely, he was about to devote more than two months to the trip to Edinburgh. Throughout this, he'd be separated from his wife and children, so the evening before he set off, he spent some precious time with Charles in the beauty of late-spring parkland. They stayed out till the air turned chilly though. A few days later, the prince fell ill. The cold air was blamed, and his early symptoms included drowsiness and loss of appetite, but his neck was bothering him too, discharge soon oozing from something on it. He was tilting his head to one side, suffering discomfort, and he failed to settle that night, partly because he was 'dry'. Then come morning, his pulse caused more serious concern. Chambers immediately called upon the great Mayerne, and Mayerne recommended more physicians, but the treatment chosen seemed gentle at first; for the 'circle of his neck', the team decided on ointment, while a special drink was hoped to reduce his temperature. Now though, Charles was vomiting. In fact, he was vomiting violently, and Chambers could hardly believe his eyes when he saw what was coming out of the 2-year-old. Before long, there was blood in it, accompanied by excruciating pangs in the belly. As more drastic measures beckoned, the doctors then targeted his intestines, subjecting little Charles to milk enemas. Unpleasant though this was, no blood appeared afterwards. However, with the toddler's 'stools corrupt' and interest in food still very low, a purge of rhubarb and senna spelled the next ordeal, on 21 May, but it had to be worth a try. Charles had been in a dire condition for days by this time, and his fever persisted.[5] For the past three years, more than 1,000 London deaths had been attributed to fever annually.[6] The chances are the prince therefore sensed fear from his attendants. Luckily, it didn't last too long. After the rhubarb and senna, he made a big improvement. This then continued so well that, twelve days later, he required intervention to stop him overeating.

His mother had been informed of his illness and approved the purge, and when his father returned, Charles was beaming, full of laughs in July. He often was, as was his sister. Their absence from the king's chamber later that month led secretary of state Francis Windebank to comment: 'mirth is suspended'.[7]

In August, it could recommence as the children passed time with both parents again, but Henrietta Maria struggled to enjoy the giggles just then. She was enduring a traumatic pregnancy. While she therefore settled into St James's in the autumn, Charles and Mary found themselves kept away,[8] and when back there, they would share their home with an adorable addition to the family. Born on 14 October 1633, their brother James was a pale-skinned, blue-eyed little bundle of joy destined to be a rather handsome Duke of York. He brought Henrietta Maria none of the shame the dark, podgy Charles engendered, and male-preference primogeniture meant James trumped Mary in status. His arrival taught Charles something about cultural ideas of gender, because having a brother was portrayed as quite a different phenomenon from having a sister. Yet fraternal relationships were nothing new for Charles.

In 1628 the assassination of the 1st Duke of Buckingham had left behind a little girl by the name Mary nicknamed Mall (born in March 1622) but also a baby boy christened George (born in January 1628) and a son in the womb, Francis (born in or before April 1629). While Mall held the title Lady and dazzled audiences at court masques in the early 1630s, her brothers had, like James, surpassed their sister in terms of succession. The elder was the 2nd Duke of Buckingham and the younger was a lord who sat as heir to the dukedom, and their first memories would involve magical playtimes with Charles, where they could handle some of the best toys the era offered.

Chapter 2

The presence of lead in some of these playthings caused little concern, few heeding a warning on lead poisoning in the much reprinted *De Architectura* by engineer Vitruvius of ancient Rome. Meanwhile gold and silver helped preserve elegance, and war featured through model cannon and model soldiers. Hobbyhorses on wheels[9] also had great potential for fun in St James's spacious apartments.

But Charles had to learn life wasn't all play. In or around 1633, Latin translator Sir Robert Le Grys had drawn up a plan of tuition for the prince and submitted it to the king. It included arithmetic, geography and 'the art of war', and it was intense, suggesting recreation also be 'instructive'. Le Grys intended to use recreation time to tell Charles stories from history and teach him about the Bible, but conversation wouldn't always be in English. Languages were the focus of the programme for the child. Much of the idea was to 'render Latin his linguam vernaculam, not [by] clogging his memory with tedious rules ... but by way much more easy'. If this continued till his seventh birthday, 'the nimblest Latinist should find him his match', Le Grys's tender claimed, and it proposed to make French Charles's 'first learned tongue' and enable Charles 'to read, write, or discourse' in Italian and Spanish.[10]

The chances are Charles would have quickly become multilingual had this plan gone ahead in his fourth year and been maintained. However, by December 1633 Le Grys had run into trouble for taking liberties in his position as captain of Cornish castle St Mawes, admitting to taking wine and timber for himself. He'd also recklessly sold ammunition, burned parts of the castle as firewood and lost the castle key. His tender for the prince's tuition was never accepted.

This left Charles at a disadvantage unforeseen in the 1630s. Nobody at that point envisaged him drifting around Europe during early adulthood, and he then needed to work to expand his linguistic knowledge. He didn't always succeed. In his mid-twenties, he was learning Italian, but he never appeared capable of putting it to great use. Examples of Italian from Charles are rare, and one is vulgar.[11] As for Spanish, Charles certainly craved more understanding there. When moving for alliance with Spain in 1656, he wrote to James Butler, Marquis of Ormond and added a postscript to request a Spanish copy of the New Testament, hoping to need the language before long.[12] However, having attempted to pen a letter in Spanish to

Portugal's queen regent Luísa in 1660, the Merry Monarch described his effort as 'the worst Spanish that ever was writt',[13] and once he'd married Luísa's daughter Catherine of Braganza in 1662, he frequently had to rely on Spanish to interact with his wife. He managed well enough. Although exposure to Welsh and Dutch may have led to disappointing results, Charles was by no means substandard as a linguist. However, as French seems to be the only foreign tongue he ever mastered with confidence, rejection of Le Grys's plan was regrettable.

Foreign accents were nevertheless familiar from the start. When Venetian ambassador Vincenzo Gussoni arrived at Gravesend in January 1632, 1-year-old Charles awaited in the nursery of St James's. Here, the prince could be seated in a special tall chair while stools of differing heights accommodated guests according to their status.[14] Indeed, even prior to great comprehension of words and sentences, Charles's mind was etched with visuals that taught him about hierarchy.

However, in light of his later love for anything of a maritime nature, probably one of the earliest visuals that stuck in his mind was an exciting toy made especially for him mid-1634. This came in the form of a ship 'completely rigged and gilded, and placed upon a carriage with wheels resembling the sea'. The 4-year-old showed immense 'joy' upon its presentation to him in St James's long gallery.[15]

Another love of Charles's would nonetheless be something quite incongruous with his excitable and yet easy-going nature. That something was the phenomenon of royal ceremony. He began to appreciate this through gradual introduction to the daunting Palace of Whitehall in the early 1630s, observing its ceremonial way of life, and church gave him further experience of ceremony, sometimes active experience. Perhaps as young as 4, he took the role of sponsor when the sovereign baptised Charlotta, the third daughter of Christabella and Edmund Wyndham.[16]

Such duties fitted with huge expectations to see the prince mature. These certainly existed, and the king seems to have demonstrated something of them when shown a new painting of his three children in 1635. Its creator Anthony van Dyck usually enjoyed great royal favour. Charles I was angry with him now though, as the portrait depicted the heir wearing children's clothes.

A skirt comprised part of the ensemble, but that was normal attire for boys of Charles's age group then, partly to avoid disastrous delays in struggles

Chapter 2

to unbutton breeches at times of urgent need. Dressing little Charles in breeches after this would therefore place him under intensified pressure to perfect bladder control and judge the timing of his body's needs. He'd no longer have Christabella to help either. Considered superfluous to his more grown-up needs, she'd be gone from his life, for now, and at the prince's new home Richmond Palace miniature chairs were readied with schooling on the agenda.[17] All round, Charles experienced quite bewildering changes at this point, but the older he got the more he realised his childhood was designed to prepare him to rule.

The 5-year-old now had greater understanding of the pecking order. He'd started learning all the titles among the clergy and aristocracy and would need to know exactly where they ranked. Meanwhile over Christmas 1635, he further acclimatised himself to feelings of superiority as his band of younger siblings expanded with the birth of second sister Elizabeth, the first family member Charles was old enough to form lasting memories of from the start. By this time, however, he was also absorbing much of the world around him, conversation no longer mere background noise, and conversation in 1636 often centred on one particular word. That word was plague.

Both typhus and smallpox had risen at alarming rates in 1634, with death tolls following suit,[18] while poor weather in the 1630s often exacerbated the prevalence of sickness in general. But plague was a particularly harrowing threat. Its visitation in 1625 had taken one in every five Londoners to the grave.[19]

Eleven years later College of Physicians licentiate Stephen Bradwell saw fit to publish *Physick for the Sicknesse, Commonly called the Plagve*, in which he declared London's 'danger is apparent' and he 'dare not be silent'. Plague, he reported, 'for the most part is accompanied with some Swelling, which is eyther called a Blayne, a Botch or a Carbuncle, or else with Spots called GODS Tokens'.[20] What he described presents mainly in the bubonic plague form, but pneumonic and septicaemic forms also exist and vary in prognosis and speed of development. In the seventeenth century, a minority of patients recovered while others lingered in their beds for days till death caught up with them, yet tales were told of the seemingly hale and hearty dropping down dead in the street as plague seized them out of nowhere. Charles heard these sorts of tales and more. There was so much more. For instance, in Cheshire in 1625 an infected heftily built man named Richard Dawson had been well enough to dig his own grave before lying in it and passing on, saving his family the difficulty of lifting his weighty corpse. Meanwhile further north in Cumberland a woman was reported as dying of plague caught from a gown delivered from London earlier the same day, and in this story the contagion had entered the residence of Lord William Howard.[21] Talk like this served as a reminder that, although plague preyed mostly on the impoverished who dwelt round vermin-infested slums, the noble were not immune to it. Added to this though, death from disease was deemed no noble death. Playing with toy soldiers may have helped Charles handle fears of dying in so-called heroic acts, but plague simply had to be avoided.

The prince was already ensconced at Richmond in rural Surrey and nearly everyone of decent wealth fled plague zones. Some of the rich, however, also numbered the powerful. For them, out of sight did not equal out of mind, or at least it shouldn't. With roughly 300 years' experience since the unparalleled decimation caused by the Black Death, English authorities knew they had to step in to achieve some control of the spread. And following a 1635 outbreak in France and the Low Countries, the Privy Council in October 1635 had stipulated that contaminated ships be sent away or quarantined. The sickness nevertheless reached London a few months later, whereupon official orders from the king saw old measures implemented and, in some parishes, expanded upon. In the process, pesthouses, occasionally fenced-off in pestfields, sprang up as temporary (but usually final) homes for the infected, theoretically separating them from the uninfected, but pesthouse capacity proved far too limited. Consequently, further ruling had many sufferers and everyone living with them confined to their own abodes instead. To prevent both exiting and entering, affected properties were physically 'shut up', and guards were posted outside. This spelled a grim plight for not just the sick but also the cohabitants. It also reduced trade and stopped employees from attending work. So came anger at His Majesty's government.[22]

Overall, the rules seemed to help though. With an official plague mortality count of 10,400 in London that year, the 1636 epidemic turned out less severe than many of its predecessors.

Plague nevertheless continued to kill Londoners by the thousand in most of the remaining years of Charles's childhood.[23] It had been doing the rounds at the time of his birth. Now the prince was growing up with its devilish potential forever hanging in the air, because nobody really had an answer for it. Two conclusions could thus be drawn. One highlighted a need to further scientific understanding. The other was all about making the most of life while it lasted.

Chapter 3

Now long past his toddler days, the temperament of the future Merry Monarch had expanded from one prone to 'musing' and seriousness, and his 'quickness' that was sparked by others around him[1] had better chance to grow.

This was partly thanks to the Villiers children. Their Catholic-born mother Katherine had abandoned Protestantism, reverted to her old religion and, in April 1635, remarried. Her new, younger husband Randal MacDonnell, Earl of Antrim from December 1636, was also Catholic, and Katherine would be living with him in Ireland from 1638 after losing a little royal favour. However, her sons George and Francis Villiers were already taken under the king's wing in loving memory of their father, the 1st Duke of Buckingham. As Charles I pretty much acted as their adoptive father now, they were even more reminiscent of brothers to Prince Charles, and their sister Mall seemed somewhat like a big sister for him, although he only saw her from time to time. One such time was 1636.

Mall was both married and widowed before her fourteenth birthday. She'd remarry too, but between husbands in 1636 she again graced the court with her presence, dressed in black to meet expectations of mourning over her spouse's recent death. As a strange result of this, Mall nearly lost her own life then, in a killing requested by none other than little Charles! At the time, however, he was somewhat mistaken about her identity. The scenario unfolded as Mall had climbed a tree in the prince's 'little' garden, intending to pick fruit. Because almost nobody was allowed in this garden, Charles never expected Mall to be there. As he looked from afar, this black creature in the branches appeared to be an indistinguishable bird, and he was intrigued, telling companion George Porter to shoot the thing down. The target was too distant though, so Porter went off to pull the trigger at closer quarters. Charles left him to it. He considered the teenaged

Porter a top marksman and imagined a cadaver would be secured as hoped. Luckily, when approaching the tree, Porter realised the creature was a human specimen of beauty. Therefore, the worst he did was shock her by telling her how close she had come to meeting her maker. The shock did nothing to subdue her though, and she was actually so tickled by the misconception that she decided Porter should not return empty-handed. Consequently, Charles found an enormous hamper carried into his rooms, with Porter describing the prey within as a 'Butterfly' so beautiful he couldn't bear the thought of killing it. At this, the prince eagerly opened the hamper, and Mall made for an 'agreeable surprize' as she flung her arms round his neck. She then acquired the lasting nickname Butterfly.[2]

Mall's retreat into the arms of her second husband James Stewart, Duke of Lennox the next summer would leave no shortage of adolescent mischief, nor indeed good looks, at court. This was not only because she'd remain a regular visitor but also because 1636 heralded the arrival of Prince Rupert of the Rhine, a remarkably tall, handsome teenager notorious for larks and capers who would often be known as *Robert le Diable* (Rupert the Devil). Yet life for Rupert was shaped by graveness. With his more reserved elder brother Charles Louis, this son of Charles's Stuart aunt Elizabeth received the king's long-term hospitality as a temporary escape from the Thirty Years' War, in which Rupert delighted in serving since age 12.[3] However, due to his family's defeat within the conflict, it was as exiles that these young men were introduced to Charles, their memories filled with horrors and escapades. They witnessed quite a contrast at the glittering Caroline court.

While the plague ravaged London in September 1636, Charles and the Villiers boys were contributing to the glitter in Surrey, performing in *The King and Queenes Entertainement at Richmond*, one of the extravagant court masques the consort was so fond of staging and Puritans so fond of decrying. This had been long in the making, encompassing specially designed scenery and costumes to create the Romano-British feel of its setting, and 6-year-old Charles appeared as heroic prince Britomart leading a group of knights adventurers. Both his parents watched keenly, particularly as Henrietta Maria had expressed a wish to see her son in a dance. She was not to be disappointed here, seeing the boy carry out two series of moves to dazzle the sea of faces before him. He was chief masquer too,[4] yet he had no speaking part.[5]

Chapter 3

In the modern head, it's easy to hear Charles speaking with the received pronunciation sometimes known as a 'public school accent', but articulation back then bore limited resemblance to this. To an extent, his pronunciation is likely to have represented northern English accents as until nearer 1700 the u sound in words such as 'bun' took the form currently retained in the north[6] and the short a sound in words such as 'bath' was deemed more correct. At the court of Charles II, something of a drawl was nevertheless fashionable, for instance turning 'what' into 'whaat'. This implies Charles spoke with at least a slight drawl, and several differences between his day and now lay in the syllable the stress fell on.[7] However, because few people travelled long distances, relative insularity brought huge contrasts in accents. During childhood, Charles was thus exposed to a diverse range of inflections and intonations as many around him hailed from far and wide. Christabella from the West Country was the person closest to Charles when his speech first developed. Meanwhile some of Charles I's spellings suggest the prince's father spoke with a vague Scottish influence.[8] More relevant though are Charles II's spellings, as is the pairing of words in a poem the Merry Monarch once wrote. This poem rhymes 'grove' with 'love' and similarly 'gone' with 'alone'.[9] Of course Charles II also used words that are now extinct, while even words still easily recognised often popped up in what these days seems a funny order. Moreover, grammar was devoid of many of its modern backbone rules and, compared with fluent Latin-speakers who habitually placed nouns after prepositions, Charles was more likely to use prepositions at the end of sentences.

In 1636, Henrietta Maria nonetheless hoped to familiarise him with Latin through one particular route: she had started taking him to Catholic Mass, and she intended to continue. For various reasons, this new experience for Charles would be terminated by the king, despite the hurt husband and wife felt at upsetting each other. Around 6 years old, therefore, the prince viewed religion as one of if not the only cause of rift between his parents. And as he learned not to cooperate with his mother on anything pertaining to the Church of Rome, he realised she could lead him into trouble.

He was quite capable of doing that himself too though. At Richmond around New Year 1637, Prince Charles and siblings were in attendance when Venetian ambassador Anzolo Correr visited and noted the king 'gently reproving' Charles for acting 'too stolidly'.[10] This wasn't the last time the boy would find his father admonishing him in full view of others, and not always would it be gentle.

But Charles I was the ruler who, in the final speech of his life, claimed: 'A Subject and a Soveraign are clean different things'.[11] For most who had any form of guardianship of the prince, the matter of discipline was tricky; how could they go about correcting or punishing the offspring of a man regarded as 'God's anointed'? Quite disgracefully, the problem was perhaps tackled through a 'whipping boy', a boy said to have received beatings on behalf of a noble boy. If so, little Charles watched to learn the error of his ways by proxy. According to nineteenth-century author Mark Twain, 'James I. and Charles II. had whipping-boys when they were little fellows', this being Twain's reason for including such a character in his famous novel *The Prince and the Pauper*.[12] In truth, however, James I was subjected to severe corporal punishment during childhood, and seventeenth-century reports of a whipping boy for Charles II are lacking. Nevertheless, in a sermon at Whitehall, poet and cleric John Donne asserted: 'Sometimes, when the children of great persons offend at school, another person is whipped for them'. This sermon was preached to Charles I two years before Charles II's birth.[13]

One of the main people to face the complexity of addressing misbehaviour from Charles was clergyman Brian Duppa, the boy's tutor. After a fairly humble start in life in the late 1580s, Duppa had excelled as a pupil of Westminster School, learned Hebrew from Westminster dean Lancelot Andrewes and achieved a series of degrees at Oxford. He'd also soaked up European culture through travelling in France and Spain during the 1610s, then in 1632–33 served as Vice-Chancellor of Oxford University. But his nonsense poem *Come Good Fiddle*[14] shows a light-humoured side of Duppa, and when already happily getting to know him, the prince was told this tutor 'hath no pedantry in him; his learning he makes right use of' and 'the purity of his witt doth not spoil the serenity of his judgment'.[15] A later description of the cleric praises his 'exemplary piety, eminent candour, humility' and 'gracefulness', while another paints him as 'a meek and humble man, and much loved for the sweetness of his temper'. No wonder Charles reacted well to a tutor of this demeanour. However, the second description, which stems from Bishop Gilbert Burnet, nevertheless declares Duppa 'no way fit' to handle educating the heir to the throne.[16]

Duppa was not expected to be a jack of all trades though. A more comprehensive education became a collaborative effort, with masters of specific fields drafted in. For instance, drawing lessons were the domain of

Chapter 3

Bohemian etcher Wenceslaus Hollar[17] during his early period of residence in England, and Charles's French tuition would come thanks to a Peter Massonnet for a promise of £60 per annum after 1638.[18] Several servants from France, the Netherlands and Germany were employed for the royal family, with Massonnet probably a French native, as was the prince's page Mr Le Grant.[19] Charles therefore had substantial opportunity to hear and even speak French in day-to-day life, and he may have bolstered this from age 6 during dancing classes with another Frenchman, Guillaume le Pierrie.[20] On paper though, the child was challenged even by English. His skills with the written word did not develop at the highest speed, and an aversion to reading and writing was germinating within him, ready to have him dodge paperwork during his reign. In light of this, it seems Duppa did insufficient to encourage Charles in at least two of the three Rs, but this clergyman was on his way to a bishopric by the time he began overseeing the prince's learning and his chief purpose as far as the king was concerned was to sculpt Charles into a pious Anglican.

Duppa was likely to do his job the way Charles I wanted. This, however, would displease other Protestants. Although moderate, Duppa could be described as a Laudian, a follower of the Puritan-persecuting William Laud. And together with the king, Laud was now well into the process of overhauling the image and practices of Anglicanism, with evermore reminiscence to Catholicism. Churches were being consecrated, statues were installed, surplices were worn and communion tables were sectioned off towards east-facing windows while repair of medieval stained glass added the finishing touches to Laud's, and indeed the king's, quest for religious beautification. In addition, worship now involved mandatory bowing at every mention of Jesus's name. In 1637 Puritan John Bastwick claimed: 'the Church is now as full of ceremonies, as a dog is full of fleas'.[21] And since Laud had been elevated to the hilt through appointment as Archbishop of Canterbury in 1633, there seemed no stopping him.

The king could deny Catholic influence till he was royal blue in the face, but his support of Laud contributed to the telling of a different story to suspicious ears. Concern for the English faith was mounting. It was stretching beyond England too, and in Stuart homeland Scotland the previous king's vision of uniting the Scottish Kirk with the Church of England would very soon be carving landmarks on the road to civil war.

To continue his father's dream, Charles I imposed on the Scots an Anglican-based Book of Common Prayer. He allowed the new book to be a Scottish version drafted with input from Scottish clerics, but he was still unaware of how deeply he'd offend. Scots intended to tell him. When the text debuted with a reading by dean James Hannay at Edinburgh cathedral St Giles' during a Sunday morning service on 23 July 1637, a stool was promptly hurled at Hannay's head as a riot erupted. And this was no isolated case. The monarch had created a recipe for disaster, but he defended his decision. Dissolving the Westminster parliament in 1629 he'd declared: 'Princes are not bound to give Account of their Actions, but to God alone',[22] and he did not regard regal orders as matters open to discussion. Yet many centres of worship in Scotland refused to comply, some on principle and some through sheer fear of anarchic tumult. The opposing multitude felt a need to take official measures. Hence in February 1638 came the National Covenant, an agreement inaugurated by several Scottish clergymen and signed by several thousand Scottish citizens, with a legal section drawn up by fanatically spiritual lawyer Archibald Johnston of Warriston. Through this monumental document, signatories pledged allegiance to Presbyterian control and, despite promising not to threaten 'the Kings greatnesse and authority',[23] shunned the changes the sovereign attempted to force upon them. Some committed with such fiery emotion, they signed with their blood.

It was in the wake of this fury against the king that Prince Charles was to be admitted into the Order of the Garter, the very highest order of knighthood. This carried considerable militant connotations from its origins with warrior king Edward III in the mid-fourteenth century, and in October 1637 Charles I and existing members wanted to let the prince join 'at the earliest opportunity', as he seemed 'to desire it exceedingly'.[24] The decision also came through the king's perception of 'joyful and pregnant hopes of your manly virtues', he told Charles on 20 May 1638 and added: 'the emulation of Chevalry will in your tender years provoke and encourage you, to pursue the glory of heroick actions'. With this letter further communicating a need to make haste to Windsor Castle 'to receive the Ensigns' the very next day,[25] Charles was thus still 7 years of age when a garter was strapped to his left leg with ceremony, and to mark the occasion, Van Dyck got to work on a portrait of the boy kitted out in battle armour complete with a pistol in his hand and his finger at the trigger. Yet within this image of grand belligerence, Charles's face is a very picture of innocent youth. Behind puppy fat still filling out rosy cheeks, his expression is furnished with serene pride as though he's poised to take a bow at a primary-school play.

In this artwork, Charles sports the longish hair fashionable in his day, cropped softly around his ears and straight along the fringe. During the late 1630s, the waviness of his locks differed between portraits, full curls sometimes appearing, and his lips were defined by curvatures while he still had something of a juvenile button nose.

Maturity was nonetheless calling. From birth, Charles had often been referred to as the Prince of Wales, but now the title was his officially, and with it came a household packed with male servants under William Cavendish, Earl of Newcastle. Some people thought this overdue. The prince had been surrounded by female influences for longer than seemed appropriate, governess Lady Dorset 'and the rest of the Underwomen' thus already removed from his daily life. Now Newcastle was to be a governor for him.[26] The earl's influence on Charles would be immeasurable, and it somewhat differed from the king's.

Chapter 4

A couple of months before he received a patent of appointment to the governorship of Charles, it was said that the Earl of Newcastle 'shall not have the name of his governor, yet he shall have that superintendency'. Technically at this time, however, Newcastle had been made Gentleman of the Bedchamber and Groom of the Stool,[1] the 'close stool' being a box housing a pot and fashioned with a big hole in the top – the toilet of the early modern rich.

The groom of the stool's job included administrative duties. Reports on the prince's bodily functions were communicated to a doctor, and monitoring of food and drink intake helped a team of staff predict when certain services would be required. After all, the portable close stool had to be ready and waiting as a luxurious relief station whenever Charles headed for it. Therefore, once he'd done his business, the pot was emptied and cleaned to reduce odours.[2] Before that point too though, somebody else performed other non-administrative tasks. This might not have been Newcastle, as the role of groom of the stool was evolving in the seventeenth century. Nevertheless, having helped with unbuttoning and divesting, the chosen person remained in the room for the duration of a bowel movement, engaging the master in conversation along the way. There was nothing demeaning about this, for either party. To be granted such intimate access to the heir to the throne was a signal honour, and not for a minute did it indicate Charles was behind in his development. For generations, kings had employed grooms of the stool to stand beside them during evacuation time. Whether the attendant wiped the royal posterior is debated, but either way, when nature called, so did Charles. This is how his life ahead was designed to be.

In fact the potty training provided for the prince demonstrates a more general side of his upbringing, because in essence he was taught self-control

Chapter 4

rather than self-sufficiency. A king would have doors opened for him, not automatically reach for the handle, and if he dropped something, a servant picked it up. Charles I would one day quite famously indicate that royalty should not be seen stooping to the floor in such instances. To paint a picture of majesty, impulse had to be suppressed and decadent dependence on others be the default. Carving, pouring and tasting were therefore all done for Prince Charles, yet his meals appeared more manifestations of restraint, not that the country at large saw them that way. While meats were rarities for the average citizen, they made substantial elements of all three daily royal repasts, and sweet treats such as tarts, custard and marzipan further strengthened the magnetism of the dining table for Charles. But breakfasts were delayed by prayers first thing and habitual early risings meant long mornings before the day's biggest feed in the afternoon, then evening fare consisted of relatively light options.[3] Gorging was frowned upon as neither the king nor the queen were big eaters, and Newcastle was much the same. He wouldn't 'add one Dish to the Table' even though it seemed 'no great one',[4] but the prince was growing into a strapping lad with an appetite hard to satisfy. What's more, the older he got, the more he dined on show, where greed would shatter refinement and ceremonious rigmaroles were played out before so much as a morsel could touch his lips.

The heir had nonetheless started recognising the significance of ceremonial. His annual inclusion in the Garter ceremony[5] was less of an irritation. In fact, this particular chivalric order meant so much to him that he'd wear the Garter star prominently throughout his adult life. However, during the late 1630s, Charles I reduced public pomp for events such as royal christenings. This was a double-edged sword for the Prince of Wales as it gave him impressive duties previously assigned to others but reduced toleration of childish fidgeting or messing around. At the baptism of his sister Anne in the spring of 1637, his 6-year-old self had played a crucial role alongside Mary, 'in the name, so they said, of their deceased grandparents', and a precedent was set for special occasions of this ilk.[6]

But every day for Prince Charles was filled with reminders of the monarchy he'd been born into, no matter what he did or where he went. At Greenwich Palace, he could observe ships passing with their topsails struck by way of salute to His Majesty – a practice the king made obligatory from 1631, with failure to comply leading to the shipmaster's arrest. However,

Greenwich now became a focus of Henrietta Maria as construction of the resplendent Queen's House was completed around 1635, essentially signalling the arrival of architectural classicism in England. While interiors featured innovative geometric designs of black-and-white marble and the mesmerising spiral Tulip Staircase, the structure was similarly breathtaking from the outside. The old red palace of Greenwich was thus left standing in shame alongside this modern shining white masterpiece from the Continentally influenced mind of Inigo Jones, the godfather of such design in England.

Tudor styles, on the other hand, dominated at other residences. The king would nevertheless spend lavishly on modernisation such as Italianate garden formations at Hampton Court,[7] built around classical statues set against the backdrop of the palace's large purply red bricks. In Hampton Court's Privy Garden, Prince Charles could also see a fountain made of bronze and marble and inspired by Greek mythology, with water spurting from sirens' breasts,[8] while a whole host of botanical wonders grew all around. For functionality too, there was a 1625 indoor tennis court at Hampton Court, helping the prince follow in his father's footsteps as a keen tennis player, and a broad-stepped ladder aided climbing of an oak tree.[9] In 1651, Charles may have recalled this particular feature of playtime in somewhat different circumstances.

Nearer the metropolis meanwhile, St James's had been built in a red of its own but with black decoration adding a striking contrast to be absorbed from the courtyards it was erected around, views from Charles's nursery days not fading from memory as he continued to spend winters here.[10] Meanwhile country excursions could also see the prince ensconced at the 100-year-old Oatlands Palace on the site of a fifteenth-century castle-like manor house with a moat still evident. The seclusion of its location outside Weybridge provided a more homely feel, and here the king kept an oak staff on which he marked his children's heights as they grew.[11]

At the other end of the scale stood the all-important Whitehall, a nucleus of regnancy. Over a space of twenty-three acres, this was the biggest palace in Europe. Yet, save for the magnificent Jacobean Banqueting House, the Palace of Whitehall was 'nothing but a heap of Houses, erected at divers times, and of different Models',[12] so didn't quite look the part. Moreover, it sat on the doorstep of the ever-expanding London, making for a near-surreal collision of classes, particularly as a public roadway ran straight through the palace grounds. With break-ins also occurring from time to time,[13] it wasn't the safest spot for the prince to rest his head.

Chapter 4

One of the good things about having so many homes was the fact they came complete with servants and families for Charles to get to know, and some of the individuals he met certainly appreciated the grand architecture on display. Living at Windsor was a boy named Christopher Wren two and a half years younger than the Prince of Wales. While burgeoning as an artist and developing scientific interests, this frail and dainty son of Windsor's dean became a regular playfellow for the big, vivacious Charles, who shared some of Wren's passions. A passion for the sea was also waiting to burst out of the prince, but in the meantime, he travelled up and down the Thames as gentle barge journeys carried him between his abodes in the late 1630s.

His base, however, remained Richmond, a favourite royal residence for centuries. In the seventeenth century, pipes supplied this palace with water from three conduits in the area. And surrounded by fields and picturesque parkland, Richmond formed a utopia for outdoor pastimes. Should they be rained off, there was plenty of space to run and play indoors too. A 1649 survey reports the great hall as 100 feet by forty feet and featuring a 'clock case' turret at the north end. Meanwhile, although bounding around during worship was of course forbidden, a chapel furnished with 'cathedral seats and pews' stood just four feet shorter in length while two galleries, one above the other, each ran to a length of 200 feet. Heights were considerable as well, making privy lodgings 'perspicuous'. These lodgings were three storeys tall, complete with fourteen turrets, and not till Charles had climbed 124 steps would he reach the top of a round 'canted tower'.[14]

The king, too, spent plenty of time at Richmond, often casting an eye over some of the masterpieces in his vast art collection. Meanwhile his eldest son would himself soon own a hoard of pictures, medals and statues together with books of drawings and prints,[15] but how much interest the prince took in them is doubtful. Thanking the Earl of Newcastle for a New Year's present featuring brass statues, a sweet letter from the child describing himself as 'very well pleased' with the gift[16] shows his much-noted politeness but may not reflect real enthusiasm inside him, with Charles preferring lively entertainment to motionless art.

So rather than the paintings at Richmond, probably more exciting for the prince was the array of wildlife there, not just the deer and other inhabitants that roamed uncaged but also more unusual examples kept under lock and key to feed his wide-eyed wonder. Antelope and such dangers as bears may have appeared in some of his most vivid childhood memories as a result, unless these were overshadowed by a bright green wickerwork aviary four yards tall installed for little Charles in Richmond's orchard in 1637. If so, ornithological pals in the shapes of pheasants, hawks, pigeons and cormorants perhaps left more lasting impressions.[17]

Of course, canine pals were so dear to Charles that entire breeds are named after him. He grew up with spaniels and greyhounds around his father, yet by proclamation in February 1638 the king forbade anyone else to keep greyhounds or mongrels within ten miles of where his court was residing. This was because the dogs hunted hares and led to disappointment on royal hunts. Gamekeepers were therefore instructed to seek out disallowed dogs and 'cause them to be presently put away, hanged up, or otherwise destroyed'.[18] Despite this, greyhounds were the king's favoured canine companions, his reason being they did not flatter.[19]

When it came to handling animals of the equine variety, the younger Charles could not have dreamed of a better introduction, for horses were central to the life of the Earl of Newcastle and the earl put his fondness for these creatures to great use. Since age 10 he'd been developing skills in the saddle. In his teens he'd trained as a rider alongside Charles I's brother Henry. And when over 50, Newcastle would see men from all over Europe flock to his equestrian school in Antwerp.[20] As Charles's governor in his forties though, he concentrated on coaching Charles. Nobody knew how this would go to begin with. Newcastle was 'the first that set him on horseback', but the child took to it so well that after two years or so he would 'ride leaping horses' and make them 'go better than any Italian or French riders (who had often rid[den] them) could'. What's more, Newcastle seemingly gave his charge the ability to work magic on almost any steed supplied. Before much longer, Charles would be getting the very best performance from horses 'the first time that ever he came upon their backs, which is the height and quintessence of the art'.[21]

Along with fencing with the earl, horsemanship provided not only a grounding in combat techniques but also a welcome alternative to the classroom, and Newcastle had few qualms about eating into classroom time. At Cambridge, he'd proven himself poorly suited to university education. Now he brought words of advice that were music to Charles's ears. Such nuggets of wisdom addressed in writing to the child included 'whensoever you are too studious your contemplation will spoil your government' and 'take heed of too much book'. The governor nevertheless felt Charles would benefit from reading history for comparison between the deceased and the living: 'the same humours is now as was then; there is no alteration but in names', he told the prince. After this, Newcastle added: 'one may be a good man, but a bad King'.[22]

Newcastle was no opponent of monarchy though and no stranger to it or its extravagance, having entertained kings at his grand East Midlands homes Welbeck Abbey and Bolsover Castle. In May 1633 his hospitality to Charles I and courtiers en route to the monarch's Scottish coronation had been so sumptuous 'as had never before been known in England',[23] but the earl was far from all show, harbouring meaningful morals. His advice to the future Charles II included 'be courteous and civil to everybody' and 'when you hear people speak ill of others reprehend them'. These words then continued with emphasis on civility towards women. Newcastle thought there should be no bounds restricting this and rhetorically asked Charles: 'what hurt were it to send them a dish from your table ... and to drink their health?'[24]

Something worth noting here is Newcastle's later marriage to Margaret Cavendish née Lucas, one of the era's few women who dared use her own name, rather than a man's, when publishing fiction and poetry as well as a range of works on matters such as natural philosophy. Flying in the face of most men of the day, Newcastle encouraged her ardently, and after he became duke (1665), she was even accepted in conversation over experiments performed for an otherwise wholly male presence at a 1667 meeting of the Royal Society,[25] the great scientific society Charles II supported.

Science certainly fired the curiosity of Newcastle, whose contact René Descartes impressed him with theories on optics and mechanics. Since the early 1630s the earl had been involved in research into both, and an informal group of enquiring minds such as Thomas Hobbes was forming around him. Known as the Cavendish Circle, or Welbeck Circle in honour of Newcastle's Nottinghamshire estate, this band of intellectuals was likewise populated by giants of the arts, however, with musicians and dramatists key members. In fact the earl himself had a future writing career already burgeoning. While Charles's governor he co-wrote three scripts alluding to the style of playwriting sensation Ben Jonson, of whom he'd been a valuable patron, and Newcastle seems to have been keen to share them with Charles. A probably late-1630s letter from the prince to the earl reads: 'I thank you for ye play. I like it so well that I desire to see it again'.[26] The genre of Newcastle's three scripts was comedy of humours,[27] which went on to shape Restoration comedy.

From even just a brief assessment of Charles II, Newcastle's influence shines through unmistakably. But none of the earl's inclinations, interests or philosophies would have had such a profound effect on Charles had they not been fortified by an affectionate personal bond. Newcastle in fact admitted that his love for his own children was measly compared to his love for Charles.[28]

The earl's love for God, on the other hand, appeared uncertain. Rumours abounded. Newcastle feared neither God nor Satan and believed in neither Heaven nor Hell, they said.[29] The king may have dismissed this tittle-tattle, but to a curious child, religion is a source of searching questions, and the governor probably received a number of these from the young Prince of Wales, whose perception and ability to read between the lines were growing rapidly.

Charles hoped to activate these skills in others too. Some months before his ninth birthday his mother wrote to him for the first time, and he did not welcome her letter, a letter apologetically but openly telling him she was 'chiding' him. The problem was he was refusing medicine. She told him: 'if you will not [take the medicine], I must come to you and make you take it, for it is for your health. I have given order to mi lord of Newcastel, to send mi word to-night whether you will or not'. Faced with this, Charles seemingly thought tactically. Although still daunted by playing scribe, he had double guiding lines ruled on paper for him, and it's thought that now was the time he wrote his governor the following note. In rounded handwriting, the child scratched: 'My lord, I would not have you take too much phisicke, for it doth always make me worse, and I think it will doe the like with you. I ride every day, and am ready to follow any other directions from you'.[30]

The domineering side of Henrietta Maria was troubling Charles, but rather than emulate her with head-on offensive, he chose to navigate around obstacles, learning a more subtle approach could produce better outcomes. Unfortunately, his father did not think quite the same way.

North of the border, Covenanters were standing firm for Presbyterian governance as outlined in the National Covenant, while in opposition to this stood similarly firm Episcopalians who believed the Church, or Kirk in Scotland, should be controlled by monarch-appointed bishops. King James's introduction of Kirk bishops had already incensed the populace of

Chapter 4

Scotland at the end of the sixteenth century, and now with Covenanters so numerous, the General Assembly of the Church of Scotland decided by the end of 1638 that bishops be ejected and regal authority therefore eliminated.

Despite the Stuarts' roots, Charles I understood even less about his Scottish subjects than about the people of England. Outraged and hurt by the Assembly's swipe, he failed to comprehend how Church appointments by election, as formed the basis of Presbyterianism, held real validity. He believed it was via episcopacy that God's wishes were met, directly through him as the anointed. Therefore, he saw no reason to negotiate. Faced with rebellion, he resolved to march on Scotland. As winter drew to a close in 1639, a Royalist army and a Covenanter army were hence preparing for the Bishops' Wars, ultimately two conflicts that would form just part of far wider hostilities.

Thus setting a precedent, the army took the king away from his family in the spring, but a stand-in filled the gap. At Charles I's insistence, the 8-year-old Charles was to inhabit the ruler's own rooms at Whitehall and take on kingly responsibilities, meeting diplomats in the withdrawing room and maintaining a presence of regality.[31] With the queen, who was recovering from the January 1639 birth and immediate death of the family's fourth daughter, the Prince of Wales essentially led the court for three months while 100 (half) of his father's military-trained guards stood around him.

But for war, the king's military men did not implant confidence. At a decade into his Personal Rule, Charles I had no desire to call a parliament to fund his efforts against Scotland. Consequently, his force was short of men, equipment and skill, with many commanding positions going to relatively untrained favourites, and bows and arrows formed the total weaponry upon some of the recruits. Initial fighting was minimal, chiefly consisting of the Battle of the Brig of Dee just south of Aberdeen as temperatures rose for the final summer of the 1630s. The Covenanters, however, took frightening victory.

Peace treaty the Pacification of Berwick was signed immediately in mid-June, but the matter was far from settled. Both sides parted only to muster more military resources. The Wars of the Three Kingdoms had begun.

Chapter 5

The future Charles II only ever had one contemporary grandparent, and she would probably never have met Charles had she not fallen out with her son Louis XIII of France. As things stood, however, Maria de' Medici was driven from France having attempted to oust first minister Cardinal Richelieu upon the Day of the Dupes in November 1630. By the end of October 1638, she'd sailed for England, and there she now resided, attempting to build bonds with her Stuart relatives. In view of the Medici Counter-Reformationist stance, she did not seem the best person to help the Prince of Wales improve his French; anything she told him could corrupt him, people thought, but she was nonetheless to receive his respect. At her arrival, she'd stepped out of a carriage drawn up in St James's courtyard and found Charles kneeling in reverence for her, beside his once again pregnant mother, then seen him standing beside his father for a grand reception in the presence chamber.[1]

Being Henrietta Maria's mother, this elderly lady had chance to see Charles I in less formal mode with family, but at official events the king made little room for anything but intense stateliness. He appeared 'more disposed to melancholy than joviality'[2] and, with his stutter still gnawing at him, had little desire to engage in unnecessary conversation with anyone outside his circle. As a barrier, an authoritarian aura oozed from him. Through reactions evident on the faces around, his son could observe the impact this had, but he also consorted with someone who would point it out in a rather unsympathetic way.

Possessing a talent for mimicry, the 2nd Duke of Buckingham had begun growing up to practise 'the art of treating persons or things in a ridiculous manner', and Charles I's 'stiffness was a frequent subject of his raillery', read later words from Bishop Burnet,[3] who knew both Buckingham and Charles II in adulthood. Burnet sometimes seems biased and deluded in his writings, especially with relation to events before his 1643 birth, but

Chapter 5

his comments here are quite believable, and raillery from Buckingham could be powerful. In the 1670s, the duke's authorship of rip-roaring play *The Rehearsal* was to prove so effective at lampooning 'heroic drama' that dramatists consequently shied away from the heroic genre, predicting they would be ridiculed as a result of Buckingham's attack on it. What's more, in pre-pubescence, Buckingham had plenty of opportunity to poke fun at Charles I where the king wasn't around but the king-to-be was.

The boys were spending hour upon hour together, and in lessons the duke sometimes sat alongside not only his brother Francis but also the two princes. This put little Charles – naturally the highest in social ranking – at the centre in terms of age, with Buckingham to look up to as the eldest pupil. On top of this, Charles shared his governor with both these Villiers sons.[4] The prince didn't want Newcastle's attention sapped away, although he'd already got used to sharing a governess with James, another attention sapper. Lady Dorset had balanced her duties to cater for James as well as Charles in the nursery, and this was particularly awkward when relatively few were employed. A letter from the governess on 1 August 1637 reveals a staffing paucity, Lady Dorset contacting the lord deputy of Ireland, Thomas Wentworth, to beg that a member of James's household be let off a call across the Irish Sea. Not even that one man could be comfortably spared, her letter claims.[5]

In childhood, the royal brothers' disparateness of character was yet to surface greatly. Both were enthused by the physical and rarely relished knuckling down to work at a desk. And because the daughters were educated separately from the sons, the future Duke of York was the sibling the Prince of Wales spent most time with, but three and a half years separated them in age. Therefore of course, when they were first playing and studying together, James needed constant guidance in areas his big brother had long mastered, and Charles's training for kingship included training for the position of head of the family.

Through the paintbrush of Van Dyck in the latter 1630s, Prince Charles comes across as a bit of a father figure. Having riled Charles I with the 1635 portrait featuring the younger Charles in a little boy's skirt, the artist quickly produced a similar painting of the three eldest mini royals with the heir sporting fine breeches and portrayed in far more adult, almost parental light. Casually propped up, legs crossed and a plinth taking his weight at the elbow, he stands at around 6 years old with an air of perfect composure, holding the tiny hand of James, who further clutches his brother's arm needily. Van Dyck's decision to paint them in this pose suggests the boys were encouraged to nurture the relationship represented, and Charles was nearly always around James whereas the king could devote less time to him.

The younger boy was nonetheless predictably jealous of his senior. When on Good Friday 1640 the Prince of Wales received an exquisitely decorated book detailing the 'life, doctrine, and actions' of Jesus Christ, the room erupted with delighted laughter as cute little James relentlessly pleaded for one of his own. He 'would have no nay; but a promise speedily to have one made for him like his brother's'. Charles, meanwhile, would not take no for an answer when offering thanks for the book, a multilingual tome covered in green velvet and fine gilt, adorned further by gold lace, and complemented by 'rare pictures to delight his eye with'. Whipping from his pocket 'a handful of twenty shilling pieces of gold', Charles explained: 'I do not give you this as any reward in recompense of your book, for I esteem it every way above much gold ... . Only you shall take this as a present testimony of my acceptance of it, and my esteem of you'.[6] And this was a child of 9.

It seems Charles neither resisted nor buckled under all the pressure to grow up. 'He hastens apace out of his childhood, and is likely to be a man betimes, and an excellent man if my presage deceives me not', Duppa had declared on 18 September 1639. Yet these words are preceded by a revelation that Charles was clinging onto memories of his infancy: 'The Prince, as he has great reason, very affectionately remembers his nurse'.[7] There can be no real doubt that the nurse concerned was Christabella, particularly as this letter was evidently written to her husband Edmund Wyndham – a man who had just returned to Somerset after the First Bishops' War.[8] Interestingly, Duppa seems to have been in regular contact with Wyndham. The opening line here reads: 'Your letters are as welcome to me out of the west as they were out of the north', and a postscript sends 'respects to Mrs. Windham'. Furthermore, this piece of correspondence indicates that Charles was still happily reunited with Christabella from time to time: 'It will not be long, I believe now, before the winter drives you this way, where your lady will be most welcome to the Prince'.[9]

Much of Edmund Wyndham's career in the 1630s had focused on money-making for the Crown, most notably through the 'soap monopoly' that saw him employed to root out soap manufactured by anyone but the company from which the Exchequer was taking a chunky profit. One of the first royalists to fight, Wyndham also had years of military service ahead of him, but with the coming of spring 1640, he found an old role revived when a phenomenon occurred that hadn't seen the light of day for eleven years – the king called a parliament.

The subsequently named Short Parliament was, to Charles I, merely a source of finance for war against the Covenanters, but as many MPs sympathised with the Presbyterian movement, the monarch found the House of Commons all but hold him to ransom. They had bones to pick with him, and they also had the perfect bone-picker. John Pym, MP for Tavistock, was well into his fifties and possessed parliamentary experience other MPs lacked. In his opinions, however, he was not unique. Risking life and limb on grounds of treasonable collusion, Pym and like-minded souls (including men as close to the king as the king's groom of the stool Henry Rich, Earl of Holland) had met furtively with Scottish commissioners as opposition to the Crown's policies grew, and across English counties Pym had ridden to encourage people to send petitions to the Commons in time for debates. Then when debates came, he shone. Just four days into the Short Parliament's session, Pym delivered a two-hour speech that went down so well it would establish him as a leading force of Parliament for the rest of his life, and it was a speech packed with grievances against the king.[10] Religion, taxation and parliamentary liberty were all subjects the MP for Tavistock highlighted, and he proposed that 'by two Statutes, not repealed nor expired, a Parliament ought to be held once in a Year'.[11] One of the greatest sources of anger towards the king concerned ship money, a medieval tax accepted for naval funding in wartime but one Charles I had reintroduced for ongoing general finance during his Personal Rule. On 4 May 1640 it was announced that he would discontinue this tax if Parliament granted him twelve subsidies.[12] But with a debate over this then ensuing and another debate scheduled for 7 May centring on the Scottish affairs, the king lost both his patience and his nerve. On 5 May he dissolved his parliament after just twenty-two days of its existence.

Some labelled him a despot, and on the surface this seems a justified accusation. However, to view him in purely despotic terms is to disregard the very core of Charles I. In his mind, his power was in fact about a subservience he saw in himself, a subservience to God. According to that fundamental doctrine known as the divine right of kings, the monarch exercised divine will on Earth, and of course he'd already asserted his belief that he was accountable to God but God alone.

Unwavering in this, the father of little Charles regarded it as a vital philosophy to instil in the heir to the throne, rendering it central to kingship preparation. On top of this, the heir was growing up around an understanding that the powers of a deity travelled through monarchs even physically. Like rulers of France, Charles I performed 'touching for the king's evil', placing his hands on sufferers of scrofula to rid them of their affliction. Scrofula made for an unpleasant sight as it brought repulsively swollen lymph glands on the neck, but it was known as the king's evil because so many people were convinced the royal touch cured it. Specially designed ceremonies of touching became highly popular. For the sovereign, these usually constituted important elements of the schedule at Michaelmas and Easter, when colder weather was hoped to lessen his risk of infection, and they stood out as rare exceptions in which he allowed the masses into his presence. To limit numbers, however, only holders of certificates were admitted,[13] whereupon the king employed himself like a demigod, just as his son would be expected to.

At the same time though, another of Newcastle's opinions written to young Charles was 'I would not have you so seared with majesty as to think you are not of mankind'.[14] Conflicting messages were being flung at the prince, and some messages he received were plain frightening.

Just before he turned 10, Charles – the boy who seldom grizzled even as a baby – was reported to have been weeping bitterly for five days straight and tormented by harrowing dreams at night. As 'no man' could comfort him, his father eventually went to ascertain what was wrong. However, quite out of character, the prince replied contemptuously: 'Your Majesty should have asked that sooner'. The king pushed for an explanation, but the words to come from his son's mouth were almost the worst he could imagine: 'My grandfather left you four kingdoms,[15] and I am afraid your Majesty will leave me never a one'.[16]

Understandably, the king wanted to know who had put such ideas into Charles's head. The culprits are unidentified, but royal households were not exclusively made up of royalists, and to on-site opponents of Charles I's seemingly high-handed actions, the Prince of Wales was a potentially useful tool for altering the course ahead. He was nevertheless a tool that would first need melting down and moulding into shape.[17] Even without such direct targeting, Charles's fears had other triggers. Writing of June 1640, monarchist John Evelyn later noted that 'London, and especially the Court, were at this period in frequent disorders, and greate insolencies were com'itted by the abus'd and too happy Citty ... many scandalous libells and invectives scatter'd about the streetes, to the reproach of Government'.[18] For

Chapter 5

Prince Charles to be so distraught, he was clearly convinced that threats were not empty, that the very foundations of everything he'd ever known could be yanked from under him if his father continued in his uncompromising way.

It's often said that Charles had a stronger father–son than mother–son relationship, but this is largely based on later evidence. Henrietta Maria was particularly attentive to her children in their times of distress, rushing to her 5-year-old when he developed even just a 'slight fever' in August 1635 and resolving to remain there at Richmond until he recovered.[19] Although one can only guess how much Charles appreciated his mother for this, he clearly resented his father for taking so long to ask what was wrong in 1640. Nevertheless, the conversation documented between the king and a tearful Charles highlights a key element of the dynamics. Resentful words were spat from the boy's troubled head, probably more than from the heart, but Charles wasn't too scared to blurt them out in his father's face, whereas he seems to have gone out of his way to avoid confrontation with his mother over the taking of medicine in 1638. Though notoriously standoffish to most people, the king was quite approachable from Charles's point of view.

Nevertheless, in his molten state in 1640, the prince merely watched on helplessly while the clouds that hung over Scotland darkened. Wentworth, Earl of Strafford from January 1640, was a Yorkshireman whose eight years as Ireland's lord deputy had demonstrated his skill in troublesome politics and now fortified him with a misplaced confidence when called back to England. It was after urging from Strafford that the Short Parliament was dissolved, unlikely to cough up funds unless appeased, and within hours of this dissolution members of the Privy Council had heard him orate with words that would later undo him, quoted as: 'Go on with a vigorous war, as you first designed, loose and absolved from all rules of government ... . They refusing, you are acquitted towards God and man. You have an army in Ireland you may employ here to reduce this kingdom'.[20] Had it not been for Strafford, the army in Ireland would have carried far less weight, but after he'd presided over an Irish parliamentary session beginning that March, a total of £180,000 was reluctantly granted to recruit 9,000 soldiers.[21] Strafford also now led a whip-round by example, donating £20,000 to put further military resources at the king's disposal, and £300,000 had rolled in after three weeks.[22] The Second Bishops' War that summer nevertheless precipitated utter humiliation on the king. Fighting him off, the Scots invaded England. Now they controlled great swathes of England's North East, and through the Treaty of Ripon signed in October 1640 the defeated sovereign was forced to pay £850 per day for the upkeep of the Covenanter army in English territory.

The king had travelled north for both Bishops' Wars, joining his men at Berwick in the First, then basing himself in York for the Second.[23] Although the younger Charles wielded swords in exhilarating sessions of fencing, he remained, for now, hundreds of miles from battle himself, but his life already hung in the balance. That September, a Scot in his service was arrested after threatening to murder him.[24]

Charles's sister Anne would not escape imminent death. She'd never been blessed with perfect health, but her 'inflammatory disposition of the lungs, accompanied with continual fever, oppression and difficulty of breathing, constant cough, and extreme debility'[25] plunged her into a particularly bad condition late 1640. Charles had periodically watched his sister growing through her toddler years. Now, at Richmond, she left him to mourn as 'suffocating catarrh' ended her three-year-old life on 5 November.[26] In July though, a healthy addition to the family had entered the world, with Henrietta Maria delivered of Prince Henry, a boy whose hair was almost as dark as Charles's. The infant was known as the Duke of Gloucester. Not till May 1659 would he officially acquire the dukedom, his biggest brother bestowing it upon him, but from the start respect for Henry was shown through use of this title, even throughout his coming ten years as a prisoner of Parliament.

Henry was the eighth child born. To Charles therefore, his mother seemed like a factory churning out offspring, yet even from his eldest sibling's birth he knew each baby was just as much his father's as his mother's. So what did the future Merry Monarch understand of how babies were made? Charles I disliked talk about sex, his attitude clear from how he behaved the first time he slept with his wife. That night, he was having none of the euphemistic air that usually preceded bedding ceremonies, which were post-nuptial traditions at other Stuart courts.[27] Bolting all seven doors, he'd locked everyone out promptly,[28] and at his court, the matter of copulation tended to be swept under the carpet. If the future Charles II had any questions about the facts of life, his father would not have welcomed them happily. The boy had something of a second father in the Earl of Newcastle, and Buckingham was probably already delighting in dirty jokes for Charles's ears, but the chances are that when approaching puberty Charles would too often be left pondering for himself about the pleasures his body was preparing for. His later openness on the subject implies he found such silent rumination unhelpful.

Chapter 6

Even before the signing of the Treaty of Ripon, the king realised that defeat to the Covenanters left the Crown in such dire financial straits that it meant recourse to another parliament before 1640 was out. With election arrangements therefore commencing on 24 September, Pym cannily set about persuading voters in marginal constituencies to turn in an anti-Royalist direction, and his endeavours paid off. When Westminster became abuzz again on 3 November, the Lower Chamber, the House of Commons, was heavily populated with MPs incensed by the king, frightened of Catholicism and determined to effect change. And it was by hunting down a certain member of the Upper Chamber, the House of Lords, that they took the first step towards this change.

If considered a militant puppeteer pulling the king's strings, the Earl of Strafford appeared a distinct threat, not least because most of the troops he'd mustered in Ireland were Catholics, and he had potential still to gain the upper hand for the Royalists and episcopacy. Future actions were preventable though, especially if past actions were punishable.

Aware of this very point, Strafford wanted a handful of parliamentary figures such as Pym charged with the capital crime of high treason for plotting the Scottish invasion of northeastern England,[1] but the earl, in poor health, proved slow to move. Conversely on 11 November, Pym declared in the Commons that Strafford was 'the principal author and promoter of all those counsels which had exposed the kingdom to so much ruin', and within just hours of this speech the Lower Chamber officially accused Strafford himself of high treason.[2] Months of preparations began for his monumental trial.

For the Prince of Wales, Strafford's trial brought new duties. The king was openly siding with the defence but found himself tucked away as a spectator, sometimes with his wife and eldest daughter. His eldest son was left to attend in an official capacity, plunged into prominence. With hatred for 'Black Tom Tyrant' Strafford widespread, all and sundry wanted to squeeze in to witness the showdown, right from its commencement on 22 March 1641. Admission required tickets bearing names,[3] and the heir to the throne was an added spectacle awaiting ticketholders. In his full robes, he sat beside the empty seat of state on each day of the proceedings, hundreds upon hundreds of eyes fixing on him when they turned towards the top of Westminster Hall. What they saw was a 10-year-old trying to follow a complicated exploration of the law in an attempt to ascertain what constituted high treason, and it seemed the definition was being stretched. Generally, this shocking crime was interpreted as an offence against the sovereign, but Charles heard an argument centring on country and subjects instead. Novel though the charges were, many classic elements of a legal case still came into play, as one man's story stood only against another's and ambiguity was seized upon, part of the prosecution hanging on one little word. When allegedly telling the king, 'You have an army in Ireland you may employ here to reduce this kingdom', Strafford had failed to specify which kingdom 'this' referred to, and he'd uttered this statement south of the Scottish border.[4] His accusers thus mooted that Strafford had intended a Catholic invasion of England. With evidence flimsy, acquittal was likely, but 'personal animosity' was seeping into Pym's performance for the prosecution,[5] and by a vote of 204 to fifty-nine on 21 April, MPs resorted to stronger stuff – a bill of attainder. Guilty or not, Strafford could be condemned to death by this bill as law. But it would only become law if signed by the sovereign, and on 1 May Charles I categorically told Parliament that, because he believed Strafford's doings had been mere misdemeanours, 'nothing whatsoever would induce him to sign the sentence of death. He had no fear of the consequences, which he would find a way of dealing with vigorously', Venetian ambassador Giovanni Giustinian reported.[6]

Vigour veered from the initial royal policy as a plan of appeasement had been in motion for months. Union with a Protestant nation could, the king hoped, dispel speculation over Catholic collusion, and the nation he turned to wasn't even a monarchy; it was the Dutch Republic. Following an old offer received, he gave the hand of his 9-year-old daughter Mary in marriage to the 14-year-old William born to Dutch stadtholder Frederick Henry. Tasks were delegated to Prince Charles here too. Back in January, he'd been put in a room at Somerset House with the restless James to meet three ambassadors from The Hague who were visiting for negotiations,[7] and Charles was to help put the bridegroom at ease. Having received him

Chapter 6

at Whitehall on 30 April, the 10-year-old took him for a walk in the garden, then led him into the presence of the bride. Now come the splendour of the big day, 2 May 1641, both Charles and James accompanied their sister at her entrance into Whitehall's chapel and escorted their new brother-in-law to a chamber to hear the sermon. With the queen and the newlyweds, the princes then aided digestion of the wedding breakfast by wandering round Hyde Park,[8] a space open to the public since 1637.[9]

But any mollification created by this union with the House of Orange was simultaneously destroyed. On the day of the wedding, a failed attempt to free Strafford from the Tower using 100 armed men was made by the poet John Suckling in league with the king, and Royalist schemes to attack Parliament by force leaked out left, right and centre, alerting the people to what's known as the First Army Plot. In fact, background machinations were becoming very public indeed. Before Suckling's rescue party could spring into action, notices scandalously reporting their plan were up for all to see.[10] With fear filling London, fired-up citizens thirsty for Strafford's blood turned to riots, furious with their sovereign for refusing them the 'justice' they felt necessary for their protection, and it was getting personal. Threatening 'the most violent measures against the state and against His Majesty's own person and all the royal House',[11] an estimated 12,000 congregated around Whitehall,[12] their capability as a lynch mob quite apparent in a sprawling palace already prone to break-ins. From the windows, Prince Charles watched in alarm. The bill of attainder dangled in front of the king, but he wept trying to reach a decision. Only indirectly could he justify signing.

Even once he had signed, he tried to reverse the decision or at least delay the beheading, sending a letter of appeal to the Lords. It was unlikely to work, but the plan had an added element to improve its chances – this letter would be delivered in person by the member of the Lords whom the king described as the 'most dear to me'.[13] He meant the Prince of Wales. It seemed Strafford's life now lay in the child's hands. This child had to move quickly though; it was 11 May and the axe was set to swing the following morning. Into a coach, young Charles was bundled, but at Westminster they 'dismissed the prince with scant civility, and refused to read the letter or the cover'.[14] The king might as well have sent one of his dogs to deliver it.

En route to the block as scheduled, Strafford received a blessing from Laud, though in rather unusual circumstances; the archbishop himself was banged up in the Tower. Given the way the wind was blowing, this was no huge shock. Backed by thousands of signatures on the public's Root and Branch Petition to banish episcopacy, oration by rising MP Harbottle

Grimston in the Commons a week before Christmas had described the Archbishop of Canterbury as 'the stye of all Pestilent filth, that hath infected the State, and Government of the Church and Common-wealth',[15] and the same day this 'stye' had been impeached for high treason. Laud was aware of how his situation mirrored Strafford's. To administer the blessing on 12 May 1641, he appeared at his cell window, his hands stretched out as the earl knelt below before proceeding to the scaffold. Laud then fainted.

With Strafford decapitated and the king an emotional wreck, 10-year-old Charles already saw Parliament as a devastating nemesis. And now this nemesis had a survival mechanism. Stripping the monarch of his power to act alone in proroguing, adjourning or dissolving either House, new legislation made these measures possible only when Parliament consented. The Long Parliament, as it's known to history, seemed more the 'perpetual parliament'.[16]

Charles would struggle enough to celebrate his birthday at the end of the month, but to make matters worse, Newcastle was summoned before the House of Lords that day on allegations of involvement in the First Army Plot, and the boy suffered agonies from a broken left arm following a nasty tumble from his horse on a gallop in Hyde Park.[17] Meanwhile vicious rumour spread. Giustinian heard that Charles was tasked with 'crushing the liberty of the country completely' by commanding forces under guidance from the Earl of Newcastle.[18]

Charles's governor was in a difficult situation, which deepened. On 24 June, Pym brought forth the Ten Propositions, a list of what could kindly be termed recommendations for the king to consider, and the fifth of these aimed to ensure the royal children be surrounded by 'persons of publique trust and well affected in Religion'.[19] To the lasting regret of both governor and charge, Newcastle resigned.

A substitute to please everyone would be hard to find, but Charles's own pleasing played little part in the decision. When William Seymour, Marquis of Hertford was appointed on 10 August, his disposition differed from the sportiness of Newcastle's and eradicated much of the fun from Charles's life instantly. For the marquis too, the arrangement was never ideal, but in case refusal of the governorship proved 'disadvantageous to his majesty', royalism spurred Hertford to accept. Crucially, however, his royalism was not seen to be of a damaging level. Hertford had grown into an ageing peer who 'cared not to discourse and argue'.[20] And thirty years after his own imprisonment in the Tower on suspicion of attempting to usurp the throne, he'd abstained from voting on Strafford's attainder. Nevertheless, while the marquis was 'conversant in books both in Latin and Greek', he was drawn to quiet country life[21] and displayed 'laziness of mind'.[22] Charles neither learned much from him nor wanted to.

Although ancient languages and history had their value, what Charles needed to understand most was current affairs, the affairs rooting themselves in the ground he would one day inherit, and not even fiscal matters could pass him by. After years of furore over ship money, this despised tax had finally been axed, and the king was painfully dependent on Parliament for subsidies. Westminster didn't want too much cash channelled the king's way though. He'd sought the previous parliament's funding as a means of firing at his Scottish enemies, and the new parliament was fast becoming his English enemy.

Indeed, revolution permeated the air. It took a toll on family life, with Henrietta Maria 'tortured by cruel distress'.[23] Pubescent Charles meanwhile would soon be expected to assume a semi-patriarchal role; he could ill afford to crumble. Yet danger lurked everywhere, shocking in its capacity no matter whom it targeted. When a smallpox outbreak was followed by plague in 1641, it ignited the usual panic but also nearly led to germ warfare. In October, Pym received a stomach-turning, bloodstained rag within a letter that explained the rag had been wiped across 'a plague sore' and sent to kill him by infection.[24]

But Pym would be alive and kicking for a little while yet, buoyed up by MPs such as John Hampden, Oliver St John and Nathaniel Fiennes, not to mention certain members of the Lords including the Earl of Holland's brother Robert Rich, better known as the 2nd Earl of Warwick, and Fiennes's father William, Viscount Saye and Sele. Collectively, Pym's most domineering force had become known as the Junto, and given the king's uncooperativeness, they were broadening parliamentary scope to domineer further. Prince Charles was now central to some official discussion, Westminster disputes erupting over whose company was best for him, i.e. for the future of the British Isles, and the boy's leisurely travels from palace to palace were to be replaced with demands for effective house arrest or dizzying pushes from pillar to post.

By November, the presence of Charles and James by their mother's side at Oatlands was stirring 'fear that the princes may be imbued with noxious ideas ... and turned away from the Protestant faith'.[25] It must be noted that the Gunpowder Plot was still in living memory, and a number of figures in Parliament, including Pym, were passionately Puritan, convinced that the Church of Rome was a national danger. The boys were therefore returned to Richmond, and Parliament instructed Hertford 'not to permit them to go to their mother in future, and not to leave the presence of his Highness at any time', under pain of beheading.[26]

The princes had already endured the past few months without their father as the king had been in Scotland for negotiations, leaving Charles behind despite initial consideration of including him in the trip. Of course, nobody had agreed on who should escort the boy. Chipping into the discussion was Puritan backbencher Oliver Cromwell, who at the time had been pushing forward the Root and Branch Bill in response to the public petition. This bill never passed, however, and despite the Junto's overarching successes, Cromwell was so discontented with parliamentary business that he was on the brink of quitting and emigrating. What persuaded him to stay was Westminster's boldest move yet.

This was the Grand Remonstrance, 204 criticisms of the king's rule that were handed to His Majesty on 1 December 1641 like a nightmare early Christmas present at Hampton Court. But the copious document brought greater division not only between King and Parliament but also within Parliament. Outraged by it, some in Parliament were becoming anti-parliamentarian.

One was lawyer-turned-MP Edward Hyde. His royalism was recognised by the king immediately, and Hyde helped him draft a forced response to the Grand Remonstrance. With Charles I opposed to change, the concessions within this response were far insufficient to appease.

Nevertheless, while ultimately ineffective here, Hyde was soon to prove his talents were almost unsurpassable, and he'd do this through his coming role with the younger Charles, for better or worse. Hyde's tendency to treat Charles II like a son would strain an otherwise good relationship to breaking point, exasperation mounting in both Charles and this father figure for about twenty-five years ahead.

In 1641, however, the paternity of Charles constituted a matter in itself. Now in the limelight, the prince was a recognisable royal figure, but among his fair-haired siblings, he stuck out like a sore thumb, and people were astonished by his large frame that continued to grow at an incredible rate while the queen was especially petite and the king only slightly taller at

Chapter 6

around five feet. All round, the Prince of Wales looked less and less like the short, slender and lighter-haired king every day. Rather unfortunately meanwhile, this child shared certain attributes with another man about the court – the tall, muscular, broad-shouldered Jermyn, the queen's most favourite of favourites.

Tongues were bound to wag, and while hearsay relates that the Marquis of Hamilton once chanced upon Henrietta Maria and Jermyn in an intimate embrace at Somerset House, another story seems more incriminating if believed. This holds that along shadowy palace corridors one night the king was discreetly making his way to his wife's quarters and was guided with a flame carried by page and famous playwright-to-be Thomas Killigrew, a cousin of Jermyn. Killigrew allegedly stepped into the queen's bedchamber ahead of his regal master, then dropped the light, spilling wax across the floor in a display of loud and farcical clumsiness that forced the king to stand waiting while the page cleared it all up and gave a Jermyn-shaped figure time to escape. By contrast, another royal confidant, again according to legend, planned to have the king walk straight in on an erotic act by cockily leading him to a room where Jermyn and Henrietta Maria were privately meeting. But the only intercourse they were found engaging in was innocent conversation.

What Jermyn was capable of in female company was nonetheless common knowledge. During 1633, he'd disgraced himself by refusing to wed the 1st Duke of Buckingham's niece Eleanor Villiers, despite the fact it may well have been his own seed planted in her expanding belly. When the king told Jermyn it was marriage or exile, Jermyn chose the latter, and only due to Henrietta Maria's persuasion was he accepted back two years later, two years in which his absence left a huge hole in the consort's life.

But their closeness began pre-1628, when the king preferred Steenie's companionship and Jermyn was equally welcomed by the queen, his fluency in French drawing him to her and often ensuring the words passing between them were uninterpretable to eavesdroppers.[27]

An affair seems unlikely given Henrietta Maria's principles. Nevertheless, in April 1659 Charles was said to be 'a bastard, and his mother Jermyn's whore'.[28] Of course if this is true, Charles never belonged in the line of succession. His mother, however, was even more jeopardised by the theory in the 1640s. If she committed adultery, she was thereby guilty of high treason.

◆ ◆ ◆

Try as they might, Parliament found no firm evidence of extramarital activity, but when anarchic violence erupted in Ireland during the autumn of 1641, Protestants were slaughtered in the name of both King and Catholicism, whereupon accusatory fingers pointed towards the queen, and the general rancour against her intensified. A Catholic manipulating the king, she was alleged to be attacking both Protestantism and English law. To topple her from her position seemed the safest thing to do. Yet those aiming to topple her had long been walking a tightrope. Just like Strafford and a section of the Junto had hoped to seal each other's fates, the queen now took Strafford's place in a parallel scenario, high treason again cited on both sides.

Five MPs and a lord were accused, but arresting men protected by parliamentary liberty was more easily said than done. Henrietta Maria thus felt a royal call to action was required: 'pull these rogues out by the ears,' she reputedly urged her husband, 'or never see my face more'.[29] This is the sort of approach of hers that later caused friction with her eldest son, though by then he had the benefit of hindsight. On 4 January 1642 meanwhile, Charles I took soldiers to Westminster and walked right into the elected's domain. He intended to arrest the Five Members in person. He'd made a seriously bad move, but not till fists were shaking at him in his carriage the next day did he realise how weighty a straw he was loading onto the camel's back. 'Privileges of Parliament!'[30] yelled enraged voices. Countering this, came hollering from his supporters as well, but Royalists were soon too scared to enter the streets. At high windows, water was kept boiling to pour onto troops searching for the Five Members, all of whom had bolted thanks to a tip-off reaching the Commons before the king had. Up went barricades, out came cannon and London descended into tumult.[31]

On 10 January, the king, queen and their three eldest children travelled surreptitiously by barge to Hampton Court. It may have saved their lives. But the suddenness of their move had them arrive unexpectedly. Beds were unmade, fires were unlit and barely a single servant accompanied them. The Prince of Wales shared one bed with his parents, brother and sister.[32] He now knew neither luxury nor life could be taken for granted.

Chapter 7

According to Henrietta Maria in February 1642, 'to settle affairs it was necessary to unsettle them first', Giustinian reported. With his own ears, he heard her utter this notion while she prepared to leave for Holland,[1] but the queen had to be careful whom she confided in; her trip was a shadowy quest to amass resources for war against Parliament. Scheming with the king, she took some of the Crown Jewels with her to pawn, and the couple struggled through a tearful farewell at Dover as they put out the story that she was merely escorting their eldest daughter over the waves to husband William. It wasn't all falsehood though; 10-year-old Mary was indeed emigrating, earlier than planned, to the Dutch court, and Prince Charles felt the absence acutely. 'I cannot enjoy that former happiness which I was wont, in the fruition of your society', Charles explained to Mary in a letter filled with brotherly love from Royston on 9 March. He then suggested they correspond so they could 'reciprocally understand of each other's welfare'. His letter-writing had come on leaps and bounds. He continued: 'we are, as much as we may [be], merry; and more than we would [be], sad, in respect we cannot alter the present distempers of these troublesome times'. Laughing in the face of adversity was clearly an early goal for Charles. He tried getting his sister smiling here, and he told her how happy she made her husband: 'who, as I conceived by his last letter, was … joyful for your presence'.[2]

With Mary easing into her wifely role, matrimony became a matter for Charles too as talk was turning to further strengthening the bond with the House of Orange through a 'double marriage', his mother proposing he marry Frederick Henry's eldest daughter Louise Henriëtte.[3] The Continent looked more friendly than England, and Maria de' Medici was already back in European territory. Her impoverished death in Cologne come summer meant Charles never saw her again. Because Parliament had less desire to see the princes leave for a mainland peppered with Catholic nations,

Henrietta Maria's wish to have her sons smuggled over was sidelined for now. Father and heir were instead bound for York, travelling a meandering journey, but some of it was very pleasant.

For instance, when the 11-year-old paid Cambridge University a call en route mid-March, he'd walk away with an honorary Master of Arts degree. Despite his accompaniment by numerous grand noblemen, proceedings during this visit revolved around Charles, with speeches addressed to him, and while 'sitting in his fathers place' he was saluted at Regent House by the public orator.[4] The boy could only guess the full extent of reverence shown. His Latin was far below the standard needed to interpret all the words he heard. After dinner, however, he was treated to entertainment in English, specifically Abraham Cowley comedy *The Guardian* at Trinity College, and 'gave all sighnes of great acceptance which he could, & more then ye University dared expect'.

A couple of days later, the king also arrived in Cambridge. Together the royals attended a banquet at St John's, where the senior Charles consumed little but took generous helpings for his son, ensuring the boy had nibbles in his pocket for later. The king was nevertheless peeved as neither the sheriff nor any of the county's gentlemen came to pay respects.[5]

It's through Cambridge University that the Prince of Wales lost yet more of those closest to him, as George and Francis Villiers were admitted in their early adolescence. Their departure wasn't the only change in the royal classroom, either. For obvious reasons, Laudian bishop Duppa was persona non grata to Parliament. He remained part of Charles's life and education, but to appease, a scribal John Earle had stepped in around the end of 1641, and despite the umbrage Charles took at the disruption forced upon him, this new tutor had great potential to gel with him. Although another Oxford doctor of divinity with a pious side as one of Charles's chaplains,[6] Earle possessed fun-loving attributes aligning with some of the tastes his eminent pupil would develop. Several poems are credited to Earle, but his most notable work was the witty *Microcosmographie*, which honed the craft of characterisation in ridiculing 1620s social morals. He was nonetheless 'amongst the few excellent men who never ... could have an enemy' except enemies of 'learning and virtue' according to Hyde, and Earle cited conversation as a source of his 'more useful learning'.[7] Charles preferred conversing to reading.

That said, in the quaint village of Little Gidding near Cambridge dwelled the makers of his wondrous 1640 book, and they had another tome for him that was mid-manufacture at the time of his journey to York. In awe of their work himself, the king insisted on a detour to see them, so with a lordly entourage

Chapter 7

in tow, the royals arrived unexpectedly in this modest setting. When given a sneak peek of the new book, however, the prince's eyes nearly popped out of their sockets as he took in its grandeur and pored over the artwork printed within. Barely liftable though it was, Charles struggled to accept he would have to leave this 'jewel' behind in its unfinished state and impatiently whined: 'But, sir, shall I not now have it with me?' As his zeal was calmed gently by his father, the boy was instead contented with apple pie and cheesecake.

He also had hunger for hunting by this age. Twilight had begun to descend as the royal party rode on, whereupon the king spied a hare and promptly shot it. Realising the animal was only wounded, the younger Charles then dashed after it on foot 'through two or three furrows of water' and, with his purpose met, unashamedly laughed as he showed his catch to the king.[8]

Shockingly few eyelids batted at cruelty to animals back then. Cockfighting and bearbaiting drew crowds, and Charles II would re-allow such savage sports after 1650s prohibitions introduced in the interests not of creature welfare but of reducing anti-Cromwellian plotting among spectators.[9] Even when not mistreated for entertainment, animals in the seventeenth century were often used more than respected, and of course equines were depended upon especially, sometimes worked to death. In 1642, however, those fit for cavalry service looked the most endangered.

Combat could still be averted, but nobody really knew how to avert it. The Anglican monarch was committed to absolutism in kingship while men embodying the Puritan leadership of Parliament wished to break the Church of England and royal prerogative, then reform both, to allow parliamentary dominance. Each side wanted the other to give far more than their respective principles permitted them to give, and expectation that it would be given indicated a mutual misunderstanding like a solid brick language barrier.

As the royal court now resided in York, the physical presence of many supporters of the king had vanished from Westminster, leaving a greater proportion of Parliamentarians to vote. Although laws could not pass without royal assent, innovative ways and means began to show that a space for the king's signature could be left blank just as effectively. The Militia Bill in December 1641 had proposed to hand Parliament military control to suppress the Irish uprisings, but because the king was not prepared to put armed forces at his enemy's disposal, he rejected this bill. In March 1642, 'King Pym' and colleagues converted it into the Militia Ordinance and enforced this as law of their own accord, the nation's defence cited for justification of their disregard of royal assent. They had taken a huge, revolutionary step here. And now the trained bands, the local militia throughout the realm, were lost to the sovereign. Parliament chose new commanders to replace those he'd installed.

Of course, that didn't stop the king appointing men of his own to lead new forces, some of which he needed for personal defence. From 20 May 1642, a variety of well-to-do northerners were recruited as his lifeguard troops before becoming part of the Royalist army, and this brought a captain's post to none other than 11-year-old Charles, nominal though it was as an experienced Colonel Thomas Byron commanded in practice. The prince meanwhile led his horse troop on ceremonial occasions such as 3 June at Yorkshire's Haworth Moor, where the king had the county's high sheriff read a declaration 'several times' to the great joy of 'three or four score thousand' if the report is accurate.[10]

Parliament were upping their own defence; placing some of their supporters in command of key towns, fortifying arsenals and seeking out financial assistance all helped, and the political boldness from Westminster continued. Dated 1 June, their Nineteen Propositions contained the bid 'That no Marriage shall be Concluded, or Treated for any of the Kings Children ... without the consent of Parliament'. The king, however, responded with '*Nolumus Leges Anglia mutari*',[11] a blanket refusal to change the laws of England. His twenty-page answer implied parliamentary rule threatened society, and he had this answer published, wanting it broadcast at English and Welsh churches. It nevertheless oozed immovability from the king.

The Prince of Wales still felt in turmoil regarding this immovability, but it seems he was shying away from bringing more of his thoughts to his father's attention; around the end of 1642, he asked Duppa to try for him. In doing so, Duppa revealed the child anxiously discussed the miseries sweeping the country and 'cannot comprehend the absolute causes; yet he gives a shrewd guesse at them'.[12] Whatever the causes though, the long-term effects depended on the short-term. Aware of this and keen to become a soldier, Prince Charles wanted nothing short of throwing himself into the fight to uphold his father's rights.

In Yorkshire early July 1642, he exercised his troops himself 'with a countenance & behaviour so full of reservednesse and manhood, that (without flattery) it much amazed the beholders'. Then he donned gilt armour and mounted a fine white steed, as if to ride into the fray.[13] Mere honorary command frustrated him.

Chapter 7

But the enemy looked more than a match for a pubescent. At Westminster on 12 July, a vote passed to raise a Parliamentarian army, and appointed head commander was the Earl of Essex, Robert Devereux, who had been a senior Royalist officer and, from July 1641 to April 1642, served as Lord Chamberlain. Essex's relationship with the Stuarts nevertheless had an acrimonious history. When a young man in the early 1610s he'd inflicted a bloody injury on Prince Henry by hitting him with a tennis racket during a row. Now Essex's offensive was bolstered by rich military experience and a commission empowering him to levy forces 'to invade, resist, repress, subdue, pursue, slay, and kill'.[14]

As levying came thick and fast on both sides, Charles's governor Hertford could no longer concentrate on Charles's care. He'd already temporarily shifted his attention to James, sneaking the 8-year-old out of rebel clutches in London and planting him in York. The pair had arrived on Easter Monday,[15] reuniting with Charles, but early August, Hertford was called to Royalist service as a commissioner of array for Somerset and as lieutenant general of southern Welsh and western English counties. This ignited envy in fellow royal favourite Lord Herbert, Edward Somerset, a scientific mind remembered today for inventing a form of steam engine. His family's astounding wealth brought great influence, and Herbert believed himself worthier of the Royalist command entrusted to Hertford. However, as a Catholic, the inventor should have known the king could not afford to favour him too openly. For nearly eighteen months, the Hertford–Herbert quarrel would build to fierce proportions,[16] but perhaps the most awkward relationship Hertford now faced was that with his closest friend, his brother-in-law Essex.[17] This was the intimate nature of the Wars of the Three Kingdoms, and Charles's governor was one of the most intimate with the enemy.

The formal start date of the wars in England is a grey area. On 4 August, Parliament had declared a necessity for military action.[18] Now, on the soggy evening of 22 August, the Prince of Wales was among the many nobility and soldiery emerging from Nottingham Castle as drums thudded in solemnity for the raising of the royal standard, a flag that billowed in the mighty tempest appropriately brewing in the sky. Raising the standard was Charles I's way of declaring the same necessity.

Prince Charles was now tasked with procuring some aid for his cause, but it was not to political negotiation that he was to rise; he simply needed to charm. His father thus sent him west, granting the Welsh a rare visit from their own prince, who in turn enjoyed a gushing reception. On 2 October the 12-year-old headed for Monmouthshire's Raglan Castle, finding grand tapestries hung for the occasion, and a welcome by Sir Hugh Vaughan described the castle upon Charles's arrival as 'a cabinet to keep and preserve the eldest jewel of the Royal progeny'. Most reassuringly for the boy, a number of gentlemen and squires also extended promises 'to assist' both king and prince and 'defend' them 'from all malignants and enemies'. A feast including local delicacies helped keep him all the happier, and Charles was lavished with gifts, the more exquisite offerings from the rich complemented by the poorer folk's presentations of farm animals and fish. The prince recognised their value in gesture. Publicly, he'd so far been a child largely seen, not heard, but as the tokens of affection flooded in, 'he could not give particular thanks unto every person'. Therefore, 'in a great assembly of lords, knights, squires, gentlemen, and many common people', he made what's recorded as his first-ever speech, beginning: 'Gentlemen, I have heard formerly of the great minds, the true affections and meanings of the ancient Britanies, but my kind entertainment hath made me confide in your love, which I shall always remember. I give you commendations, praise, and thanks'.[19] Whether the alcoholic Welsh mead metheglin consumed at the banquet helped or hindered is debatable. Like most seventeenth-century children, Charles had imbibed beer from a very delicate age, and he was similarly used to wine. Nevertheless, being privy to Royalist secrets meant inebriation was a risk he needed to guard against diligently.

By now the terms Roundheads and Cavaliers were being bandied about. The former was associated with riotous London apprentices and Puritans who sported a spherical look atop the shoulders by keeping their hair closely cropped in the early 1640s. In addition, legend states that at Strafford's trial Henrietta Maria failed to recognise Pym and asked the identity of 'that *Round-headed* Man', and this may have contributed to establishing the moniker. However, as a synonym of Roundheads, the word rebels was often used by Royalists.[20] Meanwhile, as a nickname for Royalists, the epithet Cavaliers derived from words meaning horsemen in Latin-based languages, with the Italian *cavaliere* the nearest, and was deployed derogatively by Parliamentarians as it painted a picture of marauding Catholic belligerents. Charles I soon proved resilient to this attack. Addressing his soldiers on Sunday, 23 October, he said: 'the valour of the cavaliers hath honoured

Chapter 7

that name ... it signifying no more but a gentleman serving his king on horseback'.[21]

At the time, these fighters were assembled on a Warwickshire field, cocking their pistols for the Battle of Edgehill, the first pitched battle of the First English Civil War, and both Charles and James followed their father as he rode along to inspect his troops. Adrenaline filled the air while temperatures hovered around freezing point. Still speaking of the 'reproachfull signification' behind the term Cavaliers, the king informed his men: 'ye are all designed for the slaughter, if you do not manfully behave yourselves',[22] but slaughter was more likely than expected. The next few hours saw a bloodsoaked melee that would radiate shockwaves nationwide, and the young princes witnessed it at breathtaking close quarters. There they were when Parliament's cannon began firing around 3 pm, there they were when courtiers dropped mortally wounded in the field and there they were when a fierce cavalry retaliation took off. This was led by 22-year-old Prince Rupert, the once 12-year-old soldier.

Not all men present were fighting though. The king's physician-in-ordinary William Harvey was a colossus of medicine who had discovered the basis of blood circulation, and the gory side of battle rather washed over him. Uninterested, he whipped out a book and sat reading. To immerse himself, he had to ignore distractions not only from the flashes and bangs a few yards away but also from two boys exploding with excitement beside him. He had responsibility for the safety of Charles and James, the latter only just turned 9, and the doctor was one of many underestimating the peril. However, when 'a bullet of a great gun grazed on the ground neare him', Harvey led the princes slightly further from range.[23]

The king, on the other hand, decided to get nearer the action to boost morale in the evening, but he drew the line here regarding his sons' safety, wanting Charles and James hurried away. Sir William Howard, a long-standing servant of the king, became responsible for the princes now. He brought with him around fifty soldiers.

But a body of Roundhead cavalry was charging, and Charles had no interest in his own protection. Many years subsequently, another medical man John Hinton would furnish him with memories of this dramatic moment: 'seeing the sudden and quick march of the Enemie towards you, I did with all earnestnesse, most humbly, but at last somewhat rudely, importune your

Highnesse to avoid this present and apparent danger of being killed or taken prisoner, for their horse was by this time come up within half musket shott in a full body, att which your Highnesse was pleased to tell mee, You feared them not, and drawing a pistoll out of one of your holsters, and spanning itt, resolved to charge them'. Just then, an identical urge got into one of Parliament's soldiers. This lone rider was galloping head-on towards Charles. Within minutes, the heir could have been dead. At this, Hinton fired, narrowly avoiding returning shots, and Gentleman Matthews, one of Howard's men, deployed a poleaxe to put paid to the threat entirely.[24]

For bargaining power, the prince's capture was a higher prize than his killing. If Parliament had taken him prisoner, the course ahead could have been quite different. But instead, Charles retired to lodgings at Kineton while darkness fell across a field strewn with hundreds upon hundreds of corpses. And for what? Edgehill was a stalemate.

In the wake of the battle, Charles's survival landed in the hands of Hinton long term as he was made the boy's physician-in-ordinary, and his skills were instantly required. While travelling to Oxford in November, the king and Charles were delayed in Reading when the latter became 'overtaken' by 'a heating of the blood … so violent that he had to take to his bed'. This was thought to be measles, and his father wouldn't leave him.[25] However, once the child was recovering, Oxford became the new base as wartime life took hold.

Nationwide, sieges raged, skirmishes had long been seen and deaths were mounting even among women and children as towns turned into killing grounds. Some people had hoped just one battle would decide everything, but after Edgehill, matters appeared beyond control. No longer so excited, Prince Charles found himself hit hard by the devastating reality. In fact, he was terrified of ascending the throne now. He imagined he could never 'quench the wildfire', and he took the whole situation 'to heart'. As a result, his melancholy 'may prove prejudiciall to his health and our hopes', Duppa warned.[26]

The prince was particularly alarmed by the philosophy of an eye for an eye. On 17 December the Commons had announced that captured Royalists would be sentenced to death if captured Parliamentarians were, and through Duppa, Charles begged the king to allow 'no further prosecution' of the Parliamentarians concerned.[27]

Chapter 7

Alongside James, Charles helped the king conduct a review of the troops in Oxford on 12 January 1643, with 3,000 present, but behind closed doors the 12-year-old was shedding tears frequently. He perhaps underestimated the sway he had over the king, though. Either that or it increased.

Each side in the war was forever trying to snatch the other's strongholds, and Reading fell to Parliament in late April with Cavalier colonel Richard Feilding negotiating terms of surrender. Court-martialled for such treachery, Feilding was promptly forwarded to an executioner, but this was to the chagrin of Rupert. It's remarkably telling that Rupert therefore asked Charles to have a word with the king and more telling still that Feilding was subsequently reprieved, on 13 May.

Young Charles may have genuinely convinced his father that erring on the side of leniency was best here, but the monarch knew the boy needed to be involved in regal decision-making, not fear it, especially not now. Aged 11 in 1578, King James had begun ruling without regents. In 1643, the Prince of Wales was turning 13. And his father's lifeguard troops were no guarantee of anything.

Chapter 8

When the future Charles II reached 13, he was thirty-six months past confessing his fears of being left 'never a one' kingdom. Back then, he had not only blamed his father for this risk but also been embittered by lack of attention from him. On his first teenage birthday, however, Charles was nearly halfway through a three-year spell in which he rarely left the king's side, and these three years helped the prince understand the king.

By mid-1643, Charles I had declared his belief that his adversaries wanted heresy and schism. He'd been petitioned to make peace with Parliament, by Scots he thought saw such peace as a way to exterminate episcopacy in England. And he'd learned his wife's chapel had been stormed in an anti-Catholic display of violence reflecting intentions to attack his wife.[1] Giving powers to seekers of power jeopardised everything he felt duty-bound to preserve, much of it dear to his heart, and matters weren't as simple as his eldest son had imagined.

While London was under Parliamentarian control, news poured daily into the royal home of Oxford, sometimes received by monarch and heir together. Now the adolescent had chance to observe his father's thought processes. He maybe still doubted the wisdom of the rigid attitude, but he recognised reasons behind it, and his loving bond with his father fused, never to break.[2]

Adolescence challenged this bond though. At St Mary's church one day in Oxford, Charles, Prince of Wales was seated in the vicinity of some women, and he found them rather more interesting than the service. In fact, he seems to have been flirting with them. During the sermon, he let out a laugh. Appalled, his father exercised discipline there and then, raising his cane and striking the child on the head with it. The king 'was always very severe in the education' of his son. In 1678 the Bishop of Exeter believed that if Charles I had lived to impose parental strictness for longer, 'the debaucherys of the nation' would not have rampaged under Charles II.³

Oxford was nevertheless an eye-opener in the 1640s. As the Royalist capital, it teemed with soldiers whose allegiance rested with the king, but they didn't exactly follow his example. Often drunk, they belted out bawdy Cavalier songs, and swearing was so colourful that fines of a shilling were coming to suppress it in 1644.⁴ Meanwhile rules against duelling were transgressed and loutish scraps broke out at the drop of a hat. With war underway, a sense of living for the moment prevailed. As thoughts turned to fulfilling urges, trysts were conducted by the river, while some lovers used the comparative privacy of college gardens,⁵ perhaps even those where the king and his two eldest sons took afternoon strolls with their dogs.

Either way, the unprincipled behaviour could not escape the notice of teenaged Charles. In Oxford, he travelled the streets, at his risk, and his father rode around surveying defences every few days. It seems miraculous that an assassin's gun never ended the Caroline age. However, after a destructive visit from Parliamentarians in 1642, Oxford was overwhelmingly Royalist, and citizens had been employed to fortify the town with palisades, ramparts, ditches, gates and drawbridges,⁶ while troops marched and drilled and the beat of regimental drums reverberated. In fact, sights, sounds and smells all formed memories of the war in Oxford for Charles, partly due to influx. From around the country, Royalists flocked. Even the upper echelons squeezed into hovels such as 'a baker's house in an obscure street'. It was a sanitation catastrophe. People knew this, yet 'most bore it with a martyr-like cheerfulness' as disease snatched away their lives.⁷

Indeed, many of the conflict's fatalities were indirect, and knock-on effects took their toll on the next generation, Charles II's future subjects. Trauma in pregnancy meant a lifetime of deformity in some cases. Meanwhile education fell low down the list of priorities with students abandoning university to join the ranks of their chosen side. Numerous young men would 'never be brought to their books again'.⁸

Among those who quit courses were George and Francis Villiers – now runaways from Trinity College, Cambridge. Bursting onto the scene in Oxford, they had thrown themselves into military training under Rupert and similarly gallant commander Charles Gerard, then witnessed action in April 1643 at Lichfield's Cathedral Close, but the teens' escapade was terminated after this. Although Gerard told their mother 'the more danger the more honour', she struggled to accept her sons' peril[9] and, like many seventeenth-century lads of their calibre, they were sent travelling in Europe to continue their education, leaving Prince Charles bereft of his semi-adoptive brothers' companionship again.

While his own lessons suffered despite tutors' efforts, Charles was stuck around Oxford University as the king commandeered buildings belonging to this ancient institution. New College housed vast stocks of gunpowder, an arsenal was made out of All Souls College, New Inn Hall had become the site of a royal mint in December 1642 and the Privy Council convened at Oriel College, but Oxford University also hosted the royal court.

The king resided at Christ Church, where cattle were kept in its quadrangle[10] while princes Charles and James and countless courtiers made abodes of other colleges, and lodgings were also assigned to Cavalier officers. Despite the difficulty of maintaining a majestic image here, Christmas was celebrated in style, the king's Maundy Thursday washing of the poor's feet took place in Christ Church's Tudor hall and everyday magnificence was to continue along the way, with the royals suitably attired and attended. On 21 October 1643, the monthly expenses of Charles and James were estimated as £653 7s, households and stables included.[11] Meanwhile their father encouraged them to keep active with tennis.

One reason Charles grew so close to his father while in Oxford was the fact that few siblings were around to share the patriarch. Mary remained in the Netherlands, and to the king's distress the youngest two surviving children were prisoners under Parliament's care at St James's. For the first eight months in Oxford, this reduced the immediate family around Prince Charles to just James and their father. But that changed; when on 13 July 1643 the three of them returned to Edgehill, memories of whizzing cannonballs and spurting blood were offset by a far friendlier rendezvous, reuniting the queen with her loved ones after seventeen months apart. She instantly saw how her sons had grown, Charles barely looking a minor anymore unless standing beside six-foot-four Rupert, and Henrietta Maria was back to take her maternal place as cheering townsfolk and pealing church bells greeted the royals into Oxford.[12]

The queen had actually been back in England since February. However, working to add to the aid and munitions acquired from her trip to the Continent, she'd resided for a while in York to muster soldiery, and her natural determination was taking on a militant slant. Essentially at the head of an army, she styled herself 'generalissima'[13] and opined on tactics, usually favouring action over inaction. Even in her absence the king received a barrage of her views, the couple corresponding frequently and using cipher for confidentiality – common practice in the war. 'That letter … concerning an accommodation [agreement],' Henrietta Maria tells her husband, 'is so unsupportable, that I have burnt it with joy'. She nonetheless apologised to him often, once with 'I beg your pardon if I have said anything in my letters a little passionate; it is the affection I have for you, which makes me do it'.[14] The consort may sometimes have urged the king not to concede, but she wasn't alone, especially as a few early successes in combat led Cavaliers to view victory as tangible.

Their capture of England's second city Bristol contributed to these hopes at the end of July 1643, and Gloucester lay immediately in Royalist sights. From 10 August, Charles and James lodged with their father at Matson House, a property inherited by a William Selwyn whose new daughter-in-law Margaret seemingly left in disgust as the king turned it into a royal headquarters for the Siege of Gloucester. The house was situated two to three miles from the target city, rendering the princes too far from the encounter for their liking. More than forty years later, James recalled this time: 'My brother and I were generally shut up in a Chamber on the second Floor at Matson, during the day; where you will find that we have left the marks of our confinement, inscribed with our knives, on the ledges of all the windows.'[15] Their handiwork remains there to this day, deep notches left as they hacked chunks of windowsill away in boredom and agitation nearly 400 years ago. But they missed no glory. In wet and windy conditions[16] on 5 September the boys and their father rode forlorn from Matson, following defeat.

Despite this, their faces weren't the most forlorn. After the outbreak of war, 'sadness and dejection of spirit stole upon' the king's once-vivacious secretary of state Lucius Cary, Viscount Falkland, whereupon he turned 'pale'. Falkland had hitherto dressed exceptionally well. Come mid-1643, he neglected his appearance. And his 'unreserved and affable' demeanour vanished, leaving him 'sharp', 'severe', uncommunicative and often sitting in a 'deep silence' he punctuated with sighs and repeated mumbles of the word peace. Falkland confessed the war lost him sleep, and he couldn't bear the 'desolation'.[17] Then, on the morning of the First Battle of Newbury, he appeared positive and called for a clean shirt. This, however, was so decent linen could be found upon his corpse. During the battle, the 33-year-old rode headfirst into enemy gunfire that killed him on the spot. Hyde believed Falkland had 'died as much of the time as of the bullet'.[18]

It's possible that Charles II, when insisting on fighting alongside his Spanish allies in 1657, thought about going the same way as Falkland. Duppa's concerns regarding the effect melancholy had on Charles were not overreactions. However, for someone of Charles's disposition, humour could help. It was even a means of attack.

Published weekly in Oxford from January 1643, Royalist newssheet *Mercurius Aulicus* was packed with often distasteful but amusing satire, and it gloried in its scathing comments. A lampoon once featured a Cavalier claiming the quarto killed more Roundheads over a week than battle killed over several months.[19] Since August, Parliament had started retaliating through 'unhallowed passages' in the new *Mercurius Britanicus*,[20] but this weapon was never sharpened to quite the same effect, even with propagandist Marchamont Nedham assuming editorial responsibility the following year.[21] His *Aulicus* counterpart meanwhile was notable wit John Berkenhead, who as a Laudian put his heart into ridiculing Parliament. Explaining how figures of Cavalier losses had been exaggerated for Roundhead morale in 1643, *Aulicus* printed: 'it is noticed that Sir Jacob Astley and some other chiefe commanders were lately slaine at Gloucester; (were they slain with a musket or a cannon bullet? *Sir Jacob* himself desires to know.)'.[22] Charles, unlike the father and brother around him, would soon be known for his sense of humour, and Berkenhead was clearly shaping it, his piquant turns of phrase welcomed at court.

Really though, it was all about who would have the last laugh. On 25 September 1643, Parliament made themselves more likely candidates; via a Presbyterian dream agreement called the Solemn League and Covenant, the Roundheads joined forces with the Covenanters.

Westminster was nevertheless to suffer a heavy loss, with serious revelations coming: 'Pym is crawling to his grave as fast as he can'.[23] Falling victim to cancer according to postmortem by Mayerne,[24] Parliament's leading light was extinguished on 8 December, and Oxford disgracefully erupted into celebration of feasting and bonfires.[25]

Cambridge meanwhile bore the mark of Cromwell, one of its two MPs. Cromwell had provided funds to arm Roundhead units he wanted populated by volunteer townsmen. Then he'd thwarted the king's attempt to have Cambridge University send plate for the Royalist cause. The Commons indemnified him while Charles I lost out on what was valued at approximately

£20,000.[26] In Parliament's army too, Cromwell was moving up the ranks, and a man with both political and military competence was a threat indeed.

Yet peace petitions were doing the rounds, and when the king had Royalist MPs and peers form the Oxford Parliament, it first assembled in January 1644 with the high priority of attempting reconciliation via a letter to the Earl of Essex. The Prince of Wales was one of 163 adding their names to the document then hastily dispatched, but Essex's 'cold and supercilious reply' stated an inability to present the letter officially as it was not addressed to Parliament, and the earl enclosed 'two declarations of immitigable hostility on the Scotch Parliament side, until they should obtain all their demands'.[27] The war would be a long haul still.

At court meanwhile, personal conflicts raged through emerging envies and factions, and Prince Charles watched on, weighing up the individuals concerned and observing his mother interpose to support her favourites. While a master of the revels contributed to ongoing efforts to maintain an upbeat atmosphere,[28] Henrietta Maria described herself as the only miserable person there in February 1644. She attributed her misery to the fact she was yet again pregnant.[29] By 17 April, the safety of Oxford hung in question, and she wisely left, unaware she would never see her husband again. Her eldest son joined the party accompanying her up to Abingdon before the queen went on her way to give birth in Exeter,[30] then return to France.

Meanwhile Charles had a new governor to acquaint himself with. In fact, he was having to reacquaint himself with the presence of a governor. Army command in the west meant hundreds of miles had often stood between the Marquis of Hertford and the court, but the king would no longer 'have him absent from his [the king's] person'.[31] Hertford was now Charles I's groom of the stool, removed from the prince's governorship. Ears had pricked up, with Thomas Byron's eldest brother John, made Baron Byron in October 1643, asking Rupert to secure the governorship for him,[32] and sights had initially been set on the Earl of Leicester.[33] In the end, however, the role lay with Thomas Howard, Earl of Berkshire, a father of thirteen children, but he seemed no natural governor. To Hyde, the unsuitability was obvious: 'of any who bore the name of a gentleman, [Berkshire was] the most unfit for that province, or any other that required any proportion of wisdom and understanding'. Nevertheless, Jermyn explained that 'it was of no moment who had the name and style of governor, since the King and Queen meant to be' the boy's governors in practice.[34]

Now the queen was overseas again, she could do little for her son beyond ordering him a suit of armour,[35] so the king 'had no resolution more fixed in him, than that the Prince should never be absent from him ... resolving to form his manners by his own model'.[36] Apparently Parliament felt this modelling appropriate, when they wanted to. That spring they refused to approve 13-year-old Charles as Duke of Cornwall, 'citing the example of the king himself, who never took that investiture'.[37] The child would nonetheless benefit greatly from this title when among the Cornish in times to come.

Largely around his father meanwhile, he could be found within pistol range[38] on 29 June at the Battle of Cropredy Bridge on the river Cherwell, where Cavaliers psychologically battered the Roundheads under William Waller. The result for Waller was multiple desertions. However, at the monstrous Battle of Marston Moor just three days later, the thousands of Royalist cadavers left in the field put northern England into Parliamentarian possession.

As peace-making became urgent for Royalists in particular now, some were looking to the Prince of Wales as a route towards it. That summer, he journeyed round the country. Subjects were enchanted by his manners and composure, and reception at Dartmoor proved jubilant when his father introduced him as ruler-to-be.[39] Charles I's grandmother Mary, Queen of Scots had abdicated, and ideas were turning to having Charles II on the throne early. Henry Wilmot, the king's lieutenant general of horse, attempted to carry this through, but in doing so he sought negotiation with the Earl of Essex. This amounted to arguable high treason. Wilmot was arrested on 8 August.

The plan was doomed to fail anyway. King Charles believed abdication veered from God's design, and Prince Charles harboured no intention of ruling in his father's lifetime, which he hoped would last decades yet. The boy nevertheless thought he could make a better job of ruling than his father did, actually perhaps believing Charles I too lenient sometimes. One story alludes to this: On the Oxford streets once, adolescent Charles observed a great hullabaloo and asked what was happening. Learning the people were taking 'an old rebele' to the king, he imagined a pardon would then be granted, and he wanted to intervene. 'Carry him rather to the gallows and hang him up', the prince responded, hoping to effect a fait accompli.[40] Or is this apocryphal? It contrasts sharply with his usual stance.

Aged 13, he secured a pardon for a prisoner and sped to the execution in person. The pardon was very last-minute, but there wasn't far to travel; it should have succeeded. A gibbet at Carfax in the middle of Oxford enabled public hanging of deserters and spies. However, Oxford's governor Arthur Aston delighted in hanging lesser offenders too, and he heard Charles was coming to the rescue. At this, Aston 'with his foot turned the ladder himself'. By the time the pardon arrived, the prisoner 'was so far gone that he could not be recovered'.[41]

Even if deeply dismayed by this, the prince felt recovering the Royalist cause mattered most though. Military engagements could still go either way, as he saw for himself at the indecisive Second Battle of Newbury on 27 October 1644, but Charles and his father only narrowly avoided capture here[42] and Parliament were set on course to form a more formidable 'new modelled' army.

The Prince of Wales wanted it known he was ready to fight them. From William Dobson's Oxford art studio came a colourful portrait of the heir standing bold and authoritative aged 14. With cynicism in his eyes, his childlike face has gone, his nose is taking shape and his fingers are long. Around this time, his former governor Newcastle wrote telling him: 'we have lived to see you a man',[43] and in Dobson's painting Charles sports cuirassier armour. This was made for his father in 1616, but the prince who now wore it wore it with purpose, posing with a commander's baton in one hand and a sword an integral part of the outfit.

On 6 November, not yet 14½, Charles became commander of all Royalist troops. Again, however, it fell to others to direct in the field, the king decreeing his son must not be 'engaging himself in any martial action'.[44] The boy wasn't to feel too constrained though. These instructions would coincide with his fledging.

Chapter 9

As 1645 dawned, a headsman was called upon again. With religion still fanning the flames of fury, the Church of England received a double blow on 4 January when Parliament banned the Book of Common Prayer and passed an attainder for the execution of the Archbishop of Canterbury, old William Laud. Because royal assent was no longer required in Westminster eyes, the non-consenting king felt blameless after the axe did its work on Tower Hill six days later,[1] and in August 1646 he'd write to Charles, emphasising how important it was 'never to abandon the protection of your friends'.[2] Yet in the early 1640s Charles I had warmed to Laud's bitter rival John Williams, making him Archbishop of York in 1642 and doing little to save the Archbishop of Canterbury throughout a four-year imprisonment.

Admittedly the sovereign was limited in his means of helping by 1645, and with his court just a shadow of its former lavish self, cash had become an obvious problem. An unsigned warrant dated 19 January was to permit payment of £700 for new robes for the Prince of Wales, but two major plans for the child lurked in the pipeline, and one was hoped to answer the Stuart family's financial prayers.

While nothing came of the idea of wedding Charles to Holland's Louise Henriëtte, Portugal had a potential bride of interest, whose Catholicism was not to get in the way. After a recent bereavement, 9-year-old infanta Joana was the eldest living daughter of the House of Braganza's first king, João IV, and by 20 January 1645 this Portuguese monarch had given orders for representative Don Antonio de Sousa to travel to Oxford to discuss the joining of Joana and Charles in holy matrimony. Incredibly, the don was not seen to recoil when he heard £1,000,000 mentioned as the minimum dowry wanted.[3] But what could

Chapter 9

the Stuarts offer the Braganzas in return? The English monarchy's prospects weren't exactly good.

At Marston Moor, the Cavaliers had lost the biggest battle ever fought in England. Added to the deaths, 1,500 Royalists had been taken prisoner there,[4] and Charles I now envisaged himself incarcerated following a clash to come. He nevertheless believed Parliament 'would not dare to do him harm' while the king-to-be 'was at liberty'. He also believed finding father and son together 'would be ruin to them both'.[5] The king therefore now made a U-turn in paternal thinking. This took 14-year-old Charles from his father's constant presence to sudden, total separation. And simultaneously to work.

His ex-governor Newcastle, a marquis since 1643, had commanded with Rupert at Marston Moor and couldn't bear the shame of the defeat. Having slipped off to the Continent, he wrote from Hamburg to Charles, with congratulations on a new appointment early 1645. Before closing, the marquis added: 'now it is your turn to take care of me'.[6] As just one of thousands of Cavaliers, Newcastle couldn't single himself out though, and the Prince of Wales was assuming a role that could tip the balance either way for a conclusion to the conflict. With a chance to capitalise on Royalist recruiting in South Wales, focus had turned to southwest England, giving birth to a hopeful new body known as the king's Western Association. Young Charles was placed right at its helm, with the title captain general, and so he was bound for Bristol to head not only his own little court but also a council handling military operations.

At the mooting of such a proposition in 1644, the prince had been uncooperative,[7] but now, in 1645, he embraced it, ready to put some of his training into practice. Sir Ralph, Baron Hopton served as lieutenant general of the king's western army and was posted to Bristol to 'provide a house for his highness, and to put that city into as good a posture of security … as was necessary',[8] while £100 per week and a supply of lifeguards were promised from Somerset commissioners. Much peace of mind rested on this agreement. The king's poverty meant the guards accompanying Charles would consist of just one infantry regiment and one cavalry regiment, both of which the militarily incompetent Arthur, Baron Capell was to command and raise 'upon his own credit'.[9] But this still seemed safer than keeping monarch and heir as one. When they parted in early March, a storm set in to pelt rain down on the boy as he rode away. As big a drenching from tears did not appear appropriate, particularly as the pair imagined reuniting before long. In reality though, this was farewell forever.

The West Country had been reassuringly Royalist, but when Charles journeyed towards it, Waller was on the offensive with Cromwell serving under him. In the name of the king, defences across the region were therefore being strengthened, and when the prince passed through Devizes, its castle was undergoing work to make it Wiltshire's strongest fortress. Stopping in Bath for a few days, Charles conscientiously fired off numerous letters. Some requested reports from his officers, while others were addressed to county commissioners to arrange face-to-face consultation and let them know he was approaching Bristol, imagining his soldiers and cash waiting. However, he arrived finding 'not one man or horse provided' and 'not one penny ready, nor like to be, so that he was forced to borrow from the lord Hopton's own private store to buy bread'. It turned out that the individuals who had made the agreement kept it to themselves, rendering other commissioners unaware and unable to fulfil,[10] and this applied to more than Charles's personal needs. Vulnerability descended.

Of the four counties under the Western Association, Cornwall was relatively untouched by the enemy so far, while Somerset, Devon and Dorset constituted shaky ground. Because Parliament had already taken Somerset's Taunton, the quest to reclaim it meant a siege was planned, but action got delayed as Royalist general Sir Richard Grenville refused to assist. This was indicative of the status quo. Joint command presided over the king's western forces – Sir John Berkeley and George, Baron Goring both occupied top spots alongside Grenville, and the hierarchical deficit bred a culture of unrelenting squabbles. Landed on Charles were expectations to step in with authority, but challenges prevailed. Berkeley and Grenville were fiery-tempered. In Berkeley's case, this was 'without any cause' if Pepys's musings of 1664 apply.[11] Grenville, meanwhile, was prone to establishing vendettas. After losing legal disputes, he'd had his wife's solicitor hanged under false pretences, and his name was disgracefully linked to a massacre of prisoners of war following the storming of Saltash in January 1643. However, he was a Cornishman who repeatedly proved dedicated to fair treatment of his men, particularly regarding pay. This earned him unbeatable popularity with many local soldiers despite his disciplinarian attitude.[12]

Strictness made Grenville stand out. According to Hyde, several troops in the area were 'without any discipline', leaving citizens 'exposed to rapine and violence',[13] and Charles was accountable. The prince therefore needed to spur officers into curbing the disorderliness. From this, he saw the value of character assessment, though he'd already done some of the assessing required. One of the slacker commanders was Goring, who had slipped into the place of Wilmot as lieutenant general of horse after Wilmot's arrest. Admired for his wittiness, Goring had been a popular courtier in the 1630s, aimlessly frittering his fortune away before pursuing a military career in Europe, but his penchant for indulgence was getting worse. As well as fornicating and gambling profusely, he drank to excess and did not discourage his soldiers from doing likewise. Acquiring the nickname Goring's Crew, they reputedly wreaked havoc, and complaints flooded in.

Young Charles's approach to grumbling commissioners was to try to 'give them all encouragement' by assuring them he was mindful of the problems and 'would redress them as soon as they should discern it to be in his power', a courteous reminder that the commissioners still owed money and men. He also invited these commissioners to suggest ways to address their remonstrances concerning the building of fortifications.[14] They found him far more amenable than they found one another. Like with the commanders, animosity was rife among the counties' gentlemen, and they were lobbing blame around for the myriad shortcomings and broken promises. They hoped the wonderfully cordial Prince of Wales would referee in their favour. 'Here will be no great good done,' Rupert's confidant Arthur Trevor remarked, 'the enemy being so powerful and the Gentlemen of the country so divided, that it is of equal difficulty to vanquish the one, as to compose the other'.[15] Rupert had arrived in Bristol on 11 April, and he heightened the tensions too, partly due to his offhand manners. Nevertheless, with envy more of a problem, his cousin Charles unwittingly made the dynamics worse when he consulted this Palatine prince instead of another officer.[16]

Of course, Charles also had a council, though even this added to the labyrinth of contretemps. Along with Hopton and Capell, members included elderly but brilliant military strategist Patrick Ruthven, Earl of Brentford, but two of the key performers were Hyde – both a knight and Chancellor of the Exchequer since 1643 – and baron John Colepeper, who had recently fallen out with Hyde. To the chancellor's further displeasure, Charles's governor Berkshire was also part of the outfit, and others weren't too happy about this either. Berkshire was one of the Howard family that Grenville had married into and feuded with fiercely.¹⁷ Meanwhile Charles's secretary was a competitive individual named Robert Long whose desire to fill his own purse tended to lose him friends.

So it was that Charles's induction into leadership formed a lesson in the volatility of human nature, and the child was a keen learner at this point, sitting 'frequently, if not constantly, in council, to mark and consider the state of affairs, and to accustom himself to a habit of speaking and judging upon what was said'.¹⁸ To call his Western Association rank honorary, as some do, appears misleading; teenaged Charles was actively contributing to the decision-making conducted in his name.

He'd nonetheless prove easily distracted. Adding to the woes, plague was breaking out in Bristol, so on 23 April, Charles travelled to Somerset's Bridgwater. Here he met with sixteen commissioners, one being a 21-year-old Hugh Wyndham whose father Edmund was governor of the town, but Hugh's mother Christabella was on the scene too, harbouring hopes of seeing her family climb. The prince, once reliant on Christabella for his everyday needs, now appeared to be the power that could provide for her instead. She intended to take advantage of their reunion.

This was a lady who had complained when one of her many generous gifts from the king¹⁹ had not reached her in full and a lady who would be firing a gun at the leader of Parliament's new army in July before sending a trumpeter to taunt the commander for failing to reciprocate.²⁰ Hyde believed she was 'of great rudeness' with nothing womanly about her beyond her body.²¹ This, however, seemed sufficient for Charles, whose new role starved him of female company. And his ex-nurse well knew that bits of wood could no longer content him in his bed.

Christabella is sometimes said to have taken Charles's virginity during this stay in Bridgwater, but at least two factors exist that can question the statement. For a start, there's no proof he still had his virginity. His behaviour at St Mary's church suggests he had become flirtatious by the age of 14, and his governors in Oxford had little chance to interpose; Hertford was so often away and Berkshire was so often inattentive. In 1668 a French-speaker by the name Jacques de la Cloche purported to be a son of Charles and was recorded as a 24-year-old,²² putting his conception at a date when Charles was 13 or even 12 (though La Cloche probably wasn't Charles's son really, as shall be seen).

Chapter 9

However, Charles's upbringing was steeped in Christian teachings, and because his independent thinking was still developing in his early teens, the prince is likely to have been hesitant in his initial amours. While this seems to render him relatively innocent when he arrived in Bridgwater, it also implies he remained like that when there, if inexperienced, with the second factor of query naturally being whether he and Christabella actually did the deed together. Christabella had always been a maternal figure to him, in fact one who shared several of Henrietta Maria's character traits. Yet she wasn't his mother. She was a friend whom Charles felt comfortable around, and this was long before sex with 14-year-olds was illegal. So carnal activity may have been involved. However, the now easily aroused Charles had a virtually lifelong affection for Christabella. To remain in his good books, she probably saw no need to offer herself wholly.

Nevertheless, there in Bridgwater, this beauty still in her thirties left little doubt about her familiarity with the boy. She'd sometimes 'run the length of the room and kiss him',[23] deliberately drawing the attention of as many as possible, so Charles was hardly given inhibitions regarding intimacy. Nor did he see a married woman as out of bounds. The prim-and-proper Hyde, on the other hand, reacted with disgust and was enraged to see the adolescent diverted from business.

Twenty years later, reiterated talk of Christabella would lead Pepys to comment that she'd conducted herself like 'a minister of state' and 'governed' by influence.[24] Indeed her influence over Charles usually appeared profound, but in 1645 she learned the prince was forbidden from making decisions without his council. Faction in the council, however, seemed likely to weaken the council's voice. While channelling her own voice into Charles's ear, Christabella now 'laboured to raise jealousies and dislike' among the prince's advisers. Perhaps most notably, she told Berkshire his colleagues hated him, and from then, the earl became more unaccepting of the criticism heaped on him. He further neglected Charles too. Within days, plague seemed better than Christabella as far as the council could see. Back to Bristol Charles was dragged on 30 April.[25]

Interestingly, when his eldest acknowledged son married on 20 April 1663, the Merry Monarch commented that, aged 12 and 14 respectively, both bride *and* groom were too young to spend the night together. Whatever Charles got up to in Bridgwater, he possibly regretted when older and wiser.[26]

How much of it was reported to his own father is unclear, but when the king wrote to Henrietta Maria on 14 May 1645, the letter as later printed made no reference to anything of that ilk. It did nonetheless outline another matter he termed 'a complaint' about Charles, one that indicated the boy didn't much care for instructions on whose company he could and could not keep. For the post of Gentleman of the Bedchamber, he wanted Grenville's teenaged nephew Sir John Grenville and hadn't waited for the king's consent to this appointment before making it publicly known. Refusal was therefore tricky. 'I desire thee first to chide my Sonne', the monarch told his wife and would await her advice on whether to approve John Grenville.[27]

Of more consequence than personal servants, however, were the choices for military roles, and King Charles wasn't so hesitant to reverse decisions on this score, elevating Goring when the council (so officially the prince) had given top command to Richard Grenville instead.

By no means was Goring without worth, deemed 'the most dexterous, in any sudden Emergency',[28] but while this borderline alcoholic was now directing a significant part of the Royalist effort with barely a thought for discipline, the Roundheads had introduced their rigorously regimented superior force. In the process, they did away with leadership by Essex and allowed the new leader, Sir Thomas Fairfax, to use his military expertise to choose officers himself. Known to history as the New Model Army, this stronger horde of fighters sported bright uniforms earning them the nickname Redcoats, and on 14 June they frighteningly outnumbered the Cavaliers at the Battle of Naseby amid a fight for nearby Leicester. Results were decisive. However, the casualty ratio was just one indication of this Royalist defeat. Here, a coach belonging to the king fell into enemy hands, and inside it lay 200 or so letters.[29] Some of these were clandestine communications with foreign powers, while others proved to be correspondence between King Charles and his queen. The cipher efforts would now be put to the test.

Like so often with battles though, the truth from Naseby took time to reach people, including Prince Charles. The pestilence had driven him west again. Via Bridgwater, he'd headed for Barnstaple in Devon, arriving to 'the noise and triumphs which the rebels made in those parts for their victory, without any particular information ... which left some hope that it might not be true'.[30]

As things stood, Charles struggled to ascertain what was happening right under his nose in Barnstaple. Around him lingered a young man known as Wheeler. It seems nobody much knew him, but the prince welcomed him. However, the council's attention was drawn to Wheeler when Duppa came in

Chapter 9

a state of alarm. Hugh Wyndham had reported this youthful but bold intruder for what Hyde deemed unmentionable 'beastliness', as homosexuality was sometimes labelled back then, and Duppa feared Wheeler's intentions. Described as someone of 'filthy' behaviour, Wheeler promptly became the subject of lengthy debate, in which Charles was included, and although Wheeler was then ordered to leave the town, the prince ruminated further and wanted him locked up. Before this could occur, however, Hugh Wyndham encountered Wheeler on the streets of Barnstaple, where the latter vengefully accused him of intending to 'join with the Prince against the King, and ... cut the King's throat'. When this was investigated by the lords advising 15-year-old Charles, all but Berkshire felt it necessary to act cautiously and treat Hugh Wyndham with suspicion.[31]

Needless to say, though, Charles I was at no risk of regicide by his own son's hand. In fact, he feared the youngster would make unacceptable sacrifices to protect him, sacrifices the king believed would betray God through compromise of divine rights. In the wake of Naseby, he thus sent the child a letter that made for disturbing reading, telling Charles to let him die in preference to submitting to any conditions 'derogatory to regal authority'. The sovereign then added: 'the saving of my life by complying with them [the rebels] would make me end my days with torture and disquiet of mind, not giving you my blessing. But your constancy will make me die cheerfully, praising God for giving me so gallant a son'.

By the king's further insistence, Charles secreted this document away. Until he had 'cause to use it', not even his counsellors were allowed to see it,[32] and so in his mind alone he was to turn these words over. It was an internal learning process. As he faced the prospect of losing his father to preserve regal authority, the prince recognised more inescapability brought by the beliefs held. In worry and sympathy, therefore, grew greater love.

Meanwhile the enemy was keen to expose Stuart family affection as a very negative phenomenon. Quick to act upon the Naseby acquisition of the king's letters, Parliament had decoded them and published the most damaging content, complete with annotation giving their own interpretations. Entitled *The Kings Cabinet Opened*, this work released pages and pages of effusion between the sovereign and consort, interspersed with state secrets. The king's seeking of his wife's opinion regarding the choice of gentleman of the bedchamber for Prince Charles had not been missed, adding to the conclusion that 'nothing great or small is transacted without her privity & consent'. And when permission came from the king officially, it seemed to prove the fears that had abounded for years. 'I give thee power to promise in my name ... that I will take away all the penall laws against the Roman Catholicks in England', Charles I had told his wife,[33] furnishing her with more means to acquire support from Catholic nations. Also printed here was hard evidence that the king intended to ally with the Irish Catholic Confederation. Public reaction was incendiary.

It's perhaps unsurprising that Joana never became Princess of Wales.[34] Prematurely passing away in 1653, she was denied the chance of reopened negotiations in better times, although she left behind her a sister, Catherine of Braganza.

Standing in the way of those better times, however, was the New Model Army, and by July 1645 it had already done the main work needed to win Parliament the war. While the bloodbaths continued, the post-Naseby period would see a downward spiral the king simply couldn't, or wouldn't, reverse.

Chapter 10

Unfortunately for the Western Association's adolescent captain general, the summer of 1645 saw the New Model Army concentrate great effort on southwest England, putting everything under his jurisdiction in jeopardy. And worse. On 10 July, Cavalier inferiority at the Battle of Langport in Somerset led Goring to torch the town in a desperate attempt to hold the opponents back while his troops fled. This, however, was no barrier to the Ironsides, as Cromwell's cavalrymen were known, and they promptly gave chase through the flames, killing and imprisoning several of the defeated, despite strength in Royalist numbers at the battle's commencement. Conversely in Bridgwater within the fortnight, Parliament held an advantage of eight men to one, although before fire licked through the streets there too, Christabella refused to acknowledge the power of Roundhead forces. In symbolic defiance, she reputedly bared a nipple and later declared that the breast Prince Charles had sucked would never be at Parliament's mercy.[1] Before long though, she became one of 800 or so running for their lives as Fairfax gave women and children a chance to leave ahead of the devastation, Bridgwater falling to him on 23 July.

With it went an immense Cavalier arsenal, but a wider strategic Roundhead aim was also met here. Because Bridgwater stood near the mouth of the River Parret, with Langport upstream, its capture completed a row of Parliamentarian strongholds from the port of Lyme Regis on the south coast to the Bristol Channel opposite. Royalists would struggle to cross this line, and Charles was now cut off on a peninsula, unable to forget the Royal Navy had become Parliament's in 1642.

Gobbling up local dishes like cherry pie and cream, he tried to make the best of his time in the region, but it was of course no holiday. Although travelling from town to town gave him opportunity to absorb the rural vistas, his moves were dictated by duties and threats to his safety, and uncharacteristic bouts of anger seemed to indicate his nerves were fraying.

For a start, he was losing patience with his bickering officers, necessary evils though they were, with Grenville perhaps both the evilest and most necessary. When a nasty wound in the groin earlier in the year had temporarily laid Grenville up, many of his men were lost to the cause, refusing to serve under a substitute, with discipline going out the window.

However, now a few months after his return, Grenville had been denied sufficient manpower for success when assigned to blockade Lyme Regis. In a fury at serving as subordinate to Goring, he promptly resigned without notice and soon found himself summoned before Prince Charles in Cornwall's Liskeard. There, on 25 July, the 15-year-old unleashed on Grenville a pitiless reprimanding in public,[2] and this thorn in Charles's side was ordered to make himself useful by seeking out deserters.[3]

The Cavaliers couldn't afford to see their numbers decline. But in the face of the New Model, the urge to abscond had greater magnetism, and turncoats were a constant worry. Royalist intelligence wasn't up to scratch either. On the final day of July, dawn broke to an unexpected attack by Parliament's Baptist radical Colonel John Okey, losing Charles the city of Bath.

From Wales on 5 August, the king wrote to his eldest: 'It is very fit for me now to prepare for the worst', and the letter went on to communicate a wish for the boy to go and live under his mother's care at the French court 'whensoever' capture looked probable. As Charles I's ambassador in France, Goring's father the Earl of Norwich was alarmed to hear this news, however, perceiving such a move would bring 'certain ruin to the Prince'. In discussion with His Royal Highness, advisers proposed Scotland and Ireland as alternatives if the time came to run. Although realising both were risky just then, they hoped for victory and peace, and young Charles soon sent chancellor Hyde to Falmouth, sneakily having him pretend the trip pertained to customs business and had nothing to do with a frigate secretly reserved to carry the prince away.[4] The question of its destination would see debate rage for six months in council meetings, with the king soon dispatching a stream of missives containing his thoughts and instructions.

Colepeper was responsible for the cipher in which many of the letters for the Prince of Wales arrived, deciphering them for him and then filing them, but most were also shared with Hopton, Capell and Hyde. The king's letter to Charles after Naseby was rare as a private communication. Berkshire was often left in the dark though. Few counsellors trusted him to keep secrets.

Chapter 10

Continued despair over Berkshire as Charles's governor gave reason for Charles to govern himself, particularly as one of the prime purposes for sending the prince away with his elephantine responsibilities was 'to unboy him'.[5] Hyde, however, regarded neither Berkshire nor Charles as ideal in a governing capacity. This was how Hyde adopted a semi-parental role, keen to steer Charles from 'folly and petulancy'[6] and keeping close tabs on him, but a real irony existed here. The chancellor never even wanted to find himself with Charles in the west. Distance from the sovereign diminished influence, and Hyde dreaded to think of the regal decisions made in his absence.[7] By no means was he at odds with the king's overall views. In fact, he paralleled Charles I to a significant degree. Both the king and Hyde were stuffy, principled and driven by duty, and both were committed to Anglicanism in Stuart monarchy. But now Hyde sat on the prince's council, he was also committed to teaching the prince how to be a good Stuart ruler.[8] In Hyde's opinion, the heir had previously been 'very little conversant with business' but soon 'with great ingenuity applied himself' to the lead role in council meetings.[9] Nevertheless, Charles would later complain of Hyde snubbing him 'whenever he ventured to speak at the council-table'.[10] According to the Earl of Norwich, Hyde had a tendency for 'ouervallewing himselfe and vndervallewing others'.[11] And Charles was only 15. In discussion and decision-making, the 36-year-old chancellor had reason to undervalue him compared with older voices. Consequently, Hyde developed disrespectful habits towards his teenaged master, but the real problem was the fact they were there to stay.

Against the fixed backdrop of tension in the Western Association, autumn lay on the horizon as Charles settled into another temporary home, this time in Exeter, unaware that a fallout was about to occur in his family. Roundhead siege of Bristol ended with Rupert surrendering the crucial city in September, and when this news reached Exeter it 'cast all men on their faces and damped all the former vigour'[12] before the king reacted from Hereford by stripping his capitulating nephew of commissions. Given Rupert's courage and competence, this loss was of considerable Royalist concern. Of course, the ideal situation would nonetheless be one in which military prowess had no place, as the Prince of Wales was quick to acknowledge, and the public were now aware that the younger Charles's stance didn't entirely match the elder's.

Three years earlier, Duppa's plea to the monarch on Charles's behalf had been published. This attempt for a 'speedy Accommodation' was a 'resolution' attributed to the heir, and the heir's belief it could bring a 'sudden cure' for the nation's troubles centred on clemency. He 'conceives businesses have beene transacted between your sacred Selfe and ... Parliament, with too much acrimony and violence, for ... he had gathered, that the *English* Parliaments were the best and most necessary Counsellors of the *English* Kings', it stated of 12-year-old Charles in 1642.[13] Now on 15 September 1645 the prince wrote to Fairfax to beg peace, telling him: 'we should think it a great blessing ... if we might be ... an instrument in the advancing of it'.[14]

Ironically for the leader of Parliament's army, Fairfax wasn't the most ardent of Parliamentarians. After military training on the Continent, he'd taken up arms for the king in the Bishops' Wars and been knighted in January 1641, his Royalist allegiance hoped for. As a young but prominent member of the Yorkshire gentry, he's also remembered for having a hand in the 1642 Treaty of Neutrality to try keeping his county of birth out of the troubles. But Fairfax ultimately believed Parliament worth fighting for. Had his wife felt differently, however, this somewhat quiet man, who was said to exceed 'any Expressions as a Commendation of his Resolution and Valour',[15] might never have entered Roundhead history. The whisper was that the woman joined to him in matrimony, born Anne Vere, exercised profound influence on her politically lamb-like husband, and she accompanied him round the country as battles and sieges called.

Arguably Fairfax and the Prince of Wales were two of the friendliest high-profile faces of the war, and not dissimilar ones. Fairfax's nickname Black Tom came from the strikingly dark features he shared with Charles. But while peace negotiations could benefit from friendly faces, the understanding that Charles held differing views from his father's had given birth to hopes of seeing him usurp. In the prince's eyes though, usurpation was abhorrent. His stance may be admirable, but it meant greater jeopardy. With Charles showing no signs of usurping, some Parliamentarians were convinced he needed persuasion. To them, only his kidnapping could make him that instrument in the advancing of peace, an instrument they would of course control.

By 7 November 1645, the king had decided his son should find sanctuary in Denmark, a nation ruled by the child's great-uncle Christian IV, and wrote: 'if I mistake not the present condition of the west, you ought not to defer your journey one hour'. However, as this wasn't deemed an actual

Chapter 10

command, the boy's council, cautiously confident of the area's safety, advised staying put in England and attempting to relieve Exeter.[16] While Charles remained on terra firma, he was nonetheless moving towards the coast, essentially being cornered by the New Model as they swept up more and more territory.

Goring, on the other hand, had no intention of staying put in England. On 20 November he sent Prince Charles a request for leave to retreat to France, purportedly for health considerations, and embarked from Dartmouth before permission could be withheld. Promoted into the place of this drunken commander was another Thomas Wentworth, this one made Baron Wentworth in 1640, and he bore self-importance. Now in senior command, he declared he'd take orders from nobody but His Royal Highness, as Goring had instilled in him. In fact, he mirrored Goring too much. One day Wentworth turned up under the influence of alcohol and spoke 'very offensively, to some of the council, in the presence of the Prince'.[17]

Really Grenville would have been a safer bet, although as winter neared, he proved himself no model Royalist, proposing a plan that would have changed the political map of Britain if accepted. It entailed giving Cornwall independence, setting the teenaged Charles up as its ruler and making Cornish peace with Parliament. But this plan required abdication or usurpation. The suggestion was hardly Grenville's route to regaining favour. When Charles presided over a reorganisation of the Western Association in January 1646, Hopton became top dog and Grenville was thrown in jail on St Michael's Mount after refusing a lower position.

Nevertheless, while the prince's aptitude for addressing audiences had failed to rouse enough support from the Cornish militia, Charles generally delighted his duchy's citizens, and rumours that he'd be fleeing to France led many to petition against this move. The thought he might depart England at all had caused wider consternation at public meetings too, although Charles was said to share their feelings. On 27 January, a journalist reported the prince 'cries, and stamps, and vexeth, and saith he will not leave the kingdom'.[18] But the situation was worsening daily. By late February 1646, Tiverton, Dartmouth and Torrington were in Parliamentarian hands, the Royalists gave up besieging Plymouth and Fairfax had Exeter surrounded. Meanwhile, despite the nearby Powderham Castle initially repelling attack in December, the Roundheads had brought it to capitulation the following month.

Ancient defences like that still had vital uses, and as the more modern Pendennis Castle in Falmouth was being fortified further, hopes were pinned on making it safe enough to house Charles semi-permanently. In February, he travelled there, 'to quicken the works, which were well advanced, his highness having issued all the money he could procure towards them', but as he was about to return to Truro a few days later, word came of a plot to seize him.[19] He dared not move. When he did move, it would have to be by sea. With no time left to argue, Charles and his council unanimously decided the Scilly Isles should be the destination, though even then a change of course could be taken mid-crossing. When the prince and some of his advisers boarded *Phoenix* at 10 pm on 2 March, they would nonetheless land at the Scillies' largest island St Mary's.

But they were in for a grim time. Shortly came news that Hopton had surrendered and signed an agreement to disband the king's Western army, signalling the collapse of everything the adolescent Charles had invested the past year in. Now the prince was stuck on a windswept island, battling the cold instead and forbidden to use his initiative in the war effort, still obediently following his father's orders to act upon council advice only. As ready as this was, not even Hyde was advising round the clock though. Here on the Scillies, Hyde began composing his *History of the Rebellion*,[20] one of the most informative accounts of the Civil Wars. Yet all the while, his watchful eye kept bearing down on Charles.

Lodgings for the prince while on St Mary's were the eight-point star-shaped Elizabethan fortress Star Castle, and some of his retinue were accommodated in virtually uninhabitable conditions nearby, moving in for an uncomfortable, wet stay, not to mention a hungry one. As the wife of council secretary Richard Fanshawe, a pregnant Ann Fanshawe experienced some of the misery, later recalling in her memoirs: 'meat or fuel for half the Court, to serve them a month, was not to be had in the whole island. And truly we begged our daily bread of God, for we thought every meal our last'.[21] Although the council contacted Henrietta Maria to request provisions from France, nothing ample came, and news that her son was on the Scillies met with her distinct displeasure: 'it is not sufficiently fortified, and is accessible in divers places', she pointed out, adding a reminder about Parliament's power at sea.[22]

Charles soon saw exactly what she meant. After Westminster had got wind of his whereabouts, a letter dated 30 March arrived from the Houses' speakers, inviting Charles 'to come forthwith into their quarters',[23] and within days a fleet of at least twenty gun-clad vessels were encircling the island as if to

Chapter 10

make his mind up for him. By stroke of luck, 'a very notable tempest' arrived to chase the warships away within four hours, but their arrival had been an alarming Sunday-morning sight that told Charles the enemy was targeting him with ultimatums. Particularly in light of the secret letter from his father, avoiding capture was literally vital. Under no circumstances could Charles give Parliament the upper hand through a blackmail situation; if pressed to usurp and sacrifice regal authority, he'd be under paternal orders to permit his father's death. He decided the time was ripe to let his advisers see the letter. To their surprise, he pulled it out in council, pained to share it but desperate to add weight to an argument he was making. Except for the Earl of Berkshire once again, they all then agreed the child spoke wisely in advocating a move to Jersey as already discussed.[24]

On 15 April Charles dispatched an 'artful' response to the invitation, directly informing Parliament he was heading for Jersey instead, and telling them this was where 'we may the better receive advice from you, with which we shall always comply as far as with our duty and piety we may'.[25]

The following day, he was traversing the waves again, basically chased away, but he found himself on a magical journey. This time, transport took the form of *Proud Black Eagle*, a twenty-four-gun frigate whose captain Baldwin Wake[26] stood aside to let the youngster gleefully take the helm. For a two-hour stint in 'fair' wind, Charles helped steer this vessel of 160 tons,[27] as he became ensnared by a passion for sailing that would forever remain in his heart, and he knew exactly how he wanted to spend his days ahead, soon to commission a pinnace to sail around in.

Charles had an idea of cheaper fun too. According to a series of letters written in French and bearing dates from the latter half of the 1660s, La Cloche was born later than records specify. The letters say he entered the world when Charles was around 16 and that Charles fathered him. They were purportedly penned by the Merry Monarch himself. Interestingly though, the first of these is addressed from Whitehall and dated September 1665 – a time when the Great Plague of London was keeping Charles away from Whitehall. The correspondence also speaks of Henrietta Maria as though at the English court, despite the fact she'd left forever in the spring of 1665. They are therefore indubitable forgeries, particularly given what else is understood about La Cloche. After marrying in Naples in February 1669, he was arrested the following month for suspected counterfeiting having gifted his father-in-law such an excess of coinage and jewels that their authenticity was queried. When, during his interrogation, La Cloche asserted himself as Charles II's son, this apparently got reported to Charles and had counterproductive results – a more convincing letter from the king labelling La Cloche an imposter.[28]

But the thought that Charles became a father at 16 is convincing too. It was in Jersey that he reportedly conducted his first love affair, with the object of his desire cited as a roughly 20-year-old Marguerite Carteret.[29] The Carterets were the foremost family of the island, but seemingly when around 30 Marguerite lost her respected name to marry Jean de la Cloche, son of a Jersey rector. Yet Jacques de la Cloche claimed his mother was 'Lady Mary Stuart, of the family of the Barons of St. Mars',[30] removing Marguerite from the equation.

So, the parentage of La Cloche is shrouded in mystery, a little-known perplexity of Stuart history. His death, meanwhile, theoretically links to a famous matter of intrigue in European history. Having made his will while supposedly 'sick in bed' in August 1669, La Cloche was reported dead within three days,[31] fever deemed responsible. However, twentieth-century writer Marcel Pagnol put La Cloche's passing at 1703 and averred La Cloche was the Man in the Iron Mask, a long-term captive of France who entered Pignerol jail in late August 1669 under supervision by prison governor Bénigne d'Auvergne de Saint-Mars.

Pagnol's musings also hypothesise La Cloche was a twin brother of Louis XIV of France, however. The theories of Pagnol are difficult to believe, although La Cloche may have fancied faking death and carving a new identity for himself if denunciation from Charles led him to abandon hopes of recognition.

Owning the paternity of La Cloche was nonetheless the least of Charles's worries from the forged letters. Thanks to other statements within these letters, anyone who took them at face value would believe the restored king was moving towards Catholic conversion in the 1660s.

Although the Church of Rome was yet to make a notable post-Reformation mark on Jersey, the islanders' embrace of Anglicanism had travelled a route through Calvinism, and Charles in 1646 was beginning a long exposure to spiritual and cultural customs that would spur him to form his own opinions on religion and all kinds of questionable morals.

Chapter 11

Breathing the springtime air of 1646, Charles was greeted at Jersey on Friday, 17 April by a rainbow of hues from animal, vegetable and mineral, some of which he had never set eyes on. The vibrantly coloured western green lizard, for instance, was no generally familiar sight north of the Channel, and beyond the archipelago's fine pale sand and jagged rocks stood woodland that had an exotic look to someone brought up in England. On the Sunday night, what's more, the landscape was dotted with bright orange bonfires of rejoice for the royal visitor's arrival. It was all such a pleasing sight and, having 'taken an account' of the island, Charles was satisfied his surroundings were safe[1] as well as scenic.

This was good news for many other people too. In the prince's tow were approximately 300 attendants, with the higher-ranking also employing their own while some brought families. Alongside numerous military officers and guards, the retinue included lords, knights, gentlemen, clergymen, physicians and tradesmen such as tailors and shoemakers, plus household staff to keep everything running and suitably ostentatious. With the Western Association's fall in March, young Charles had released Richard Grenville from prison to allow him to escape the enemy, but while this ex-commander had fled to Brest, his nephew John Grenville remained by the prince's side, as Gentleman of the Bedchamber; in the end, the appointment had been allowed, and the boy was joined by not only his pick of servants but also some friends. For example, there was Mr Walton – son of an early wet nurse of Charles's, with records suggesting she was the Welsh nurse deemed necessary for the heir's Welsh-speaking prospects. Because of his link to Walton, Charles affectionately referred to him as 'my brother'.[2]

Those closest to the prince were making their homes with him at Elizabeth Castle, an imposing piece of architecture with relatively modern commodities after construction had begun towards the end of its namesake's reign. Its location bolstered its safety too. Near Jersey's capital St Helier, the fortress stood on an islet in St Aubin's Bay, off the south coast, and a half-mile causeway connecting it to the main island emerged at low tide only, so Charles was afforded mesmerising views of the waves on all four sides.

Meanwhile the sizeable overspill of his entourage was anything but cut off, forced to lodge with local townsfolk. Despite no expectation to pay for the guests' upkeep, landlords and families were somewhat obliged to admit them, and with hundreds of extra mouths to feed, farmers and butchers would soon be commanded to bring their goods to the market hall by 9 am each Wednesday, whether they wanted to or not. Then, till noon, they would be forbidden from selling to anyone except the purveyors serving Charles and his most esteemed lords, usually leaving just the lower-quality produce for everyone else although price limits would soften this blow slightly. A proclamation was also coming to compel fishermen to vend their catches at market, while for the remainder of the week the people of the country parishes were to supply Elizabeth Castle daily with sheep, pigs, chickens and goslings (two of each), a calf, a lamb, twenty-four eggs and two pots of butter.[3] Royalist though it now was, Jersey had been a Parliamentarian zone for a spell in 1643 when controlled by Major Leonard Lydcott as deputy to the Roundhead Earl of Warwick,[4] and its allegiance to Parliament hadn't vanished entirely. If the prince's presence on the island caused too many problems, it could turn rebellious feelings into rebellious actions.

But on his first Monday in Jersey, Charles did something that would instantly endear him to citizens with Parliamentarian leanings. After the island's Royalist recapture in November 1643, the Crown had seized several jewels belonging to St Helier's Roundhead wives and daughters. Now the Prince of Wales was there, the 'extreme hardship of the case' was presented to him, and in the blink of an eye he 'issued peremptory orders' that the confiscated gems be returned to their owners. Charles rather liked this idea, finding it earn him 'golden opinions from all sorts of women'.[5]

He nevertheless understood the value of his popularity with all, and he knew he could do better than give directions from behind closed doors. Over the next few days, he therefore held levees in Elizabeth Castle's great hall, where 'chief functionaries' were invited to approach him, bend on one knee and kiss his right hand. Yet he simultaneously gave the impression he was beneath such fawning. People were 'fascinated with his "benign" demeanour, and the affability with which he gave them audience',[6] but of course he'd identified the errors of his father's haughty ways.

Chapter 11

Now in regal mode, Charles was departing from his father's decisions slightly, too. On 24 April he not only made Baldwin Wake a sir but had also decided that the knighthood granted, by the king, to Jersey's lieutenant governor George Carteret was insufficient. Although ceremoniously dubbing Carteret a knight, the prince took the further step of making him a baronet.

Here was the germination of one of the strongest governmental relationships Charles ever had, but this relationship demonstrates how, as monarch, he sometimes relied too much on specific individuals. He'd be unable 'to whip a cat' unless 'I ... be at the tayle of it', Carteret commented in 1665, five years into his tenure on the Privy Council. And according to Pepys, Charles openly agreed the baronet was indispensable.[7] A passionate monarchist, Carteret was even handy at Charles's 1661 coronation, standing in for absent almoner the Earl of Exeter in the grand ceremony at Westminster Abbey.[8]

The ceremony of knighthood at Elizabeth Castle paled into insignificance then, but for the Jersey populace in 1646 meanwhile, it was hypnotic. They had never seen anything like this, and their love of ritualistic grandeur was blatant. Charles intended to use it to his advantage.

By the end of April, he also intended to use the church to help with this. An announcement was thus made that he'd be attending a service in St Helier, and the locals dropped everything to welcome him. Excitation abounded as they carpeted their house of prayer, decorated it inside and out with pretty flora and installed a chair of state alongside cushions for the royal elbows and knees. Then, when the boy set off on that Sunday morning, roughly 400 men guarded him as drums thudded and flags fluttered, and his route was crammed with beaming faces. 'They neither speak English nor good French', Ann Fanshawe claimed of Jersey's people.[9] Yet specially for His Royal Highness, English was used throughout the service, and an English chaplain would now officiate every Wednesday, Friday and Sunday, with much the same pomp accompanying Charles each time. That's until the hassle of regularly venturing off the islet became too irksome and the priory there was hence converted into a chapel royal.[10]

But the desire to gawp at the prince was fulfilled in other ways, not least when he chose to make a public spectacle of dining. This ritual commenced with him standing in reverence while a blessing was pronounced by a doctor of theology, after which Charles put on a hat and took his seat at the top of the table. Lords, gentlemen and the theological doctor then stood around him, and a page knelt with a napkin and basin of water. Having rinsed and dried his hands, Charles selected the comestibles he wanted from the 'massive' dishes displaying them, and with meat or fish to begin, his choice was carried to the carver Mr Palmer, who sliced and tasted it before His Royal Highness received it. Beverages were provided by cupbearer Mr Smyth, who also tasted the drink and on bended knee held another receptacle under the prince's chin in case a drop dribbled down. To finish the show after the final dish, the chaplain said grace before Charles disappeared, leaving the menial servants to clear away the dazzling silver.[11]

The part the prince played was work to him though. He'd rather have stuffed his face without a care for dignity, but he was disciplining himself by second nature now, albeit as a spendthrift. And it was just as well the islanders derived entertainment from all this. Having 'lent' him 1,500 pistoles within a week of his arrival,[12] they were basically footing the bills themselves.

However, he wasn't spending it all on himself. Soon he'd be gifting Jersey's Royalist soldiers a total of 900 livres, announcing this at the end of a 'grand militia field-day' on 29 April. For this event, Carteret had 'ordered all men capable of bearing arms, from fifteen to seventy years of age, to muster', and an estimated two-thirds of the population was flocking to attend. That morning, the prince traversed the countryside en route to the east coast's thirteenth-century castle Mont Orgueil. Gunfire salute heralded his approach, and from 2 pm he was playing commander again, inspecting each battalion 'in detail, company by company'. After this, he rode along the line of troops, who yelled '*Dieu sauve le Roi et le Prince*' as he raised his hat and bowed in appreciation, though none of the loyalty proved any battle skills. Before the day ended, the dragoons nonetheless performed a symbolic show 'across the sands, charging an imaginary enemy'.[13]

In Oxford, on the other hand, the enemy was very real indeed and had been closing in on the king directly. At 3 am on 27 April, he'd therefore slipped quietly away, his hair cropped, beard trimmed and face shadowed by a peaked cap as he masqueraded as a groom named Harry. He'd been informed that barbarity would be exercised on him if the disguise failed to convince, so James was left behind with common citizens in the Royalist capital as the New Model began besieging it.[14]

Parliament's stalwart army had been formed mainly by the War Party, a section of Westminster intent on fighting till they secured victory without

Chapter 11

great concession, and these men had hoped that Scottish assistance in accordance with the Solemn League and Covenant would help achieve this. By now, however, the Caledonians sided more with the Peace Party, which wanted negotiation with the king to end the hostilities. As a result, many in the War Party were now anti-Scots Independents and at loggerheads with pro-Scots Presbyterians, meaning the king could crush one by uniting with the other. And the Scots and English Presbyterians were clandestinely offering him a deal to preserve some of his powers. They expected nothing more than mediation to begin with, so it was to their astonishment when he turned up in Nottinghamshire's Southwell and promptly surrendered to the Scottish army on 5 May. But he had no intention of meeting the exact terms of the deal. His side of it, if accepted, would force him to abandon episcopacy and commit to the Covenant. Refusing, he was dragged to Newcastle upon Tyne, separated from his servants and incarcerated in the governor's house to experience Presbyterian worship. Between the services, lectures came thick and fast from Scottish commissioners tearing their hair out trying to talk him into signing the Covenant.[15]

In the meantime, others felt that the Irish could better help the Royalist cause, particularly as its Catholic Confederacy had signed a treaty, on 28 March, agreeing to provide military support to the king. Along to Jersey had now come George, Lord Digby, a walking disaster of a royal adviser who steered Charles I away from compromise, not to mention the fact this lord had advocated battle at Naseby, dismissal of Rupert and probably the king's trip to the Commons to arrest the Five Members. Now Digby wanted to take the teenaged Charles to Ireland to launch an attack on England, largely Parliament-controlled as it was by this time. Of itself, the plan had merits in the youngster's eyes. 'I wish action were as ready for him, as he is for it', read words from Hyde to Jermyn on 20 May,[16] but Charles delicately told Digby that no such course should be taken without the king's approval. Tactics of persuasion were unlikely to work, as Digby could see. He quickly turned his thoughts in a devious direction. Remembering the boy's new maritime enthusiasm, he hatched a plot to lure Charles aboard a frigate as if for a viewing but would then, the peer hoped, promptly up anchor and carry him off to the Emerald Isle. Having communicated this to a council member though, Digby realised he wouldn't get away with it. He therefore took ship to the palace of Saint-Germain-en-Laye near Paris, to try coaxing Henrietta Maria into backing his Irish plan for the prince. She, however, was hellbent on receiving her son in France.

For many months, Charles had been counselled on the opposite side of this argument and seemingly possessed 'the greatest averseness and resolution against going into France'.[17] But the king now shared his wife's feelings, wanting his heir delivered to Saint-Germain. With this, Henrietta Maria told the boy: 'your coming hither is the security of the king your father; therefore make all the haste you can, to show yourself a dutiful son ... otherwise, you may ruin the king and yourself. ... Parliament will, with all their power, force you to come to them'.[18]

This was a blinkered viewpoint. 'I command you ... to be constant to your religion', the king had written to his eldest son in March, at the time thinking Charles already in France![19] But nobody could guarantee the prince would follow this instruction, and he still sat destined to become ruler the moment his father passed on. Jersey was British, Protestant soil. If the young impressionable heir passed into Catholic territory, more and more of England would believe Parliament a better governing option.

To most of the council, the answer for Charles was not to seek refuge in France but instead to make Jersey impregnable. Carteret, besides endeavouring 'to entertain his Highness and Court with all plenty and kindness possible',[20] was already working towards this, with ramparts being erected and cavalry patrols conducted day and night, but the prince was also heavily involved in meeting defence needs. His own efforts included paying fifty pistoles for repair of the outwork St Aubin's Tower and sending for a skilled engineer to oversee construction of various fortifications.

Charles nevertheless usually followed advice; he shouldn't be credited for what were really counsellors' or officers' decisions, but he was eager to learn how to make creditable decisions himself. On his birthday, in fact, he went surveying coastal defences, somewhat immersed in the task despite great jubilation round the island. Volleys had echoed from coast to coast that morning, and the day unfolded with sumptuous feasts before nightfall triggered a spectacular light show. All to mark the completion of the prince's sixteenth year, bonfires on hills were hence complemented by illumination at windows while flickering lamps hung from rigging for a blinding panorama of St Aubin's Bay.

However, as gratifying as this was for Charles, he'd find far greater excitement awaiting him on the water. On 8 June, his pinnace arrived, complete with a magnificent paint job, an emblazoning of his armorials and cushions for comfort. But its sublime features were nothing compared to its functionality, especially as it boasted not just two masts but also twelve pairs of oars. To his delight, Charles could take his pick between sailing and rowing, unless the weather decided it for him, and henceforth he wanted to travel between islet and mainland at high tide only, not by the boring dry land of the causeway. Moreover, by his further insistence, he'd be the one steering.[21]

Handily for the prince, there appeared no shortage of men who could teach him the art of handling vessels. Present in Jersey were twelve of the king's naval officers, and on top of this Charles was attended by Sir Henry Mainwaring, a former pirate but, in 1618, 'the foremost and boldest sailor and sea captain that England possessed'.[22]

Having quickly got the hang of basic seafaring, the prince was king of his pinnace, becoming incredibly tetchy about it. He couldn't bear for anyone else to tamper with the tiller, and the ship was nearly as hard to separate from him as his beloved chunk of wood had been fifteen years earlier. For hour upon hour, Charles took his grand new toy round and round the bay, finally experiencing mental escape while the island's immense security gave him little reason to flee physically.

But the matter of his removal was turning very political. The monarch of France was now a 7-year-old Louis XIV, whose mother Anne of Austria acted as regent while chief minister Cardinal Jules Mazarin reportedly 'directed all that was to be done and dictated all that was to be said', and Mazarin believed Charles's presence in France was 'of the highest importance to their affairs'. The cardinal had now informed Digby that France never wanted to see Charles I 'at the mercy of his own rebels' and was willing to declare its own war on them. If Parliament refused demands made by the French court, Mazarin's plan was to provide an army for the Prince of Wales to lead over to England, making it 'absolutely necessary' that Charles be in France for this assault on the enemy to take place. And as if this weren't enough incentive, Mazarin also told Henrietta Maria he 'had intelligence from London that the Prince was to be given up by some of his own followers for £5000'.[23]

The queen would stand for no more procrastination and sent her dearest Jermyn over to Jersey, expecting him to return with her son. Arriving on Saturday, 20 June, Jermyn was supported by the voices of several gentlemen and lords accompanying him, including Digby and even Colepeper – the only one of Charles's advisers favouring French residence for the prince – and the air quickly choked with tension as Charles called a meeting in his bedchamber. From the start, the council objected to the presence of the queen's party during the discussion, while the queen's party claimed the council had no right to advise their young master on this matter since Their Majesties' orders were clear. Yet this was queried. Extracts of letters from the king were there, one of which had been transcribed by Jermyn's hand,[24] but was this proof of a command from father to son? If not, the council were accountable for the prince's actions. Nevertheless, they could only guide him.

Over two days' heated debate, Charles listened to the myriad points made and heard his mother's representatives question why he would deprive his father and himself 'of so great fruit' as offered. The army awaiting Charles numbered 30,000, and 'France had no reason to embark themselves so far in the King's quarrel if the Prince of Wales should refuse to venture his person with them'.[25] When Charles declared his decision, however, he said it was based on an understanding that his parents were in fact instructing him. He was therefore resolved to go and could tolerate no further argument. The last thing he wanted to do just then, though, was offend the counsellors who had fought to keep him out of the Gallic Catholic nation. But as he expressed desire that they attend him in France to continue as his advisers, every one of them declined.

So, Charles was to wave goodbye to Capell, Hopton, Brentford, Berkshire and Hyde. For the past sixteen months, they had basically been his trusted family, the people on whom he'd relied in practically his every move. Now, with the weather delaying departure till 25 June, they watched helplessly as an agitated Charles grew so fixed on complying with his real family's wishes that he forbade any of the travelling party from leaving the castle in case the wind dropped and they missed a chance to embark.

During this agonising wait, Charles was at least blissfully ignorant of his brother's situation. Oxford was capitulating, and into the possession of the Roundheads fell 12-year-old James. If they couldn't get their hands on the Prince of Wales, they wanted to make a puppet king of the Duke of York. While his father was a prisoner of the Covenanters, James thus became a captive of Parliament as the First Civil War drew to a close. Nobody knew a second would soon unfold, yet there was an awful lot of unfinished business.

Chapter 12

'This is rather to tell you where I am, and that I am well, than to direct you anything,' the king began a letter to Charles on 2 June 1646, ironically continuing: 'having written fully to your mother what I would have you do, whom I command you to obey in everything, (except in religion ...) and see that you go no whither without her or my particular directions'.[1] When Prince Charles landed at Brittany's Saint-Malo a few weeks later, he was an exceptionally tall 16-year-old whose experiences in charge of the Western Association had catapulted him into maturity of mind, and for the past sixteen months he'd led an isolated royal court, only ever surrounded by people below him. Now he'd be bowing to Bourbon royalty and living in the clutches of his mother at Saint-Germain, where there was no escaping a certain reliance on her. For the upkeep of Henrietta Maria, France supplied her with a daily 1,200 francs.[2] For the upkeep of Charles, however, they simply increased this allowance by twenty-five per cent,[3] paying it all to her. The sum seemed inadequate, especially as the consort sent a lot of it off as means to help her husband, but not even the largest sums could sweeten a situation whereby the prince had to go begging to his mother, a woman whose natural hot-headedness was currently exacerbated by continuous anxiety as well as continual toothache.[4] On top of this, the fact Charles no longer had a governor gave the queen more reason to involve herself in her son's life, and this was a son she had spent just a few months with since his pre-teens. She barely knew her eldest now, having missed much opportunity to mould him.

Saddened, she wasn't going to let this happen with her youngest. Not anymore. After giving birth to Henrietta on 16 June 1644, Henrietta Maria had suffered temporary blindness in one eye coupled with 'paralysis' and, 'tightly squeezed in the region of the heart', felt as if suffocating. But 'shifting for one hour's life longer',[5] she'd surreptitiously fled to France the following month, leaving her baby behind with governess Lady Dalkeith, another member of the Villiers dynasty.⁶ Two years later, the queen was still experiencing health problems and a dainty Henrietta had started growing up with one shoulder lower than the other, as Charles would now see as this blue-eyed chestnut-haired toddler was smuggled across the Channel herself, still easily young enough for a French upbringing. She'd be raised Roman Catholic, and the name acquired at her Anglican baptism was now Gallicised to Henriette, with Anne added to honour Louis XIV's mother. Charles, however, sometimes called his sister Minette, a pet name reflecting her tininess.

Something that made Minette seem particularly small was the presence of the towering Prince Rupert from around this time. He'd now made amends with Charles I, and the future Charles II greeted him enthusiastically, though can't have enjoyed seeing Rupert subsequently handed command of the 1,400 English troops in France.⁷ After all, the expectation had been for Charles to lead a French army to Roundhead destruction in England. But France was at war against Spain. Could the French really spare the resources to attack Parliament too? The answer was no, or at least not when the New Model Army looked so strong. Had Charles I met Covenanter demands and joined forces with the Scots, his English opponents might have weakened enough to start turning the tables. As it was, Mazarin and his queen had more sense than to send troops to probable defeat, so withheld the army allotted for Prince Charles. Besides, if he was detained at the royal courts of France, nobody could easily capture him. Ergo, enemies of the French weren't getting him. Mazarin and Anne just preferred to keep that consideration hushed.

As chief minister and queen regent respectively, this pair enjoyed a partnership so close that it sparked rumour they were married. Due to their like-mindedness, both strove to remain relatively detached from the English affairs, but they had a conundrum on their hands now the Prince of Wales was there, expected to meet their monarch. If the child king and adolescent prince were introduced officially, France would be linked too closely to the Stuart cause. A chance encounter seemed best, albeit with meticulous planning.

The setting chosen for this choreographed scene in August was the Forest of Fontainebleau, where the coaches of Charles and Louis crossed paths and the boys stepped out with their mothers. As introductions proceeded, the prince kissed the hand of his reigning 7-year-old cousin and that of Anne, before she returned the compliment by pecking Charles on the cheek. But much further respect for Charles would be shown – practically nonstop for the next three days. During this time, the Prince of Wales found himself treated with such privilege at Fontainebleau that he was seated in a chair with arms that was almost identical to Louis's, he sat and walked on Louis's right and he wore a hat when strolling with Louis.[8] The little king himself gave Charles permission for all this, yet there was no real connection between the boys. Courtier Madame de Motteville noted that both were shy and appeared 'embarrassed by each other's presence', but relaxing around Louis was hard. Even at this age, he oozed dignity and seriousness. Nevertheless, comedies were among the entertainments Charles witnessed, and he was also taken on 'excursions'. 'The unhappy state of his affairs', Motteville mused about Charles, 'made every one regard him with the tenderness that accompanies pity, and … his good qualities received greater lustre'.[9]

Perhaps it's no surprise that he was admitted to the *petit lever*, the earlier part of the French king's ceremonial rising in the morning, though it was an honour indeed; only the most select were invited into the royal bedchamber for this. Its ritualistic focus on dressing drew Charles's attention to some of the differences between English and French fashions. However, the most striking difference in clothing existed between the king and his brother Philippe. Despite being breeching[10] age when Charles had met him with Louis in the forest, Philippe would remain dressed like a girl in frocks for a long while yet, quite contrary to custom for males much over 5 and of course contrary to Charles's own experience, as Van Dyck could have verified had he not passed away in 1641.

But there was also a notable *lack* of crossdressing. Upon the Paris stage, skirts had female bodies parading around within them. By contrast in England, women were prevented from treading the boards, meaning male actors filled female roles and costumes.

Puritanism nonetheless frowned on theatre altogether, and Parliament had London playhouses shut since September 1642. With Westminster feeling a call to protect the populace from unhallowed merry-making, restrictive laws loomed, most notoriously banning so-called popish festivities marking Christmas, as well as Easter and Whitsun, from June 1647. Meanwhile MPs were to treat 25 December like a working day in 1646, sitting in the Commons in accordance with an anti-Catholic agenda for English citizens.

Earlier in 1646, however, an English exile consumed much of the Houses' attention. Parliament had stated that 'under pain of rebellion' the heir wasn't to leave the kingdom without their permission. Because he'd done so, they had mooted he should be made to repent, and now they were threatening to exclude him from the succession, if it still stood; they were also debating whether to declare England kingless should Charles I refuse the peace propositions put to him.[11]

Few argued for this though, so others hoped the Duke of York would reign instead. This captured pubescent was based at St James's Palace, sharing the lives of 6-year-old brother Henry and 10-year-old sister Elizabeth, and he was a much bigger, feistier handful than either of them, now also proving himself quite a different character from Charles. While James indignantly asserted his esteemed position, Charles was noted for 'a sweetness of nature', and 'the French were as familiar with him as could be imagined'.[12]

Some of the people most familiar with Charles in France were figures from his English past. For instance, life in Europe had taken the Marquis of Newcastle to Saint-Germain. It was thanks to this move that, in 1645, the widowed Newcastle had utterly charmed and married Margaret Lucas, one of Henrietta Maria's everyday attendants known as maids of honour, and he didn't regret it. Ignoring disapproval from his friends, Newcastle had hereby made a decision that brought him true happiness. Charles was observing change and development in more of his closest circle too, though not always for the better. Also around him again were the Villiers lads, now with three years' Continental travel behind them. According to Burnet decades later, the elder brother Buckingham had, by 1646, 'got into all the impieties and vices of the age' and set about corrupting Charles, the cleric claiming Buckingham found the young prince 'enough inclined'.[13]

Another man Burnet said had influenced Charles from this time was philosopher Thomas Hobbes, engaged as a mathematics tutor for the prince although the appointment triggered complaint. Rumour had it that Hobbes was an atheist. Yet after the words 'Teacher of the Prince of Wales' were added to a portrait of Hobbes in preparation for an edition of his partially political text *De Cive*, Hobbes himself objected and would deny their accuracy in March 1647, afraid to appear overly partisan.[14] Burnet's writings state that Hobbes fed Charles's brain with 'his schemes, both with relation to religion and politicks, which made deep and lasting impressions' on his royal pupil.[15] Meanwhile Charles is said to have remarked that, of all the men he'd ever encountered, Hobbes was the oddest.

Chapter 12

Judging by the 'Mechanical Head' Charles had upon his shoulders,[16] it's safe to say he listened to Hobbes about mathematics at least, but the prince's education struggled to recover the time lost to the war. Main tutor Earle was reading with Charles for only an hour a day – the same amount of time devoted to mathematics – and opportunity for distraction was immense. Despite the presence of the Villiers brothers' tutor William Aylesbury in Paris, the prince's lessons were again shared with budding wit and rake Buckingham. Meanwhile the king remained more interested in his son's spiritual development. He had assigned, in August, a Dr Stewart to be Dean of the heir's chapel[17] and previously placed Duppa in charge of religious guidance for young Charles while in France.

Charles I was labouring to surround his son with Church of England influences to outweigh the French adherents to the Church of Rome, Henrietta Maria included. She restrained herself remarkably well though, making little or no attempt to turn the boy into a Catholic. Marrying him to a Catholic, on the other hand, would be easier to get away with, especially a Catholic who happened to be considered the wealthiest heiress in Europe.

This heiress was Henrietta Maria's super-confident niece Anne-Marie-Louise d'Orléans, Duchess of Montpensier, an intimidating buxom blonde living at the Tuileries in Paris but a familiar face at Saint-Germain. She was learning to abhor the world, her memoirs reveal, and she constantly declared her intention to wed a man of highly exalted status. Following the birth of Louis, she called the infant 'my little husband'.[18] A practically penniless powerless prince seemed no ideal substitute. That is unless love conquered all, fake though it would be in this case. To stir romantic desires within the duchess, she was thus given to understand that Charles was desperately in love with her and talked about her ceaselessly, but once Henrietta Maria had told her this lie, the prince was required to make it convincing.

Known as La Grande Mademoiselle, the prospective bride was tall like Charles and shared his star sign Gemini, born almost exactly three years before him. Charles and Mademoiselle had little opportunity to discover what else they had in common, however, because Charles conveyed the notion that he was incapable of conversing in French. In January 1649, his father would add an English translation when telling him 'I had rather you should be Charles *le bon*, than *le grand*',[19] but the translation seems more for emphasis, and during childhood the heir was surrounded by Frenchmen to start him speaking his mother's language. Charles was perhaps now stretching the truth by claiming ignorance of French.

In addition, Motteville reported that when the prince did try speaking, he stuttered. Although nerves may lead anyone to do this, Charles isn't generally known to have struggled this way, even in imposing company. So, was this also part of an act avoiding conversation? Charles was a decent imitator and had of course been growing up around a father who stuttered, not to mention Buckingham and his penchant for both mimicry and ridiculing Charles I. The chances were the prince could feign a speech impediment. But Henrietta Maria would have known if her son's behaviour constituted feigning, whether in stuttering or in handling French. Maybe his reticence was no facade at all. Alternatively, it could have been a facade she encouraged.

Reflecting on memories of one occasion, characteristic words from Mademoiselle translate as: 'It pleases me to believe that ... his silence resulted from an excess of respect for me'.[20] And Henrietta Maria did all she could to create this impression. One day she dragged Charles to the Tuileries and had him act like a lowly fawning servant, the prince holding a candle while she helped do Mademoiselle's coiffure. He also carried out such gestures as escorting the would-be bride in and out of her carriage and sat with her throughout plays at the Palais-Royal.[21] Rather than offend his vain cousin or incense his matchmaking mother, Charles adopted the veneer of a wanton but gracious gentleman, all the while cannily keeping Mademoiselle at an emotional distance that helped exclude nuptial desires. He knew she could bring the Stuarts little more than money, and money wouldn't buy all they needed. Plus, in early 1647, the Venetian ambassador in France had been told that Parliamentarians wanted a law passed to ensure English princes married only members of the religion 'professed by the state'.[22]

It was therefore fortunate that, by the spring, Mademoiselle had her heart set on marrying Holy Roman Emperor Ferdinand III, and Charles's eyes descended upon court beauty Isabelle-Angélique, Duchess of Châtillon. Henrietta Maria saw her powers of persuasion failing on her niece and son, but their failure on her husband was more concerning.

The consort had been advising him to sign the Covenant, even before he was imprisoned. Early 1647, Charles I's refusal continued though, and his Scottish captors were out of patience. Therefore, on the promise of £400,000, they had handed him to Parliament. Apprehensions festered under the surface. In discussion beforehand, Parliament's Independents had made ominous reference to the execution of Mary, Queen of Scots.[23] But it wasn't as a reigning monarch that this grandmother of Charles I had been decapitated. Although shadowy murder threatened the king, his official regicide seemed unthinkable. Besides, Parliament was now predominantly Presbyterian; the Independents such as Cromwell were a minority. They were nevertheless a minority controlling the New Model Army, and after abduction plots were suspected, this formidable force successfully secured the king as their own prisoner in June. Now Charles I met Cromwell face-to-face, yet a pleasantly personable atmosphere was maintained. Then Cromwell 'wept plentifully' having witnessed James, Elizabeth and Henry meet up with their father in July. Talk that he harboured 'sinister opinions of the King' amounted to unprecedented abuse, the Puritan claimed.[24] In fact Cromwell and his Puritan son-in-law MP Henry Ireton were some of the senior New Model Army members known as the Grandees who were seen, by a few, as dangerously willing to concede. Those few included the Levellers, a new egalitarian sect pushing for electoral reform that jeopardised Parliament as well as King, whoever the king might be.

The Levellers were far less radical than factions such as the Diggers, whose philosophies allude to communism, and the Ranters, who advocated nudity, but all three factions exemplify the phenomenal social movement England experienced in the 1640s–50s. This movement makes Charles's understanding of the 1660s English zeitgeist especially impressive as Charles spent less than three months on English turf over the thirteen years preceding 1660. In 1647, Parliament considered sending a deputation over to coax him back to his homeland. But although he occasionally accompanied his mother to another residence at the Louvre, Saint-Germain was where the young hopeful largely remained that year, finding himself at a loose end. Court theatre and balls were dazzling, while hunts provided some invigoration, but he missed his pinnace, and he was enduring a long period of dashed martial hopes.

In Ireland, lord lieutenant the Marquis of Ormond had surrendered Dublin to Parliament in June, strengthening the Roundheads further and giving Mazarin even less reason to entrust the prince with a force to attack them. The Protestant Ormond had been attacked himself by Irish Catholics for concessions he made through the treaty promising Irish aid to the Royalists in March 1646,[25] and it was now a year since Charles had resisted Digby's suggestion of heading Irish forces provided through this. Restless at all the inaction, the boy developed a yearning to join the French army and canter off to Flanders to do battle against Spain, defying his mother's refusal as he wrote to request his father's permission for this,[26] but with Mazarin determined to hold young Charles in France, the Spanish remained safe from the Prince of Wales, and vice versa.

Duels proved to be the closest Charles got to bloodshed at this point, though not as a combatant. In fact, his role at one was merely preventative. After Rupert challenged Digby to a duel to take place in the Forest of Poissy in October 1647, Henrietta Maria was determined to intervene, and Charles arrived to arrest the challenger before weapons could be drawn. Following this, Rupert duelled when Charles was off hunting alongside 'meniall servants'. Lord Percy, a verbal troublemaker the previous day, ended up with Rupert's sword through 'the fleshie part of his right side'.[27]

Meanwhile the Scots were infighting, dividing in opinion, and Charles I made use of this division. On 26 December, he signed an agreement called the Engagement. Countersignatories and their supporters were thus known as the Engagers, making a third Scottish sect alongside die-hard Covenanters and Royalists, and the Engagers believed it unnecessary that the king himself commit to the Covenant. As Covenant embracers themselves though, the Engagers were still committed to Presbyterianism while opposing the politics dominating in Westminster. The Engagement therefore saw Charles I agree to impose Presbyterianism in England for three years and Engagers promise men and arms to supress Parliament. But the king had negotiated this in secret, and revelation of the underhandedness lost him further trust, not least from Cromwell after interception of a letter between monarch and consort.

It was again time to try putting the heir on the throne. Or was it? On 1 February 1648 overtures were said to be on their way to Prince Charles and his mother in France, but a newsletter featured scribblings by a Roman correspondent in England claiming that ideas of crowning the prince were a pretence. A republic was dreamt of instead, the correspondent believed, his words published on 7 January 1648.[28]

Either way, via the Vote of No Addresses the same month, Parliament ceased parley with Charles I. Then they issued an explanatory declaration in February to intensify hatred for him after his surreptitious dealings. At the same time, however, the religious restrictions and financial strain that Westminster placed on England meant anti-parliamentary uprisings were brewing, as was another war.

Chapter 13

As the Second Civil War loomed, previous plans for the Prince of Wales resurfaced. Agents from the Irish Catholic Confederacy turned up at Saint-Germain in early 1648, hoping he'd this time join with them in Ireland to invade England. Meanwhile, through a clause in the Engagement, Engagers promised safe, kind reception for the heir, and in the spring, having clandestinely asked him in 1647, they were again arranging to invite him to Scotland for invasion of England.[1] Rather than the Catholic, this Presbyterian option would soon be pursued, but in March 1648 Charles feared that, if he put himself into Scottish hands, 'he may be sold as his father was'. Therefore, looking for assistance elsewhere, the prince hoped he'd be permitted a trip to Christian IV in Denmark.[2]

Even if this great-uncle of his couldn't help win the war, Charles as Mazarin's quasi 'hostage'[3] would feel a sense of victory just by getting out of France. The Villiers brothers had already left Paris to go and fight in England, and even the jailed king had absconded from Hampton Court. Slipping away in November while assumed to be silently writing letters in a locked room,[4] Charles I had made it right over to the Isle of Wight before his recapture and imprisonment there at Carisbrooke Castle. Now the Duke of York was busting out of St James's Palace.

On 22 February 1648 the monarch had instructed Royalist intelligence agent Colonel Joseph Bampfield to organise an escape for James. Bampfield obliged, but the duke himself became a major co-plotter. Every evening for a fortnight James played hide-and-seek with siblings Elizabeth and Henry and found such obscure hiding spots that he usually made his whereabouts unknown for thirty minutes at a time. During the game on 20 April therefore, nobody questioned his disappearance till too late. Having also tricked the gardener into giving him a treble key, James was gone. Via Bampfield, a made-to-measure female disguise waited, and the next morning the disguised duke was on the high seas, bound for his sister Mary in The Hague. Bampfield stood like a hero beside him.

The previous year, Mary's husband William had become Stadtholder following his father's death, and the couple were now Prince and Princess of Orange. Glory failed to bring Mary happiness though. As she was hostile towards the Dutch and refused to learn their language, her popularity suffered, and her mother-in-law Amalia appeared to hate everything English, including Mary,[5] while William proved more enamoured of other women than of his wife. He nevertheless shared Mary's desire to assist the Cavaliers. Hopeful, Charles planned a Dutch detour for his mooted trip to Denmark, but nothing was coming to fruition in early 1648.

Then, before summer, a setback befell Parliament; their complete control of the Royal Navy started crumbling. Six years since they acquired it, this was a major turn of events, and when mutineers docked nine ships at Holland's Hellevoetsluis in June, they had declared for the king and needed a Royalist commander. To Charles, the opportunity here was irresistible. It also tied in with another. Because Scotland could be easily reached from the Netherlands, the latter would be useful for beginning an Engagers-assisted advance into England, and Henrietta Maria concurred with advisers in believing her son should sail for Holland. Not even Mazarin detained Charles now. France's own civil conflicts of the Fronde were brewing so significantly that the cardinal had bigger fish to fry.[6] Remembering the Engagers had split from the harder-line Covenanters who had 'sold' the king in 1647, Charles thus bade farewell to the royals in Paris around Midsummer's Day and weighed anchor at Calais on 6 July,[7] eager to fight with army or navy.

Harsh reminders of the risks of combat were coming. During a skirmish just outside Kingston in Surrey the following day, 19-year-old Francis Villiers had his horse slain under him at the head of his troop, and as he backed against an oak tree, he was trapped. When, 'with nine wounds in his beautiful face and body', the young lord perished,[8] Charles lost one of his closest childhood friends.

Yet unaware of this, the prince was filled with Royalist hopes on his way to Holland. Sailing buoyed up his spirits further, and for the very first time he had neither a parent nor a governor or governess watching him. Although his entourage included old counsellors Colepeper, Hopton and Brentford, Hyde wasn't among them for now, but the frolicsome Rupert was.[9] On top of this,

Chapter 13

Charles relished the thought of reuniting with his eldest brother and sister. Six years had passed since he'd shared the company of Mary. She was now 16 and had suffered a miscarriage in October. Meanwhile James stood at around the king's height. These siblings, in turn, saw quite an adult-looking Prince of Wales reach the Dutch court. At 18, Charles appeared a 'trimme person, and of a manlie carriage',[10] and portraiture of him from this period shows a youthful but far from childlike figure, his signature swarthiness slightly accentuated by a thin moustache. So, crossing into what seemed full adulthood thanks to his new independence, Charles looked the part, but his prompt decision to act the part by exercising a certain seniority would highly displease James.

This obstinate[11] duke was 14 (the same age Charles had been when last around him) but since age 4 had held the post of Lord High Admiral, looking forward to when this titular role would be translated into tangible command. Now with warships at Royalist disposal, James felt the time ripe to take that command, and Bampfield had persuaded the mutineers to place themselves under the duke. Building on the escape's success, this had Bampfield believing 'he should be able to govern both his highness and the fleet',[12] but he wasn't wrong, already cajoling James into appointing specific officers. The Prince of Wales arrived to find the fleet in 'faction and disorder'.[13] He swept in with alacrity, removing Bampfield and making James's role merely nominal again. To the 14-year-old, this was outrageous. Hurt by the distrust, James claimed it left him no freer than as a prisoner. He also asserted he'd been robbed of his birthright, and accused Charles of disrespecting the king's wishes.[14] Perhaps it was partly to console James that his appointment of Lord Willoughby of Parham for Vice-Admiral remained, despite Willoughby's distinct lack of naval experience. This is nonetheless indicative of how Charles would appoint commanders for the Restoration navy, placing more significance on the person than on their capability. As stroppy teenaged James seemed slightly too incapable though, Charles delighted in taking the armada for himself in 1648 and resolved to lead an expedition forthwith.

Preparation for this was intense. Although Rupert had a knack for subduing rebellious seamen and helped ready the ships, Charles directed operations closely, super-busy for a week, yet it was actually during this short, frenzied period that a moment's leisure time saw Charles furnish Stuart history with one of its biggest talking points. He didn't do this deliberately though, nor on his own.

◆ ◆ ◆

Aged approximately 18 like Charles, Welsh gentlewoman Lucy Walter was 'insipid' according to Evelyn. She nevertheless appeared 'brown, beautiful, bold'[15] and frisky, and she utterly fired the taste buds of the Prince of Wales. Lucy may have been in a relationship with Cavalier colonel Robert Sidney, Chamberlain to the Princess of Orange, but James's memoirs aver that Charles 'found means to get her from her Collonel, she not being averse to so advantageous a change',[16] and just days after Charles's arrival in Holland, Lucy was pregnant with Charles's famous son, the future Duke of Monmouth.

This lends credence to speculation that Charles had already explored female bodies. However, there's little proof of sexual licentiousness from him before this. How far he went with Christabella is uncertain, and La Cloche is no convincing evidence of anything between Charles and Marguerite or any other woman. As for Isabelle-Angélique, her husband somewhat sat in the way having won her heart.

In fact, Lucy's *might* have been the only female body Charles was familiar with during his father's lifetime, though possibly from pre-1648. Memoirs by Restoration courtier Marie-Catherine d'Aulnoy report that Lucy 'charm'd and transported' Charles 'when he first saw her in *Wales*'[17] (although she moved to London before he set foot in his principality in 1642) and that 'amidst the Misfortunes which disturbed the first Years of his Life and Reign, he enjoy'd no Satisfaction or Pleasure but in loving and being beloved by this charming Mistress'.[18]

The idea that Lucy was more than his mistress is nevertheless hard to believe, for most. During his reign, claims that Charles had married Lucy accompanied attempts to alter the succession. A few months after his death, they helped drive a bloody rebellion. And even now they pose question over who should really have ascended the throne after Charles and who should therefore rule today. Nobody, however, has once brought into the limelight any proof of this marriage taking place, let alone where or when.

Although the main conjecture revolves around a secret wedding on the Continent, one suggestion has it that Charles and Lucy married in Exeter before the prince ever left England. Such a marriage spelled dangerous disrepute for the Stuart family in the 1640s, and neither theory is likely, but Exeter prompts interesting consideration. When Charles resided in Exeter, he was 15, more liable to being sucked into nuptials than his shrewder 18-year-old self might be, and both love and sex had potential to lure him. Obvious speculation could involve Lucy withholding herself unless made his queen-to-be. However, straight after fourteen years' upbringing at his father's prudish court, Charles perhaps even possessed reservations about sex outside wedlock; adolescent Charles was not the Merry Monarch he would become. The obedience of Charles as a son is nonetheless one of many factors lowering the probability he married behind his parents' backs, although 1645 may have given him a political reason. If union with the Braganzas' Joana was against his better judgement, wedding Lucy could have seemed an inviting way to terminate the plan. Yet with this very argument lies a far more credible counterargument. The option of marrying Charles into a powerful ruling dynasty was a lifeline. Unless planning bigamy, Charles knew he'd be closing the door on immeasurable assets if he became Lucy's husband, and bigamy could land him in very deep water.

Literally heading for deep water towards the end of July 1648 though, the prince left an embryo beginning gestation and embarked on his naval expedition – not yet to Scotland, but speeding towards England's east coast in the wake of Royalist risings in his homeland. Before scudding off, he'd penned letters to whip up further support of this nature and explain what he was doing. 'We conceive it to be our duty to lay hold of all means that may probably conduce to the restoring of the King ... to his liberty and just rights ... and the settling of a well grounded and happy peace', he'd told the Mayor and Corporation of Kingston-upon-Hull. 'We have therefore thought fit to invite you to partake with us ... if you shall do, we assure you and the whole town of a full pardon and indemnity for all that is past'.[19] Although no such partaking occurred during an initial anchorage off Great Yarmouth, the fleet wasn't too disheartened as it advanced towards Kent to bolster Cavalier garrisons at the castles of Deal and Sandown, and before long it was gifted an extra ship. This came thanks to, and along with, seasoned mariner William Batten, a Presbyterian who had led the attempt to snatch Charles from the Scillies but more recently waved goodbye to commanding positions in Parliament's navy. He'd now been working to reopen negotiations with the king before partly instigating the recent mutiny, and the Prince of Wales promptly knighted him and installed him as Rear-Admiral.[20] In a flash though, Batten was arguing with Rupert and others about strategy, meaning the best the armada managed was to capture merchant ships and gain £20,000 ransom from London.[21]

On the plus side, the Scottish plans were progressing, albeit with provisos. On 16 August, Charles received an official invitation 'to Scotland or to the Armie or wher the forces haue the power', whichever he thought best. But the document inviting him was the first of three letters outlining expectation he not only leave chaplains and certain servants behind but also, while among the Scots, worship the Presbyterian way 'established by law in Scotland'. Essentially, Charles could either maintain principles or obtain soldiers. He chose the latter. Via written declarations, he promised to comply with those expectations, agreeing to requests word for word. Pressure had been applied in person. Engager John Maitland, Earl of Lauderdale was a Scottish representative tasked with persuading the 18-year-old to yield and had joined him onboard, then cornered him alone,[22] but things were quite harmonious, and Charles was here meeting a man he'd raise to dizzying heights of power through the Cabal, a Restoration innovation in government ministry. Lauderdale meanwhile wrote of his 'great opinion' of the prince having met him.[23] Charles always made friends easily. Many servants, for instance, genuinely cared about him.

Now with eleven ships, the fleet had roughly 300 guns,[24] and in London a story circulated that Charles was 'hurt with powder', prompting Hinton to run to the Downs and jump aboard *Admirall*. This physician who had defended Charles from the charging enemy at Edgehill had also attended Minette in Exeter when she'd suffered convulsions after birth, the prince sending him to her in 1644, but the lifesaving doctor now brought news of mass killing. Presenting Charles with a copy of a letter from Cromwell to Parliament, Hinton revealed that, at the Battle of Preston on 17 August, the Roundheads had inflicted 'totall defeat' on the Engagers' army led by James, Duke (previously Marquis) of Hamilton. Charles was to serve with this army. It was destined for bloodbaths, and by now Buckingham had come along, as Francis's bereaved brother.[25]

However, far from recoiling in fear, Charles grew in bellicosity. As August neared its end, Parliament's Earl of Warwick sailed his own fleet towards the Royalists'. Then came a summons from Warwick calling himself Lord High Admiral of England and instructing removal of the royal standard. To this, Charles replied that only His Majesty could make a Lord High Admiral, and Charles's communication offered pardon, pay and protection to men who left Warwick's command. The prince even promised to receive Warwick 'with sincerity and affection'.[26] However, Warwick still hostile, both sides now had opportunity for an episode of the Civil Wars at sea. And when Charles, to 'great acclamations of joy' from his crew, declared his intention of seizing this opportunity, he was jigging around in zealous anticipation.[27] As he soon awaited the booming of cannon, he

Chapter 13

planted himself on deck, demonstrating how his honour meant more than his protection. He also silenced anyone urging him to take cover from the expected onslaught. Brandishing a pistol, he announced he'd exterminate Warwick personally. This Roundhead, on the other hand, wasn't so trigger-happy just then and decided to hold off fighting till further ships arrived as support, but waiting was the last thing the Royalists could do here. Charles had already been highlighting the problem of dwindling supplies, so when signals for battle finally came, it was no great loss to find the skies deliver a storm forcing the adversaries apart and sending Charles steering his way back to Hellevoetsluis in early September, everyone with him on the brink of dying of thirst.[28]

Although Warwick followed, Dutch ships literally intervened to prevent battle, anchoring themselves between the Royalist and Parliamentarian vessels, and there they stayed. Not for two months would Warwick retreat. The Prince of Orange meanwhile wanted to help the Royalists more, but the governing States-General weren't so keen. As Stadtholder, William possessed limited powers, and Charles was now ensconced in a republic, observing how it worked. Settling into The Hague's court, Charles used his genial manner to good effect though, so it was unfortunate all round when he curtailed significant face-to-face interaction, coming down with one of the seventeenth century's deadliest infectious diseases.

Rendering the heir 'overtaken by a fever'[29] in October, smallpox was a sickness that brought vomiting while producing blisters characterised by a dent in the middle. These threatened to scar Charles for life if he survived. Depending on how it developed, the illness could also leave him blind. He had a lucky escape, reappearing after 'a long convalescence',[30] but soon would come challenges to his mental well-being.

During the prince's sickness, Parliament had been debating how to proceed following their victorious end to the Second Civil War, 19 August's Battle of Winwick having drawn fighting to a close. An impasse still prevailed, but some thought this could be conquered via retribution. In this vein, a set of proposed demands by Ireton came to prominence. One stated that 'the Prince of Wales and the Duke of York should be summoned to surrender for trial on pain of being declared incapable of governing, and sentenced to die without mercy if found in England or its dominions'. Another, meanwhile, centred more intently on the king. So he could be 'speedily brought to justice for the treason, blood[shed], and mischief' he was accused of, a plan was now set in motion to place His Majesty himself on trial.[31] Approval of this plan was far from unanimous, but now came Pride's Purge – here, Colonel Thomas Pride took New Model Army soldiers to Westminster on 6 December, whereupon forty-five disapproving members were arrested and another 186 excluded. Then, after more left of their own accord, MPs in the remaining Rump Parliament, as it's later known, passed an 'Act' (without agreement from the Lords) on 6 January 1649 that dictated King Charles appear before a specially convened High Court of Justice, a court unauthorised by the sovereign. The law wasn't designed this way. Cromwell pushed the scheme forwards, but Fairfax wanted no part of it, and getting someone to agree to act as presiding judge took till 10 January. Now though, a nervous Chief Justice John Bradshaw would be expected to sentence the king to decapitation in the event of a guilty verdict.

By this time, the House of Orange could no longer afford to keep both Charles and James, and the latter had set off to their mother at Saint-Germain, while the former remained in the Netherlands with virtually 'nothing to live on'.[32] More problematic than lack of money, however, was lack of information. News from England took time to reach Holland, so only well into January did Charles hear his father's trial was to take place. With advisers, such as Hyde again, he immediately attempted to halt it all, but he needed outside help. In person, he rushed straight to the Dutch States-General. Then he beseeched the French powers, writing: 'it tends to the security of all kings to oppose examples of such evil consequence'.[33] As January progressed, a French envoy in England was ordered to assist, and two Dutch envoys set off for London together with Sir Henry Seymour, an emissary sent by Charles. But more direct action from the prince existed in the form of a letter he'd written Fairfax's Council of War on 13 January upon receipt of the frightening news. Aiming to remind them they had a choice, Charles affirmed that, if they permitted the king's execution, they would be 'the authors of misery unprecedented in this country [England], by contributing to an action which all Christians think repugnant … . I therefore conjure you to think seriously … and I doubt not you will … preserve and defend the King'.[34] Though not entire, this absence of doubt was all he had to see him through as the cold days passed without a word from London.

When his chaplain Stephen Goffe engaged him in conversation in early February, Charles thought still no news had come. Goffe seemed to have none. He was touching on other topics as if chatting aimlessly. Middialogue, however, the chaplain dropped in two little words; he addressed his royal master as 'Your Majesty'.[35] In the silence that followed, Charles processed what Goffe was telling him and, despite quickly comprehending, appeared 'much astonish'd'. Men in attendance watched a 'sad dejected countenance' cloak Charles as he declared: 'woe be unto the Kingdome of England', and tears started gushing from his eyes.[36]

It had happened. Revolution had stolen his father's life. Late November, his father had told him: 'if God give you success, use it humbly and far from revenge'.[37] Only time could tell whether the new king would comply with this.

Chapter 14

Despite the past decade of anger at Charles I, what had now come to pass was stupefying. Labelled a 'Tyrant, trayter, murderer, and a public enemy',[1] the convicted sovereign had been led onto a scaffold for all to see just three days after his trial and beheaded in accordance with the sentence passed by the High Court of Justice. But the proceedings had all taken place in defiance of the reminder that 'the King *could be tried by noe court*'.[2] The dubious judicial nature of Charles I's journey to the block therefore rendered this act of regicide unique. Virtually nobody had envisaged it, and previous fears did little to prepare Charles II for the sudden reality: 'he knew the desperate state his father was long in, yet the barbarous stroke so surprised him, that he was in all the confusion imaginable'.[3] Failure to foresee it deep down was a particularly crushing factor in Charles's bereavement as it generated inescapable regret. While loitering off the Kent coast during the summer of 1648, he'd had opportunity to sail a rescue party to his father at Carisbrooke Castle, and he'd prevented Bampfield from attempting this. Then in January 1649, did scribbled words and foreign envoys represent unyielding effort from the Prince of Wales? Options had been limited, and anything too bold might have provoked the enemy, but Charles was now to live with the memory of treading so carefully he left just faint footprints on a blocked path towards his father's preservation. Underestimating the Rump Parliament's capability, the famously perceptive Charles II had fallen under a spell of imperception.

So, he was in a state of sombre shock when he robed himself in purple mourning as befitted his now kingly status, while courtiers donned black, and black hangings surrounded him, the Prince of Orange sympathetically footing bills to deck out Charles's rooms appropriately. The following month, Hyde would prepare a declaration from the new monarch 'upon the inhumane and impious murther of his late father' but find it rejected in council.⁴ With 'amazement' part of the reason behind the silence, several months passed before a declaration went public.⁵ Meanwhile Hyde composed a letter on Charles's behalf to Henrietta Maria as Charles was delaying getting in touch, yet this was similarly never sent. It maybe didn't say what Charles wanted to say, his attitude to his mother changing.

There weren't many people the new king could discuss his feelings with just then. He characteristically gratified the Dutch by telling them 'his sole comfort ... was to find himself among them',⁶ but his household had been reduced through financial constraints and sister Mary was his only close relative in Holland. Moreover, he began eating 'like a king', 'alone and no longer with his sister',⁷ though effecting this regal aura did have healing properties, for his father's execution had been accompanied by further injurious developments.

As the hour of the condemned's own choosing,⁸ it was just after 2 pm on 30 January 1649 that a single swing of the axe had ended the life of Charles I outside his beloved Banqueting House at Whitehall. There on the scaffold, he'd divested himself of a diamond-encrusted carved onyx example of a 'George', the badge of the Order of the Garter depicting St George's slaying of the dragon, and handed this to trusted prelate William Juxon to send to the 18-year-old Charles as ascending sovereign.⁹ But that morning, the Commons had passed what it termed an Act stating that, on penalty of death, 'no person or persons whatsoever do presume to Proclaim, Declare, Publish, or any way promote Charls Stuart ... commonly called, The Prince of Wales, or any other person to be King ... of England, or of Ireland, or of any [of] the Dominions belonging to them'.¹⁰

Unsurprisingly, Charles assumed the title of King immediately. By birthright, 'fundamental laws' meant the crown was his, he professed.¹¹ And, together with his followers, he was hellbent on restoration. Therefore, to stop him 'sinking under the burden of his grief', 'those who were about him besought him to resume so much courage as was necessary'.¹² But he needed advice too.

He thus formed a Privy Council comprising experienced men. Charles I's treasurer Francis Cottington and lord keeper Richard Lane were included, while much of the nucleus of advice from the old Western Association days got in, Brentford, Colepeper, Hopton and Hyde all appointed.¹³ One of their ex-colleagues, however, couldn't join them. Lord Capell had surrendered to Fairfax in August and following escape from the Tower was executed by Parliament on 9 March together with the Engagers' army leader Hamilton and old turncoat courtier the Earl of Holland who had more recently defected back to the Royalists. With Cromwell at the fore, MPs were dictating all, and they had to deal with threats. Ten days after the peers' executions, the House of Commons abolished the House of Lords, although the 'Act' that occasioned this was overshadowed by another. This other one, on 17 March, constituted the abolition of the monarchy.

That was south of the border though. In Edinburgh, the Scots had proclaimed Charles king on 5 February. But they would only accept him in a governing capacity if he met certain demands. While the Engagers under Lauderdale and the new Duke of Hamilton (William, brother of the executed James Hamilton) were Covenant signatories demonstrating malleability, the dominating force in Scotland was the more stubborn Covenanting faction known as the Kirk Party led by a worryingly adroit Archibald Campbell, Marquis of Argyll. These particular Presbyterians were disparagingly nicknamed the Whiggamores or Whigs – the sobriquet applied to the Duke of York's opponents nearer the end of the seventeenth century – and, like the later Whigs, had rigid ideas about the beliefs their monarch should hold. They wanted a Covenanter on the throne. They had handed Charles I to Parliament for refusing to become one. Now in March 1649 a group of their commissioners was travelling to his eldest son for negotiations at The Hague's Binnenhof palace.

From the off, Hyde was outraged by them: 'In their proclamation and letters they express no detestation of the murder or murderers of the King' and spoke of the regicide as though it had been 'an ordinary accident', and that was only when they mentioned it at all.[14] They weren't even very forthcoming on the matter they were there to discuss. At first, they focused on little beyond calling for Charles to punish the leading Scottish Royalist, James Graham, Marquis of Montrose, though such a request was no surprise. This marquis had inflicted bloody defeat on the Covenanters in a series of battles during the mid-1640s, capitalising on hatred driven partly by clan feuding. But, from the royal perspective, he was both a military mastermind and a monarchist of unrelenting support. Just then Montrose was busy acquiring eleven diamond rings from Denmark. Charles decided to be firm. He told the Covenanters he'd agree to nothing until they had revealed everything. When they did, he learned their conditions not only entailed his signing both Covenants (the National Covenant and the Solemn League and Covenant) but also that he promise to establish Presbyterianism

Chapter 14

by law, refer all ecclesiastical matters to the Kirk's General Assembly and leave all civil matters in the hands of Edinburgh's parliament. Unable to appease with halfway measures, Charles would decline.

But he'd graciously received a book containing the Covenants and other Presbyterian texts and bitten his tongue amid the inadequate respect shown by the commissioners, leaving their minister Robert Baillie describing him as 'one of the most gentle, innocent, well-inclyned Princes ... in the world'.[15] Not all Scottish hopes were lost, and Charles was lining Montrose up for military action to coax the Kirk Party into submission. Anyway, there seemed no need to rush with Scotland; in January, Ormond had signed the Second Ormond Peace, another treaty with the Irish Catholic Confederates, and soldiers awaited Charles in Ireland. However, the current plan of journeying to them required money, when finances were cripplingly low.

Like Montrose, counsellors would soon travel hundreds and hundreds of miles to pursue monetary aid from foreign powers. Meanwhile Charles was sending circulars begging cash, but he also combined business with pleasure to address the funding crisis. Dallying with Palatine princesses had become an enchanting feature of his life in The Hague. Through this, he was showing real warmth for Sophia,[16] Rupert's youngest sister. By her husband Ernest Augustus in 1660, Sophia would give birth to the royal known now as George I, the 1714 successor to Charles's niece Anne when the Hanovers supplanted the Stuarts. Not even Charles could predict that, however. In 1649, he and Sophia were great friends and often attended church together, but a walk at Voorhout didn't go too well. Here Charles showered Sophia with such intense compliments that she suspected underlying motives, and their relationship crumbled as his interest in her focused that bit more on her purse than her person. His attraction to Lucy, on the other hand, was no secret as a physical phenomenon. With a baby James, fondly known as Jemmy, appearing from Lucy's womb in Rotterdam in the spring, the new king acknowledged paternity, apparently unperturbed by confessing sins of the flesh, no marriage intimated.

But a more shameful incident was coming as May dawned. Just arrived in The Hague was Isaac Dorislaus, an envoy for the new English regime who had been denouncing regal authority since the 1620s. More notably, he'd also helped draw up the treason charges against Charles I, and as this anti-monarchist settled into Dutch lodgings at an inn on 2 May, a group of Cavaliers burst in with Colonel Walter Whitford, a Scottish courtier of the young Charles's, determined to take revenge. Dorislaus stood no chance.

As his head was 'cleaved' with a broadsword,[17] it was instant murder, and one that put Charles dangerously close to implication.

Because this made the move to Ireland urgent, Charles sought money from the governor of Flanders and further contacted the emperor of Germany before presenting himself to the Dutch States-General, hoping for a loan of £20,000 and some ships. Not that the latter were needed yet. The Celtic Sea south of Ireland provided the best way to Ireland, but sailing into that sea was risky as Commonwealth vessels prowled to its east. A route by land to the western French coast thus seemed safer. Moreover, it would take Charles through Flanders in the Spanish Netherlands, and it therefore brought prudent timing of secret propositions put to Spain, including a promise to attempt to repeal all laws 'made to the prejudice of English Catholics'.

With preparations nearly complete, a 'solemn fast' was to be held two days before Charles's scheduled departure.[18] Saying goodbye to Mary and aunt Elizabeth in Breda, the Stuart monarch then found events went gratifyingly in Flanders, where from 11 June he spent around forty-eight hours in Antwerp with palace accommodation and received 25,000 gold crowns courtesy of Felipe IV, King of Spain.[19] Charles was 'royally entertained' in Brussels too. Then came ceremonies as he passed through Valenciennes.[20] But a longer stopoff would occur in France, heralding some interesting behaviour.

A league from Compiègne, Charles was greeted by 10-year-old Louis and queen regent Anne and chatted in French as hunting was discussed.[21] However, when topics of conversation put him on his guard, he sometimes 'opened his teeth only to devour fat meat', and he suddenly appeared unrefined in the process, maybe on purpose. During a banquet held by the regent, Charles was observed tucking into a shoulder of mutton and an 'enormous' piece of beef 'as if he had never eaten before', showing himself up further by meanwhile declining the highly regarded delicacy of ortolans. With La Grande Mademoiselle concluding he had 'somewhat indelicate' taste,[22] this was perhaps another attempt to keep Mademoiselle at arm's length.

Reaching Saint-Germain soon after this, Charles was irked by more of his mother's schemes to make this ambitious duchess his wife, but Henrietta Maria needed to remember that the occurrence of the regicide meant a transposition in the Stuart family. The former queen consort was

Chapter 14

now the queen mother, and her eldest boy, as king, had risen above her. Over their first two to three days together, mother and son reflected in solidarity, pouring out their grief with tears for the martyred monarch, but the atmosphere soon turned. As Henrietta Maria enquired 'what course' he planned for restoration, Charles evaded questions. Ultimately, in fact, he told his mother to keep her nose out of it, and he didn't even apologise. While promising to 'perform his duty towards her with great affection and exactness', he informed the widow he'd be following his own judgement so had no mind to discuss business with her. After this, he took to plain avoidance where possible and often walked out on her abruptly.[23]

Nevertheless, with Charles's coldness unexpected, blame was laid on someone else. New groom of the bedchamber Thomas Elliot was an overly confident individual who now rarely left the close side of Charles but had been separated from him for ill influence in 1644–45. Regaining influence now, Elliot was forever whispering words into Charles's ear, including a message outlining how 'the most unpopular thing' the king could do was to allow himself to be 'governed by his mother',[24] but Charles already understood the dangers posed by an image like that. It was lucky the maternal figure of Christabella stirred less political controversy, because Elliot's sway over Charles perhaps centred more on her. This groom of the bedchamber was Christabella's son-in-law, and meanwhile the man Charles hinted at to fill the role of Secretary of State was none other than Christabella's husband Colonel Edmund Wyndham, who possessed not a jot of qualification for the job. If real sexual air existed between Charles and Christabella, it seems to have provoked no jealousy of her husband, Charles dismissing concerns about inexperience and asserting Wyndham was an honest man.

But the good-natured side of Charles was exploited through this juvenile misguidance. One day, the roughly 70-year-old Cottington mentioned to Charles that an elderly falconer who had served the late king deserved recognition. Deadpan, Cottington strung Charles along to think a genuine request was coming but then, in front of several courtiers, asked whether the falconer could get a chaplain's position, explaining him to be as suitable for it as Wyndham was for Secretary of State. Nobody could stop themselves giggling, and the story was quickly passed round 'in all companies' as the king grew so red-faced he felt forced to disappoint Wyndham.[25] Secretary duties were left with Long, meaning more reminisce to the distressing Western Association period, but Cottington easily got away with humiliating his royal master.

If Charles wanted to hide on occasion, he had the arms of Lucy to retreat into, at least in August 1649. Lucy's record nevertheless implies she struggled to curb her friendliness with other men, so the possibility Lucy cheated on the king is no unlikely catalyst of his perpetual infidelity. Either way, Charles was almost certainly cheating on Lucy when he began an affair with Thomas Killigrew's sister Elizabeth Boyle, a married woman eight years his senior who bore him a daughter in the early 1650s. Christened Charlotte Jemima Henrietta Maria, the girl would get the surname Fitzroy, indicating her royal paternity.

Amours aside, Charles again wasn't having the best time in France. He'd intended to stay just ten days, but Ormond had written to inform him of Cromwell journeying to Ireland with an army, halting the move west.[26] Charles edged a little nearer though. Returning to Jersey in late September, he stepped onto British soil for the first time since the monarchy's abolition, yet Jersey seemed safer than France in a sense. The king's resolve to take the Duke of York with him was considered a decision made 'to annoy his mother, with whom there is little love lost'. However, the goal of removing her influence from the duke was added to by concern Charles felt regarding loyalty from the French: 'he fears that they mean to deceive, to divert the wrath of parliament', reported Michiel Morosini, Venetian ambassador in France, who therefore believed that the elder brother was unwilling to leave the younger 'exposed to the caprice of those who would think nothing of sacrificing him'.[27]

So, James also now witnessed the Royalist fervour in Jersey, a land where Carteret's proclaiming of Charles as king had been met with passionate embrace on 16 February. However, despite exultant welcomes to the sounds of pealing bells and sights of bonfires, this sojourn bore a subdued feel compared to that of 1646. Charles chatted to charmed faces looking up at him, and he smiled to acknowledge the respect shown at every turn, but his countenance betrayed despondence within him, and the royals appeared in their mourning dress, the king consequently cutting a grave purple figure. With dogs and armed guards at their side, they nevertheless jaunted around. Every Sunday, they rowed from Elizabeth Castle to attend church at St Helier, and Charles returned to sailing his pinnace when he wasn't out shooting. Both brothers threw themselves into hobbies like this, with Charles in January 1650 describing his suits 'for horse-back' as 'so

A 1629 painting by Daniël Mijtens (Metropolitan Museum of Art, New York): Charles's father Charles I with orb, sceptre and state crown. Little did he know most of the Crown Jewels such as these would be destroyed in the aftermath of his death.

A 1630 jeton (Rijksmuseum, Amsterdam): commemorating the birth and baptism of the future Charles II. The obverse features symbols of England, Scotland and Ireland but also France. In a tradition originating with the Plantagenets, Stuart monarchs nominally claimed to reign over France too.

After a 1632 painting by Anthony van Dyck, a c. 1660s mezzotint by Wallerant Vaillant (Rijksmuseum, Amsterdam): Charles the toddler. Mainly due to his dark features, Charles was considered 'ugly'. Remembering this, artists perhaps portrayed him inaccurately. In some early 1630s artwork, his hair appears fair.

A 1636 painting by Anthony van Dyck (Metropolitan Museum of Art, New York): Charles's mother Henrietta Maria with arms cradled. The pose implies she was pregnant, and the following year she gave birth for the sixth time. Through childhood, Charles was accustomed to seeing her pregnant.

After a 1636 painting by Anthony van Dyck, a 1752 mezzotint by James McArdell (Rijksmuseum, Amsterdam): George Villiers, 2nd Duke of Buckingham and his brother Lord Francis Villiers. Charles viewed them like his own brothers, growing up with them, but Buckingham seems to have been a bad influence.

A 1637 painting by Anthony van Dyck, photographic reproduction (Rijksmuseum, Amsterdam): siblings (from left) Mary, James, Charles, Elizabeth, Anne. The dogs were just two of several the children were growing up around.

A 1638 etching by Wenceslaus Hollar (Metropolitan Museum of Art, New York): Richmond. The palace was Charles's main home at the time, and the king is in the foreground with his sons. Age 4 to 5, James already wears breeches. This helps indicate Charles was 'breeched' at that age.

Right: Artwork in Newcastle, Margaret, Duchess of, *The Life of William Cavendish Duke of Newcastle*, ed. C. H. Firth (Internet Archive): William Cavendish, who was Earl of Newcastle when Charles's governor. Newcastle's scientific, theatrical and sporting interests seem to have influenced Charles distinctly. Lack of spirituality in the earl may also be significant.

Below: A 1641 etching by Wenceslaus Hollar (Rijksmuseum, Amsterdam): the trial of the Earl of Strafford. Each day of the trial, 10-year-old Charles sat as a lone royal on show while John Pym argued for the prosecution and sickly Strafford defended himself.

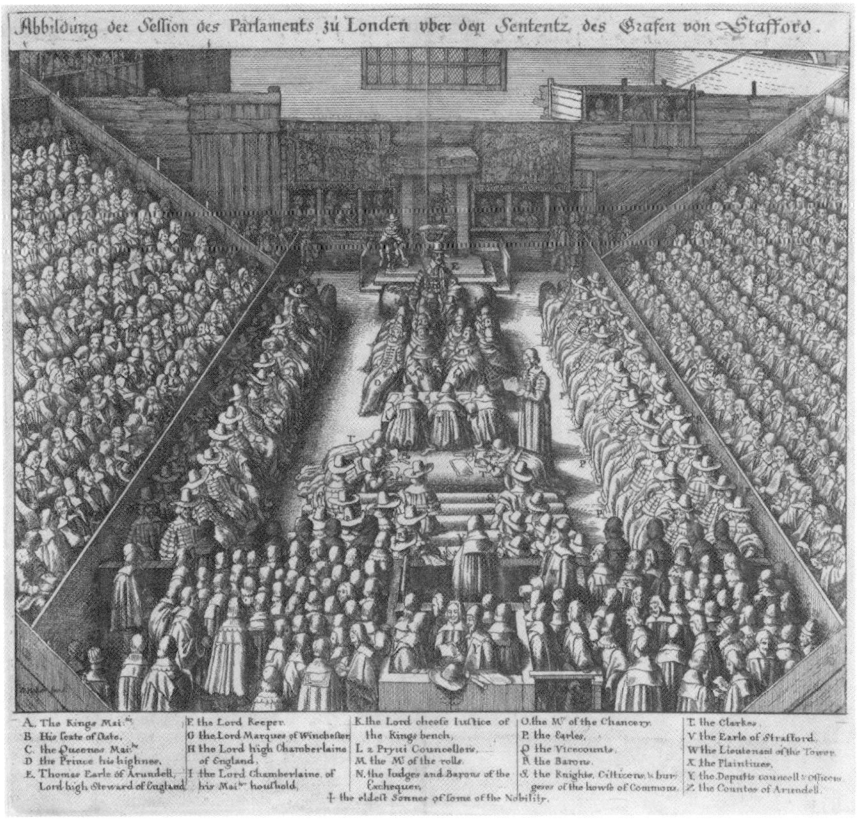

After a 1641 painting by Anthony van Dyck, a 1649 etching by Wenceslaus Hollar (Rijksmuseum, Amsterdam): Charles looking characteristically mature aged 11. However, the etching is post-regicide, and its background includes Banqueting House, the site of the regicide.

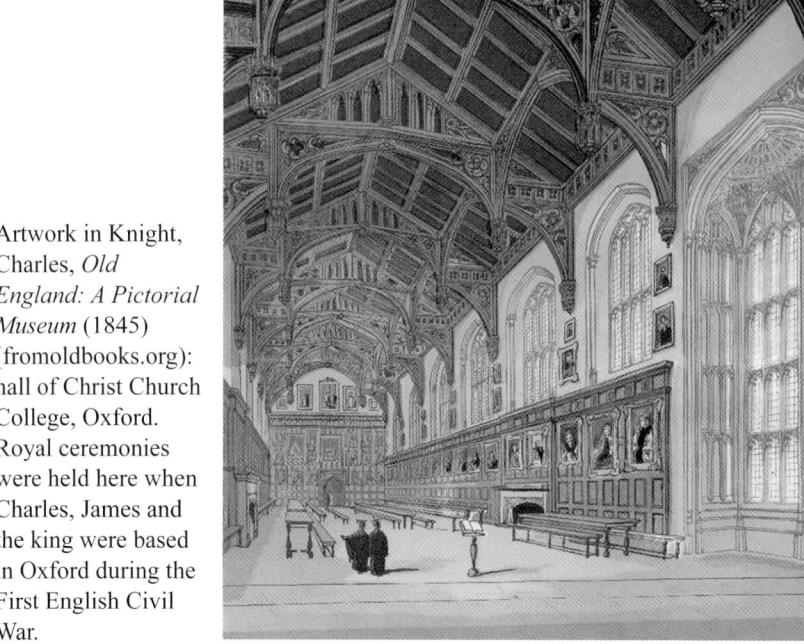

Artwork in Knight, Charles, *Old England: A Pictorial Museum* (1845) (fromoldbooks.org): hall of Christ Church College, Oxford. Royal ceremonies were held here when Charles, James and the king were based in Oxford during the First English Civil War.

A modern-day photograph (Wikimedia Commons): Pendennis Castle, Cornwall. Hearing of a plot to kidnap him having arrived here in early 1646, Charles did not dare leave the premises until he was fleeing England, heading for the Scilly Isles that March.

A mid-seventeenth-century engraving (Rijksmuseum, Amsterdam): Louis XIV shortly before Charles first met him. Louis had a serious temperament in childhood and did not click with teenaged Charles, despite mutual respect.

A mid-seventeenth-century engraving (Rijksmuseum, Amsterdam): Charles's potential queen 'La Grande Mademoiselle', Duchess of Montpensier, in artwork paralleling the Louis artwork. Extremely self-important, the duchess didn't much entice Charles, but he spent many months courting her, at his mother's insistence initially, then tried to marry her for her vast wealth.

A 1647 painting by Gerard Van Honthorst (Rijksmuseum, Amsterdam): Charles's sister Mary and her husband William II, Prince of Orange. Charles benefitted from much generosity from William in 1648–50 and received compassion at the Orange court when news of Charles I's execution came.

After a regicide-era painting by Adriaen Hanneman, a 1650s miniature by Nathaniel Thach (Rijksmuseum, Amsterdam): Charles sporting the Order of the Garter sash. Miniatures enabled people to carry pictures of family, and pictures of Charles took a similar place in the hearts of some Royalists.

A 1656 etching by Wallerant Vaillant (Rijksmuseum, Amsterdam): Charles's cousin Sophia of the Palatinate. Around the time Charles became a father by Lucy Walter, he conducted a teenaged romance with Sophia, until she terminated it. All British monarchs since George I are descended from Sophia, but not through Charles.

A modern-day photograph (Wikimedia Commons): Elizabeth Castle, Jersey. With land access impossible at high tide, Charles loved it when he had to row or sail to and from the islet on which the castle stands. Deemed a secure fortress, Elizabeth Castle was his residence during 1646 and 1649–50.

A c. 1651 engraving and etching (Rijksmuseum, Amsterdam): allegory *The Scene of English Misery*. Charles is primed to fight for the English throne. On the right is a seven-headed dragon of Parliament beside the severed head of Charles I, whose execution fills the background.

Artwork in Knight, Charles, *Old England: A Pictorial Museum* (1845) (fromoldbooks.org): the Battle of Worcester. As King of the Scots and head Royalist, Charles commanded and fought in the thick of it, throwing himself into some of the worst bloodshed of the Wars of the Three Kingdoms.

Above: A c. 1700 snuffbox (Metropolitan Museum of Art, New York): Charles in the oak tree. He is depicted among the leaves, with an angel presenting him with the three Stuart crowns, and below ride two Roundheads seeking him out. Such souvenirs were produced in many forms.

Right: After a 1640s–50s painting by Adriaen Hanneman, an eighteenth-century mezzotint by Thomas Johnson (Rijksmuseum, Amsterdam): Sir Edward Hyde, later Earl of Clarendon, arguably the most competent man in Charles's councils. From age 14, Charles had him as a leading adviser, tolerating constant berating from Hyde till 1667.

A c. 1653 painting by Adriaen Hanneman (National Gallery of Art, Washington, DC): Charles's brother Henry. From infancy in 1642, Henry was imprisoned by Parliament for roughly eleven years. However, on the Continent afterwards, he shared the life of Charles, who helped bring him up as dutiful prince.

A 1655 print (Rijksmuseum, Amsterdam): relief of Arras (1654) in the Franco-Spanish War, with France's chief minister Cardinal Mazarin bottom left. As Mazarin allied with Oliver Cromwell, Charles joined Spain in this war and led new Cavalier regiments. Today's Grenadier Guards descends from one, Lord Rochester's regiment.

A late-seventeenth-century painting by Gerrit Berckheyde (Clark Art Institute, Williamstown, MA): Cologne. Avoiding the expenses of owning a coach, impoverished Charles travelled on foot and often took walks for pure pleasure during his Cologne residency, familiarising himself with the city.

A 1660 engraving attributed to Pieter Philippe (Rijksmuseum, Amsterdam): Charles addressing the Dutch States-General before his 1660 departure for England. The meeting formed part of the rapturous embrace of his restoration.

spotted and spoiled' that he'd be ashamed out wearing them anywhere else.[28] Indoors, he nevertheless applied himself to business, if with a little persuasion, and derived some pleasure from drawing a map of Jersey, with which he impressed officials thanks to its accuracy. But anything that cost much was unattainable. While the royal party's presence again caused a food supply problem on the island, a meagreness in the dishes served[29] at Elizabeth Castle resulted from Stuart poverty, and Charles made yet more servants redundant. He also resorted to selling sections of the island. Meanwhile Privy Council members and other men the king relied upon were rewarded with lands in America.[30] Yet many Covenanters regarded the Privy Council as Charles's main problem. Sent by the parliament of Scotland amid (well-founded) fears Charles was ordering Montrose to invade, George Winram, Laird of Libberton had arrived in Jersey in late 1649 and mused that the king's 'deuillish Counsell will suffer him to starue before they will suffer him to take the League & Covenant'.[31]

Charles preferred to avoid both forms of suffering though. Every day he hoped for favourable news from Ireland that would theoretically enable him to reach Ormond's Catholic army and render the Covenanters superfluous to needs. By 1650, however, his Irish prospects looked hideously bleak. Cromwell had begun a conquest of the western realm that already included shocking massacres at Drogheda and Wexford, and Charles realised a Scottish army instead was vital. He decided to recommence discussion with the Kirk Party.

With Breda in Holland set as the meeting place, Charles prepared to leave James in Jersey and make him feel important going solo. However, while transferring the island's official governorship from Jermyn to the 16-year-old duke, the king told Carteret to keep 'a very strict eye' on the boy secretly.[32] James was correct in thinking his eldest sibling had little confidence in him.

Some bad influence was nevertheless removed from James when the king left Jersey. Retracing his steps to a degree, Charles trekked back through France en route to Breda but now stopped at Beauvais, where his court displayed 'such extream debauchery' that it was 'hardly' possible to believe. Against this backdrop, the king lodged in a house with his mother and showed 'very great respect' to her and Jermyn. However, Henrietta Maria was constantly pressing her son to take her advice, and after three hours with him just before parting in March, she emerged 'red with anger'.[33]

Charles was far less provocative with officials. When he met the Scottish commissioners on 16 March though, he came with scant bargaining power, and Argyll's men were still fixed on the terms proposed a year earlier. In September 1649, the king had added to the Privy Council. Now it included 1630s overseer of ship money collection, Edward Nicholas, whom Charles I had recommended for Charles's service but Henrietta Maria disliked. Desire to please father but defy mother may therefore have swayed Charles II to accept Nicholas. Either way, he didn't take great heed of Nicholas's advice in 1650. Like Hyde, Nicholas was devoted to Anglicanism and episcopacy and appalled by Kirk Party demands. Hyde would have backed Nicholas in person, but since the autumn Hyde had been in Madrid with Cottington, seeking help from Felipe, and remained on Spanish soil for now. Meanwhile Engager Hamilton and unspiritual favourites Newcastle and Buckingham were admitted to the Privy Council, and Lauderdale and the Prince of Orange bombarded Charles with reasons to give in to the Kirk Party.[34] Through a month and a half of tense talks Charles nevertheless strove for compromise regarding England particularly and tried to resist pressure to annul the Second Ormond Peace. But what he achieved was a draft of the 1650 Treaty of Breda, and Edinburgh's parliament repudiated this draft on 18 May.[35] Despite his odd display of 'bitter execration' at the commissioners, a spy report claimed he 'strokes them till he can get into the saddle, and then he will make them feel his spurs ... and they ... will not agree he shall back them with his heels armed'.[36] Charles didn't yet know the treaty had been refused, but the reality was the Covenanters were poised to strap their king into the harness.

Chapter 15

On his twentieth birthday, Charles II was informed of a gruesome event that blackened his name. From Edinburgh, the news had taken more than a week to reach him in Holland, but slowness of communication applied both ways, and this was part of the problem. By advancing from the Orkneys and attempting invasion of Scotland, the Marquis of Montrose had been obeying the king's orders, a situation leading to his defeat at the Battle of Carbisdale on 27 April 1650, but he'd acted without knowledge of developments at the Breda talks that month. From these talks, the king agreed to disavow Montrose's campaign; in official terms, he made Montrose guilty of treachery. Rather late, Charles had instructed him to disband and disarm. However, failing to receive the instructions, 'the Great Marquis' was doomed after capture near Loch Assynt in the Highlands on 4 May. Without trial, he suffered ignoble hanging on Edinburgh's high street on 21 May before Charles could interpose. Then, following three hours in a gibbet, Montrose was quartered, and the four sections plus the head were distributed for display across Scotland.

One communication Charles perhaps should have delayed was his letter of condolence to the marquis's eldest surviving son. It bears the date of Charles's twentieth birthday and appears self-centred. 'Though your father is unfortunately lost, contrary to my expectation,' the sovereign wrote, '... I shall have the same care for you as if he were still living and as able to serve me as ever'.[1] The disavowal had helped get Charles invited to Scotland, and he didn't yet regret what he was doing.

Thanks to the provision of vessels from the Prince of Orange, he boarded a man-of-war and set sail with relative optimism in early June. Then, mid-crossing, the weather forced a stop off Heligoland, and news of the repudiation of the Treaty of Breda draft was broken to him here, original requests thrust in his face. The king was so incensed that he threatened to swivel round for Denmark[2] and deny the Kirk Party what it sought – regal backing in governance. His little convoy nevertheless proceeded towards Caledonia, and upon anchorage on the Moray Firth near the village of Garmouth,[3] the Scottish crown dangled like a bejewelled carrot. As successor, he had key duties in continuing his father's cause, but it seemed impossible to fulfil them simultaneously. Without power, he could do little for episcopacy anyway, and the Kirk Party appeared his only route to power. So it was that within eighteen months of his father becoming a martyr for episcopacy, Charles subscribed to Presbyterianism, unconditionally. He signed both Covenants on 23 June before being allowed ashore, and the final version of the Treaty of Breda moved towards ratification as a massive white flag of surrender.

That's because Charles was promising to confirm Acts already passed in Scotland's Covenanter-led parliament, acquiesce to both this parliament and the Kirk in future, annul the Second Ormond Peace, penalise Catholics, attempt to enforce Presbyterianism in England and ensure Presbyterian practice in his household and family. What's more, such rules should not upset him, some thought. One of the commissioners was Alexander Jaffray, voted representative for Aberdeen in the 1640s, and he'd advised Charles not to sign unless spiritually inclined to. By signing, Charles conjured the illusion of becoming Presbyterian in mind, not just name. But to an insider it was 'clear and demonstrable' that the king abhorred the pact.[4]

For outsiders, however, his feelings were concealed,[5] with his new Covenanter status leading Scots to sing, dance and lob furniture onto celebratory bonfires while the Kirk Party limited his contact with the populace. Now on his way down to the ancient royal residence of Falkland Palace in Fife, Charles was nonetheless to make numerous stops. Therefore, moving on to the Bog of Gicht for a day or two, he reportedly wrote from the mansion of Shulagreen in Culsalmond to invite himself to Pitcaple House a few miles ahead. This story goes on to relate that he was entertained at a ball held on the lawn at Pitcaple, during which a female known as the Good Wife of Glack piped up with bold words. Argyll 'helped to tak off your father's head,' she allegedly told Charles, with this foremost statesman seated right beside him; 'if ye takna care, [he] will tak aff yours neist'.

Aberdeen nevertheless welcomed him, using public funding to cover his expenses and gifting him £1,500 in Scottish currency, but Edinburgh's parliament quickly forbade further burghs from making such gestures.[6]

Chapter 15

Introducing him to Caledonian customs wasn't frowned upon though. Having proceeded to the shoreline castle of Dunnottar near Stonehaven, Charles became a guest of David Carnegie, Earl of Southesk, at Southesk's family estate of Kinnaird House on 29 June,[7] and was here persuaded to perch one leg on a door bolt to honour tradition while downing a goblet of wine.[8] Scotland was foreign territory to Charles. Near the river Ury en route from Pitcaple, he'd commented that crops at a farm evoked memories of 'dear England',[9] but over the coming months he would form an overarching preference for the southern kingdom, setting within him a lifelong aversion to the Scots despite his Stuart ancestry.

Although July began with a hospitable three-day stay at the medieval tower house Dudhope Castle towards Dundee, Charles then crossed the Tay to arrive outside St Mary's College in St Andrews where a Principal Rutherford pontificated in Latin about regal responsibilities, warning that cooperation from Scotland would cease if the king dishonoured the Covenants. Then within hours, Charles visited prominent Kirk minister Robert Blair, who stopped his wife bringing their royal guest a chair. His Majesty could get one himself, the clergyman asserted.[10] Blair was friendlier than some though. When Charles I had been captive to the Scots, forced into Presbyterian worship he'd chosen this minister as his chaplain. Now the General Assembly assigned Blair as chaplain to Charles II.

By this time, Scottish officials were well into organising the king's circle and wanted to oust nearly all the gents and nobles young Charles had brought from Holland, perceiving a large proportion to be anti-Covenant 'malignants'. Brentford and Long went, as did Scots Hamilton and Lauderdale, which angered Charles immeasurably, but these Scots both led the Engagers and represented the Hamilton and Maitland clans respectively; they were major rivals of Argyll, whose loyalties divided between the Kirk Party and the Campbell clan, and Charles now had to remember the history of clan warring. Understanding it could help him navigate the challenges ahead. In fact, he needed to understand more than ever now that some of his advisers were barred from him, yet his autonomy didn't look likely to see the light of day.

Given new servants, the king was suitably provided for. His 'table was well served, and there he sat in majesty, waited upon with decency'. Meanwhile when out, he appeared in regal style, but he could only go where permitted, when permitted.[11] The 20-year-old was treated like a spoiled but grounded pubescent who required discipline and removal from bad influences. Presbyterian ministers never left him alone, sometimes turning up in his chamber to lecture him. And despite adopting 'the humblest postures', they 'reprehended him very sharply if he smiled' on Sundays 'and if his looks and gestures did not please them, whilst all their prayers and sermons, at which he was compelled to be present, were libels and bitter invectives against all the actions of his father, the idolatry of his mother, and his own malignity'.[12] This was tough treatment to take. At its most intense, Charles experienced a blasting of these sermons into his ears several times a day. He also experienced restrictions akin to English laws just then. With gaiety banned, the king was severely berated if caught dancing or playing cards, and more sinful pleasures could bring worse. Having, at a window, been spotted 'fondling' a mistress, he was nearly forced to 'doe public penance ... and suffer a rebuke from the pulpite'. In the end, a sympathetic cleric handled admonishment for this privately, telling the youth that when one was 'inclined to kiss his neighbour's wife, it was proper to shut all the doors and windows!'[13]

But sympathetic characters seemed rarities. Scottish parliamentary votes fundamentally dictated the punishing life Charles now lived, even though Argyll recognised the value of having him on side and worked to limit the misery. In his forties, this magnate was a short, slender, mild-mannered individual with a squint, and in person Charles got on with him well, delighting in the noble's conversation. Even the lowly ranks found Argyll approachable, yet he was Scotland's most powerful man. The king meanwhile found himself forbidden input in government. Outside intense hours of compulsory prayer, Charles therefore languished, but his preference for instant contentment on Earth rather than eternal happiness in Heaven says something about him as he knew death could be just around the corner.

Although he had no promise of military help from the Covenanters, he hoped it was coming. He wanted to be soon conquering England with Scottish soldiers, and Fairfax had been poised to retaliate, but many others in the New Model Army felt prevention was better than cure. Their plan was to invade Scotland before Charles could reach England. In 1649, Fairfax had crushed Leveller mutinies and ordered merciless executions, but now, probably at his wife's persuasion, he refused to wage war on Scotland – 'to whom we are engaged in a solemn league and covenant', he explained. With that, Fairfax had resigned as head of the New Model Army, and into his place had ascended Cromwell on the same day, 26 June 1650.[14]

The Covenanter army meanwhile took orders from Lieutenant General David Leslie, a Scottish serviceman whose career had begun in Sweden around 1630 before having him train guns on the Cavaliers. At Marston

Chapter 15

Moor, Leslie and Cromwell had combined their skills, but now they were pitched against each other. To stop Cromwell's advance, Leslie was ordering fortification, as Charles witnessed by turning up among Covenanter troops. He'd been asked to stay away, though. The request he ignored came from the Committee of Estates, the body Scotland's parliament was replaced with when not in session, and the soldiers' cheers at his arrival explained the Committee's desire to keep Charles detached from the army; he was capable of seizing control of it.[15] Meanwhile Charles was trying to detach the Committee from the army. On 19 July he'd asked Argyll to prevent the Committee from giving Leslie orders and leave decisions to Leslie's judgement.[16]

Initially, this judgement seemed sound as a fresh war began with the New Model blocked throughout 1650's wet August and pushed back to the southeast Scottish coast. However, on 3 September Leslie's army met catastrophe at the Battle of Dunbar, depleting its numbers by thousands. This was the army Charles desperately needed, but he loathed the Kirk Party more each day. He also imagined their losses would soften them to the idea of Royalist and Engager involvement. Privately, his reaction was mixed. He 'comforted' Argyll and company,[17] but Cromwell was told the monarch dropped to his knees to thank God for the defeat.[18]

Publicly though, Charles had to apologise to God. On 12 September, General Assembly moderator Robert Douglas told Charles: 'Wee pray the Lord to give your Majestie the grace of repentance and reall humiliation, that all the Lord's controversie may be taken away from you and your Royall family'.[19] Hearing the sermons wasn't enough; Charles himself had to say much the same things. Scotland wanted him shrouded with Stuart guilt for all to see. In August, the Kirk Party had already pushed Charles into signing a declaration denouncing himself and his parents, and his Covenanter alliance brought serious family consequences.

Although Henrietta Maria recommended cooperation with the Covenanters, she resented the concessions made by Charles and had declared herself 'disabled to serve him'.[20] In addition, though very indirectly, his Scottish move had even led to Stuart tragedy. Due to Charles's presence in the British Isles, a report from Westminster's Council of State in the summer asserted that, in the event of insurrections, 'the late King's children ... may be made use of to the prejudice of the public'. Therefore, Elizabeth and Henry, still as captives of England's parliament, were moved from Penshurst Place in Kent to their father's 1648 Isle of Wight prison Carisbrooke Castle, much to the distress of Elizabeth. The regicide had taken a dreadful toll on Elizabeth's psychological welfare, but at least her respiratory problems had improved at Penshurst. Conversely at Carisbrooke, she'd fallen alarmingly ill following a soaking in sudden rain. The island's Dr Bignall possessed limited expertise, and the result was devastating, leaving Charles to learn his 14-year-old sister had passed away on 8 September.[21] It was eight years since he'd seen her.

The king had now reached a severe low. These were still early days for coming to terms with his father's execution, restoration was nowhere in sight and, by joining with Presbyterians, he alienated quite a few Royalists. Meanwhile Continental powers continued quailing at the thought of the Rump Parliament's wrath should they support him. Little came from the many countries approached. Colepeper had recently secured a three-year loan of 20,000 rubles' worth of fur and corn after going to Moscow[22] and kissing the robe of Russian czar Aleksey Mikhaylovich, but it was negligible. Then there was Lucy. It seems the king had grown to distrust her quite seriously and instructed Elliot to have Jemmy abducted some months earlier. Lucy had hence been sent into at least ten days' panic looking for the precious baby she'd born by Charles.[23] Now Charles was suffering an oppressive daily existence in the hands of Presbyterian clerics, he decided on rash behaviour here as well.

His Scottish physician Fraser had been with him since at least 1646, and Charles trusted him so much that he'd started using Fraser for secret liaising with Engagers and Royalists. As a result, the king was preparing to flee his current quasi prison in Perth in central Scotland and head to the Highlands to lead an uprising against the Kirk Party. At least 11,000 were reportedly waiting to join him,[24] and so began an episode known as 'the Start'. By now, Buckingham was cunningly well in with Argyll and, as one of few allowed to remain at court, helped steer Charles away from this risky idea, or so the duke thought. The king called it off but then became highly distressed and cursed the advice of Buckingham before falling into a huge argument with him. It was 3 October, the day scheduled for the insurgence, and Charles thought there was still chance to revert to Plan A,[25] albeit perhaps twenty-four hours late. Around 1.30 pm the following day, he therefore jumped on a horse, taking just a handful of men and not so much as a change of clothes.

Chapter 15

Interestingly, he went with something indicating his scientific enthusiasm – a set of Euclid's mathematical problems that he probably carried around in the thin riding suit he was wearing. At this point, however, his own problems preoccupied him. Needing to explain his disappearance, he met Engager Lord Balcarres and sent him to the Committee to say His Majesty had gone to raise troops for Scottish defence. The Committee knew better though, maybe informed by Buckingham, and soldiers mounted steeds to give chase. Despite dropping in at the homes of allies along the way, Charles ignored advice to turn back and made quick work of forty-two miles, staying ahead of his pursuers, but he'd also overtaken his messages cancelling the uprising's initial cancellation. He consequently met disappointment at the destination of Glen Clova, no vast numbers bearing arms. So, with darkness descending like his spirits, the monarch retired to the Laird of Clova's very humble cottage as he pondered his next move. He wouldn't have long to think. Here, at dawn, the Covenanters caught up with him, officers Boynton and Nairn finding him lying 'over-wearied and verey fearfull' on a makeshift bed in a 'nastie' room. As instructed, they offered him indemnity, and their superior Montgomery soon joined them, assuring the monarch that a rumour of giving him up to Cromwell was untrue. This threat, Charles said, was his reason for what he'd done,[26] but the Covenanters perceived they had pushed him too far – to the point of losing him to rivals.

And Charles capitalised on their fears. He faked remorse for his escapade, but nobody could guarantee it wouldn't happen again, as he claimed others, such as Fraser, had led him astray. In response, the doctor would soon be banished from his own country.[27]

Springing to mind as a possible repercussion is the fact Charles and Fraser weren't exactly pally in the late 1650s, although they were pally when again at Louis's court in the early 1650s. They appear particularly close in 1653 as Fraser helped Charles through a difficult illness, and Charles praised him. Among the Merry Monarch's brilliant people skills sat the ability to make individuals feel valued. Notably, he had Fraser's friendship when he wanted it, and with approachability Charles could make friends of strangers too as almost everyone he met believed he was listening to them. As with many of Charles's skills, this one seems to have been innate in basic form but consciously developed through lessons learned. After all, Charles better understood the importance of feeling valued once Scotland had him so undervalued.

Following 'the Start' though, he began engineering a turning of the tables. Because the Covenanters knew that improving his life might ensure they held onto him, he was finally admitted to governmental meetings from 10 October and took a more operative role. Some of the most passionate Presbyterians, with a new force in western Scotland, issued a remonstrance decrying Charles for underhandedness, but Argyll supported him,[28] and king and marquis had more reason to work together. Although new sects weakened Argyll's somewhat, the marquis hoped to regain strength through Charles, in part by aiming to become the monarch's father-in-law. Having deftly referred this matter to Henrietta Maria, Charles would successfully keep the consort space available as political bait. But with smallpox killing the Prince of Orange on 6 November, the king lost an asset. Now progressing towards Scottish power, he vowed to stick with the Covenanters, painful though this could still be.

Such pain would be endured at his Scottish coronation on 1 January. This took place at Scone, the site of coronations for centuries before, but a Covenanted king was a new phenomenon, and this coronation, the last in Scotland, had its own flavour. From his bedchamber, the king was initially escorted into the presence chamber at Scone Palace to hear a speech outlining Scottish subjects' desire to be governed by him but provided he upheld the Covenants. In response Charles delivered the words 'I do esteem the affection of my good people ... and shall be ready, by God's assistance, to bestow my life in their defence'. A procession of commissioners and nobles then accompanied him in style to Scone abbey, the coronation regalia conveyed for all to see, and the main event began with a sermon from Douglas, packed with attacks on Charles's family and including a wish for the king to be 'truly humbled for *his own sins, and the sins of his father's house*'. Prayer was then followed by a reading of both Covenants, after which further prayer preceded the most dubious element of it all. Here, Charles knelt, held up his right hand and swore commitment to the Covenants, then signed promises he'd break. As the proceedings continued, the Lord Lyon King of Arms asked the people: 'are you willing to have him for your King ... ?' The monarch walked to each corner of a stage erected, showing himself for approval, and soon heard the affirmative reply 'God save the King'. After consequently swearing the coronation oath dating from his Scottish grandfather's day, he was divested of the 'princely robe' upon him and dressed in 'royal robes'. The Lord Great Chamberlain took care of this and was swiftly followed by the Lord Great Constable handing Charles the Sword of State for Presbyterian defence and 'punishment of all iniquity and injustice'. Having clutched the weapon briefly, the king returned it to its bearer, and into the equation now came the crown.[29] Adorned with such treasures as garnet, amethyst and nearly seventy freshwater pearls, this was just over 100 years old, made of gold and weighed 3.6 lb. Once Argyll had placed it on Charles's head, the congregation, hands aloft, swore to 'live and die' with their Covenanted ruler, and before lords knelt to pledge likewise and kissed the king's left cheek, the sceptre was delivered into the royal right hand, by the Earl of Crawford, after which Charles took his seat upon the throne, receiving a blessing at the end. With suitable solemnity after all was complete, the sovereign returned to Scone Palace, the crown still on his head and sceptre in his hand[30] as he awaited a feast where 'CR' was to be found embroidered on damask serviettes.[31]

As a Presbyterian ceremony, his 1651 coronation was modest, lacking music and anointing with oil, but the subject of it all provided theatre, acting his way through the event. His serious and devout demeanour meant nobody doubted his sincerity, it was reported.[32] Charles was becoming a master of deceit.

Chapter 16

It's generally Charles I who's considered Cromwell's nemesis, but Cromwell didn't turn actively republican or regicidal till the late 1640s. After January 1649, he was left with Charles II as an archenemy. Seventeenth-century Scottish chronicler John Nicoll reported that Cromwell used all means to get Charles II 'cutt af ... evidencit by ane Englische man callit Mos ... sent out to poyson the King'.[1] Meanwhile, when master falconer Alexander Hope advised Charles to negotiate with 'Old Noll' Cromwell and abandon pursuit of restoration, the king wanted Hope 'hanged at one end of a rope, and Cromwell at the other'.[2] This was mid-January 1651, and the Roundhead invasion of Scotland meant Old Noll was gaining ground, yet young Charles was simultaneously on the rise.

Since 'the Start', more respect had been shown for His Majesty, with banished courtiers allowed back, and he was making real impact in Scottish politics. So much so that Argyll found himself losing influence in debates, which the monarch could attend in Scotland. Arguing adeptly, Charles persuaded Edinburgh's parliament in March to set up a commission for military affairs, and it comprised Kirk Party members and their opponents alike.[3] He was gradually bringing peace between the nation's factions, but his intentions were far from peaceful. The more he united the Scots under him, the more he'd have for invasion of England. And by the end of the month, he'd been made commander-in-chief of the Covenanter forces. A whirlwind of activity, Charles was 'adventuring his Person ... upon every shew of danger, riding continually, and being up early and late'.[4] He dashed between government and garrison, holding authority in both before his twenty-first birthday, and he made the principal military camp his home, often inspecting troops as he watched his efforts in levying contribute to growth of his soldiery.[5] Then, in June 1651, he succeeded in repealing the 1649 Act of Classes, which had barred Royalists and Engagers from public

Chapter 16

office, army included. Cromwell was taking Scotland bit by bit, and when the Roundheads concentrated manoeuvres further from the border, Charles decided the time had come to move on England. Although Leslie advised against this, the king was adamant, but he didn't realise Cromwell had set him a trap, deliberately enticing him in. This was how the Parliamentarian would see off his royal adversary.

If Charles could gather enough support, he'd stand a chance, but Cromwell was already on the case regarding this. In March, Cavalier captain Isaac Berkenhead, brother of *Mercurius Aulicus*'s John, had been captured carrying papers with details of anti-Commonwealth plots; Cromwell had him imprisoned in London and a planned uprising in Liverpool never took place. Other consequences arose too. The seized correspondence revealed Thomas Coke, ex-MP in the Oxford Parliament, as a leading conspirator against the Rump Parliament.[6] To save his life, Coke confessed practically everything he could, resulting in roughly 2,000 arrests. These reduced Charles's numbers, as did desertions. The king imagined English subjects would flock as he began travelling down the west, approaching Carlisle on 6 August. However, the New Model Army was well trained, well fed and well armed while Charles couldn't even afford stockings or shoes for his soldiers. He offered pay to Parliamentarians who would join him, but execution threatened them if they did. He also promised Presbyterianism in England, fooled by Scottish thinking that English support for the Covenants was strong. In reality, the prospect of fighting alongside Scottish Presbyterians repelled many Englishmen. Charles had disastrously misread the mood in England. In Lancaster, he was proclaimed king, but Shrewsbury refused him entrance, and his presence in Stoke, Market Drayton, Tong and Kidderminster[7] proved largely fruitless. As he ceremoniously passed through one of Worcester's city gates at midday on 23 August, a pistol shot ripped through the mouth of a local. It was possibly aimed at Charles.[8] The region's allegiance was debatable, and not even 200 would be recorded as turning up in response to royal demand for all the county's able-bodied males aged 16 to 60.[9] Ultimately, the king's army failed to exceed about 16,000, most of whom were Scottish Covenanters.

The plan had been to march on to the capital, but Worcester provided good protection around narrow streets, and there were two rivers – Britain's longest, the Severn, flowing down by the west of the walled city, and the Teme running into the Severn further southwest. Giving his troops much-needed rest, Charles stayed put and began preparations for battle right there. The Covenanters had come with sixteen leather cannon, but musket balls were to be quickly manufactured by melting down lead lifted from local roofs,[10] and – like with the summons to muster – urgent need to improve defences got the king trying to use authority he didn't have in practice. For instance, on 24 August his words to Salwarpe in mid-Worcestershire were: 'You are hereby required to send ... 30 able men to work at the fortifications ... and ... to begin tomorrow morning (Monday) at five o'clock'. Fort Royal near the road to London was quickly developed into a bastioned star-shaped earthwork,[11] ditches were dug and city gates were blockaded. Charles also ordered the destruction of bridges. Cromwell, however, had been journeying down the east and arrived with a force double the size of Charles's, whereupon the Roundheads began forming pontoon bridges, lines of boats across the water with decking and ramps to enable crossing on foot or horseback. In the meantime, violence ensued, but Cromwell delayed full fighting till the anniversary of Dunbar.

So it was 3 September 1651 when the king took a council of war to the top of Worcester Cathedral's tower, ready to watch men kill and be killed in his name. A wide panorama of the whole scene was available from here, and the clear day lent itself to immaculate vision. Charles had situated plenty of Leslie's cavalry in Pitchcroft field to the city's north, just east of the Severn, and placed many infantrymen nearer the Teme, under officers Thomas Dalziel, William Keith and Colin Pitscottie, who were taking orders from Montgomery. One such order assigned Keith responsibility for holding Powick Bridge – the site of the first-ever significant skirmish between Roundheads and Cavaliers, where the latter had triumphed in September 1642. Now, nine years later, Parliament's Major General Charles Fleetwood had launched a northerly advance along the Severn's west bank at daybreak, and the New Model was on its way to taking Powick Bridge as part of a fierce assault around the Teme. To help, Cromwell led three brigades across the Severn, targeting his attack on Pitscottie's Highlanders. In doing so, however, the great general left vulnerability for Parliamentarian artillery bases to the east. These were across from the cathedral. Adrenaline rushed within the king. He saw a chance to win the day.

Chapter 16

With the troops he could spare, Charles therefore rode resolutely to unleash an onslaught on the Red Hill base while Hamilton went for that of Perry Wood and Buckingham headed further cavalry support. It was the first (and only) time Charles led at the frontline in England, and he seemed to shine at first as the line of foot collapsed, New Model artillery was seized and the king's men wielded their pikes when their ammunition ran out. They also deployed their muskets like clubs to bludgeon. But then Cromwell and his brigades returned. From here, it all turned Parliament's way.

Charles made a dash to join soldiers in the streets. At Sidbury Gate his path was blocked by an upturned wagon, so he dismounted. He crawled through the wheels to continue forward, but he wasn't so determined to continue on another level.

This may have been the case for quite some months. The Covenanters recognised 'the Start' as an attempt he made to escape his life at the time, and they improved his situation immediately, but the suffering didn't stop altogether. In Scotland, Christmas 1650 was officially ignored while that 26 December was devoted to fasting for atonement, the reason given being twelve criticisms of the king and his immediate two predecessors. Scottish calls for Charles to repent on his family's behalf were frequent, and he again submitted publicly on the day concerned. Privately though, he commented: 'I think I must repent too that ever I was born'.[12] His words are open to interpretation. Charles was never averse to sardonic wit and could have been implying the Covenanters wanted him to repent over so much that they would make him apologise for his own birth. However, the repeated repentance was embarrassing, and it constituted his own betrayal of his family. With Charles deeply unhappy when he made this remark, it seems to have reflected dark feelings within him. Later evidence somewhat aligns.

Shortly after reaching Worcester, Charles said: 'For me, it is a crown or a coffin',[13] and by the time he'd squeezed through the wagon at the battle, the chances of a crown were slim. His men were falling victim to carnage at every turn as panic took over. Grabbing another steed, he rode around frantically, doing all he could think of to increase morale and calling officers by name to demonstrate familiarity, but just before this, he'd removed the metal armour on his torso. Doing that left him with the limited protection of his buff coat, an ineffective barrier against firearms. That day, he charged multiple times and 'hazarded his person much more than any other officer of his army',[14] says a witness's report. Everything was resting on this battle, but Charles was watching it all slip away, watching his hellish Scottish experience and signing of the

Covenants simply end his dreams. As allied troops surrendered around him, he declared: 'I had rather that you would shoot me, than keep me alive to see the sad consequences of this fatal day'.[15]

Fatal indeed. Approximately 3,000 of Charles's fighters lost their lives at Worcester. The Parliamentarian death toll is recorded as 200. Deemed, by Cromwell, to have wrought 'marvellous salvation',[16] the clash signalled total victory for Parliament, and it brought combat to a close in England. Nobody could have predicted the end of these vicious wars would take place right at the spot of their active commencement, Powick Bridge.

Although military action wasn't yet over in Scotland or Ireland, the defeat also lost Charles his Scottish sovereignty as Caledonia headed towards Commonwealth rule. Yet Scotland was safer than England for the king, many of his officers thought. It was certainly safer than Worcester just then, blood running in corpse-filled streets.

Charles nevertheless needed persuasion before he made a final decision to flee. With diversion created by Royalist charges down Sidbury Street and High Street, he slipped through St Martin's Gate at 6 pm but then continually stopped on the initial road north, wanting to turn back for a last-ditch counterattack.[17] He had to be begged to move his horse on. Hamilton was left behind, bone in his leg shattered by musket shot that would kill him on 12 September, and Leslie had appeared dazed, escaping separately but destined for imprisonment. Some officers nonetheless made it away with the king, Buckingham for one. There was also Wilmot, the man arrested in 1644 with hopes of having Charles I abdicate. However, made a gentleman of the bedchamber in 1649, Wilmot was a trusted servant of the younger Charles by 1651. Another member of the runaway party was James Stanley, Earl of Derby, who had just been in a similar position having bolted from enemy attack on his troops near Wigan on 25 August. He'd then taken refuge with Catholics at a remote Boscobel House in Shropshire's Brewood Forest. In fact, among the lower ranks with the king was Charles Giffard, a member of the family that owned the house, and the whole band retreating from Worcester comprised hundreds. As they neared Droitwich, however, they were about to lose Major General Edward Massey. The pre-battle assaults left Massey with horrendous injuries. Now he had to give up the ride and find a bed, a probable deathbed. Upon his farewell, the king broke down in tears.

Chapter 16

This release of emotion may have helped pull Charles into the reality of defeat and take stock of his situation. 'Lord blesse and preserve us both', he said to Massey,[18] but the decision not to return to Worcester was somewhat forced, routed Royalists unwilling to fight again. Charles would later claim: 'though I could not get them to stand by me against the enemy, I could not get rid of them, now I had a mind to'.[19] The reason he eventually had a mind to rid himself of these few hundred men was simple; his concerns were beginning to centre on avoiding recognition, avoiding capture. Failed invasion was how Montrose had ended up hanged and quartered after capture by his long-time adversaries. A similar fate was highly likely for the king – the leading traitor, some would call him. However, the worry of blackmail still existed in the event of Charles's capture. In addition, Charles thought James incapable of governing Jersey just eighteen months earlier. If the king died now, James would lead the entire restoration effort. Personal survival was no sole motive in Charles's resolve to escape.

Making an icon of an oak tree, this escape proved to be one of the most monumental events in the monumentally eventful life of Charles II, but the main reason it left its mark on history is that it made an everlasting impact on Charles. Even three decades later, he recalled minute details, and he told the stories so many times that courtiers were sick to the back teeth of listening. However, in October 1680, Charles sat Pepys down with a pen during one of many royal excursions to Newmarket and dictated an account for posterity, spending a total of six hours reliving the memories over two sessions.[20] Shorthand systems had been taking off in England over the past 100 years, and Pepys was proficient in Thomas Shelton's tachygraphy dating from the 1620s, so kept up with the probably fast flow. From reading the words, the king's excitement is evident, and there's little denying that what he saw, heard and felt during those six weeks on the run were crucial factors in forming the Merry Monarch's character. Yet, to see the escape's full significance for Charles, it's important to consider his frame of mind at the time. This was a Charles who had just expressed a wish to die.

'Shift yourselves, gentlemen!' he barked to the vast train tagged onto him from Worcester. And, pared down to a less conspicuous sixty or so, they threw people off the scent by speaking French when passing through Stourbridge.[21] Whatever his main motive, the king seemed committed to the quest of evading capture. The Continent therefore beckoned once more, and he secretly (telling only Wilmot) hoped to reach it via London,[22] unconvinced by suggestions to head for Scotland. But Charles was in the West Midlands. London lay over 100 miles away, so where was safe in the meantime? The hunt for the king would already be on.

Derby suggested Boscobel, whose Catholic occupants had treated him very kindly, and Giffard naturally offered His Majesty shelter. Within a mile of Boscobel, what's more, sat an even more secluded Giffard property in the forest. This was Whiteladies, a large house on the site of a priory dissolved under Henry VIII's early-Reformation rule, and it provided a roof over the heads of several Catholics. Charles understood followers of the Church of Rome could be his saviours. Some recusant homes contained priest-holes for hiding their clerics when such men risked capital punishment in Elizabethan and Jacobean times, and Catholics had been mastering the art of concealment for generations, often needing to masquerade as others.

Hiding the king's identity would be a challenge though, for various reasons. Whether sitting, standing or walking, Charles carried a permanently regal bearing, 'majestie beeing soe naturall unto him, that even when he said nothing, did nothing, his very looks ... were enough to betray him'.[23] Only when he was asleep or pretending to sleep would this giveaway diminish, and still he'd be discernible. Artist David des Granges had become limner to Charles in Scotland and, around the time of the 1651 coronation, painted a 6.3-cm miniature of the monarch, whose boldly swart features can clearly be seen from the artwork. By 21, the king had striking black eyebrows and quite a large nose protruding from a round face, his head sizeable but looking all the bigger with a mass of black curls surrounding it. Such a dark visage was a rare sight in England, rendering Charles famous for it. In addition, having reached an astonishing six foot two, he was over half a foot taller than his homeland's average male.[24] Not only did this make him stand out; it also made him difficult to fit into premade garments, but he needed a very plain ensemble.

Losing their bearings some hours earlier, the party finally made it to Whiteladies towards sunrise, where servant George Penderel opened the gate to Giffard and of course also admitted the fellow arrivals. Derby then had George's brother William, a housekeeper at Boscobel, brought over and, trustful of the company, introduced Charles as none other than His Majesty. Once the shock had passed, Whiteladies was eager to help, and so began the task of transforming the king into a peasant. Workaday breeches, shirt, doublet and shoes were found that Charles just squeezed into while a brimmed hat would help cast him in shadow. In the meantime, he shed the cascading locks over his shoulders as Wilmot hacked away with a knife before agricultural shears did a better job in the hands of another Penderel brother 'Trusty Richard', a tenant farmer from nearby Hobbal Grange farm, who had now been rushed across too. And with soot rubbed over hands and face for a grubby look, Charles took on the guise of a woodcutter.

Appearance alone didn't make an alter-ego, however. Despite his decent attempts at a West Midlands accent, the king was no expert in its nuances and needed others to speak on his behalf. Yet his entourage had to go, many of lordly demeanour, and hiding more than one or two seemed impossible. Even his horse was too magnificent to avoid suspicion. That was waved off too.

So, the sovereign, who had relied on hundreds of attendants to provide opulence in palaces most of his life, was suddenly stranded in an ordinary rustic setting populated by a mere handful of ordinary rustic folk. And because Whiteladies had no priest-holes for him, he dived straight into his role. William, Richard and George had two other brothers assisting, both of whom resided at Whiteladies. One was John, now leaving with Wilmot, while the other was Humphrey, a miller, who took on lookout duties with George as the king picked up a weighty tool akin to a giant billhook and trekked half a mile with Richard to hide out for the day in Spring Coppice.

Less than an hour after Charles set off from Whiteladies, a Parliamentarian detachment came knocking, asking whether anyone had seen him. Having only just met the inhabitants, the king hadn't really managed to sum them up. He was relying on virtual blind faith, and through various attempted routes to the coast over the next six weeks, this would come into play repeatedly. Anyone found helping Charles Stuart was liable for the death penalty, whereas anyone enabling his capture would be eligible for a colossal £1,000.[25] The odds were stacked against Charles in no uncertain terms.

Chapter 17

In Spring Coppice the morning after the Battle of Worcester, rain pelted down as the king, in his woodcutter disguise, hid near the highway, alert for oncoming threats but unaware of fortune smiling upon him. Of course it was no obvious smile, not least when an enemy troop 'immediately' hove into view.[1] Parliament were seeking out any of the defeated who had fled Worcester, but eyes were especially peeled for a tall, dark and courtly young gentleman. To this gentleman's relief, however, the searchers merely rode on, and after a day's soaking, he'd learn the downpour hadn't fallen elsewhere around, only the Spring Coppice area. He believed this deterred them from venturing his way.

Significant relief wasn't likely unless he made it to the Continent though. Being in such landlocked territory was therefore inconvenient, and while chatting to Richard in the forest, Charles lost hope of reaching the coast via London. Instead, he fixed on a port, such as Swansea, in Royalist-strong Wales, 'a way that I thought none would suspect my taking', he'd explain.[2]

That evening, Richard's wife Mary cooked for the king as he visited Hobbal Grange farmhouse, but what he really needed was sleep. He had been on his horse most of the night before the battle[3] and of course the night after it, then bypassed bed to trudge into Spring Coppice. A blanket had been brought to him there, but he'd spent considerable time practising the local accent and trying to effect an ignoble gait. What Charles did as darkness fell, however, was set off for Wales, on foot. Requiring stealth, he'd be avoiding roads, consequently crossing challenging Shropshire terrain full of obstacles, and a horse wasn't an option.

Even for Charles, this terrain meant torture. His shoes, supplied by a William Creswell at Whiteladies,[4] were stiff and fitted so inadequately that soreness from blisters increased with each stride. And to remain inconspicuous, his entire support system that night constituted Richard alone, who couldn't carry a six-foot-two man. At least the pace could be gentle, mostly.

Around midnight the pair came to Evelith Mill, hoping they would be undetected under the pitch-black conditions, but a man in white menacingly called: 'Who goes there?' Thinking quickly, Richard claimed he and Charles were local neighbours, whereupon the man, probably the miller, demanded they show themselves – 'or I will knock you down', he threatened. Their subsequent retreat convinced him such violence was fair. 'Rogues!' he yelled, and a whole gang emerged in pursuit. In a panicked burst of acceleration, the king scrabbled up a 'very deep and very dirty' lane and vaulted over a hedge. With Richard, he then lay there panting.

Silence around them nevertheless gave the trekkers courage to creep on after half an hour, and before dawn they reached the mining town of Madeley a mile from the Severn, which they intended to cross by ferry. First though, they headed for the Catholic home of Francis Woolf, an elderly friend of Richard's, who revealed Parliament was diligently guarding the Severn to prevent Royalists slipping into Wales. The entire ordeal had been futile. Charles and Richard spent the day nestled behind hay in Woolf's barn, but gone twilight, they turned back, Charles set for another night's agony on feet missing much of their skin. An alternative route also heightened infection risks. To dodge Evelith Mill, the king insisted on getting wet crossing the nearby water, promising to swim Richard over if it proved deep. So, in stepped Charles. Immersed only to the torso, he simply took Richard's hand reassuringly as the pair waded through,[5] but his supportive demeanour masked the diminishing of his strength.

By early morning, Charles could barely stand having reached Boscobel. William Penderel's wife Joan was alarmed by his condition, so she opened up his blisters and washed his feet, providing some ease. Nobody, however, eased his mind effectively.

At Boscobel he met another runaway from the battle. This was Major William Careless, whose monarchism was intense. Entering the royal presence that morning, he wept, and Charles followed suit.[6] The king's emotions fluctuated during his escape. So far, he'd amused Richard's little daughter on his lap by the fire at Hobbal Grange and, at mealtime that same evening, passed light-hearted comments accusing Richard of gluttony.[7] But during the cross-country walking, Charles had 'many times cast himself upon the ground, with a desperate and obstinate resolution to rest there till the morning'. His endurance continually vanishing, he'd sometimes 'prefer being taken' by the Roundheads at this point.[8] Again, Charles seemed to be willing death on. And at Boscobel he'd arrived melancholic.[9]

Quite literally, he didn't know where to turn. Cromwell's forces were scouring with scrutiny, and Careless told Charles that Boscobel might well be searched high and low that day. The best hideout, the major suggested, took the form of a tree in the surrounding woods. It was a mighty oak with wondrously dense foliage, and Careless knew it concealed; he'd already hidden in it. So, at 9 am, both fugitives ensconced themselves up high in what would later be dubbed the Royal Oak. However, with pillows, the exhausted Charles was getting comfortable. Resting on Careless, he fell into a deep slumber.[10] Therefore, while eyeing Roundheads sniffing about, the major had to prevent the king plummeting to the ground. A problem fast developed. The weight of Charles was deadening the nerves, and Careless couldn't support it much longer. He needed to wake the king urgently. But soldiers had now reached the tree. There they were, right below. Even whispering was risky. Careless had to break codes of conduct. He pinched the king between finger and thumb, relieved to find him stir quietly. Heart-stopping moments nevertheless kept coming. Joan, pretending she was simply collecting sticks, roamed around with vigilance and distracted a horseman whose gaze was fixed on the tree, but troops were seen throughout the day, and Charles heard some describe what they would do to him if they caught him. At dusk, however, the coast seemed reasonably clear, so the king and Careless descended the trunk, Charles ready to answer as William Jones if accosted.

A cramped priest-hole would make sleep challenging that night, and Charles wanted comfort food for the next day. Bread, cheese and beer had provided sustenance in the tree, but the king was accustomed to meat. He now requested mutton. He either didn't know or didn't care that the average citizen could rarely afford it, and he maybe even condoned William Penderel's resultant smuggling of a sheep.[11] The fact the king himself sliced and fried the meat does not redress this, but it's just one way Charles embraced a 'when in Rome' philosophy, irrespective of the social class.

By contrast, Wilmot was so unwilling to integrate that he refused to adopt a disguise. And Charles planned to cross the Channel with Wilmot. In the meantime,

Chapter 17

both men were about to shelter together. John Penderel had secured refuge for Wilmot at another Catholic property, Moseley Hall north of Wolverhampton, and the soldiers' omnipresence around Boscobel rendered Moseley safer. So, on the rainy evening of 7 September, Charles was on the move again. This time, his feet were spared, with Humphrey Penderel's mill supplying a workhorse, but the king grumbled as the animal showed itself uncooperative. However, explaining the horse was carrying the weight of three kingdoms, Humphrey's jokey retort appealed nicely to Charles's sense of humour.

At Moseley, Wilmot introduced the esteemed guest to his host Thomas Whitgreave and to John Huddleston, who was a 43-year-old priest but also tutored three boys[12] at the hall; his Catholic clergyman status could be concealed. However, the only residents allowed to see the king, or even know who was there, were Whitgreave, Huddleston and Whitgreave's elderly mother, and Charles was confined to just a few rooms.

Receiving him in the small hours of 8 September, Whitgreave and Huddleston showed him the priest-hole readily awaiting. Charles then sat consuming biscuits plus the fortified white wine known as sack, after which he'd grow 'very chearful',[13] and he wasn't perturbed when blood suddenly emerged from his nose. He often suffered nosebleeds, he explained, but Huddleston tended with a handkerchief. He and Whitgreave also washed those painful blistered feet and supplied Charles with slippers, fresh stockings and a clean shirt. Both men doted on him nonstop. And at Moseley, the king went to bed. He had almost forgotten what a proper bed was. Twenty-four hours after his arrival, he slept soundly as Huddleston guarded him in the room while Whitgreave played sentry outside the door, but during forty winks on 9 September, a maid's cry of 'Soldiers, soldiers' had the king diving into the priest-hole. He might still have been discovered had they entered the property, though. Among them was a 'great priest-catcher' named Southall.[14]

Charles had now spent nearly a week living with English Catholics, experiencing the conditions forced on them by national hostility. And to Huddleston that night, he explained he knew him to be a priest but there was no reason to fear admitting it to him. The king even went on to say that, if restored, he'd ensure worship according to Rome be freely permitted. He was readying to leave Moseley at this point, but during the morning, he'd wandered into Whitgreave's study and perused a copy of the Catholic catechism *Manual of Controversies* by theologian Henry Turbeville, then said he'd be taking it when departing, seeming keen to read it.

◆ ◆ ◆

By this time, a great plan had been hatched. To tackle Charles's invasion, some Royalists were barred from straying beyond a five-mile radius of their homes. However, while seeking to secrete Wilmot's fine horse, Moseley's Catholic neighbour William Walker had trotted four miles southeast to Bentley Hall, residence of Cavalier Colonel John Lane whose sister Jane Lane, it had transpired, held a pass for travel to Abbots Leigh, near Bristol, as she was wanted at a birth.[15] And a servant could accompany her. Having arrived at Bentley Hall in the early hours of 10 September, 'woodcutter William Jones' thus became 'manservant William Jackson', donning a plain grey suit, and Moseley had already answered his footwear prayers, providing boots. Charles couldn't exactly relax though. The slog to Abbots Leigh would be undertaken in daylight, with stopoffs, and the king was now to mingle properly while playing an actively subordinate role. Things didn't bode well when he 'offered his hand the contrary way'[16] to help Jane into the saddle, but at least the undisguised Wilmot wouldn't cause direct concern; Charles was constantly separating from him, with meeting places carefully agreed. While Wilmot therefore made his own way towards Bristol, Jane's cousin Henry Lascelles rode alongside the mistress and manservant, who were sharing a horse, Charles taking the reins with Jane mounted sidesaddle against his back. Both cousins knew the attendant's identity, but not for a minute could they appear reverential.

Before the journey was even two hours old, the double-saddled horse lost a shoe. The travellers consequently sought shoeing services in what the king called 'a scattering village, whose name begins with something like Long', and here he held the hoof steady while it was worked on it, the blacksmith apparently hearing nothing too odd in his customer's accent as conversation ensued. Using this conversation to gather information, Charles asked the blacksmith whether any Englishmen on the Scots' side had been captured. 'He answered', Charles's account reports, 'that he did not hear that that rogue Charles Stuart was taken … . I told him, that if that rogue were taken he deserved to be hanged more than all the rest'.[17]

Having ridden straight through a set of Cromwellian cavalrymen in Wootton outside Stratford-upon-Avon, the trio arrived for the night of 10 September at Long Marston, lodging with John Tombs, a kinsman of the Lanes. But as 'William Jackson', Charles was set to work. This put him face-to-face with a jack, a device for turning spits. Clueless, he nearly broke it, winding it the wrong way, and so came a tongue-lashing from the cook.

But Jane spared Charles such scenarios at the Abbots Leigh residence of George Norton and wife Ellen, her cousin the expectant mother. Reaching this

Chapter 17

destination on 12 September, Jane claimed her manservant was recovering from ague so needed rest and a good bed. Unfortunately though, this meant doctor Thomas Gorges turned up in the bedchamber, feeling a pulse and asking questions. Charles 'answered in as few words as was possible' while edging from the candlelight,[18] but his alarm wouldn't have been so acute if he hadn't known the doctor; Gorges had been a chaplain to Charles I. Ally or enemy, the more people in on the whole secret, the higher the chances of discovery. Nevertheless, the ruse of fake illness delighted Charles, particularly as Jane plied him with food aplenty for regaining strength. Despite the permanent anguish, Charles's appetite (especially for meat) rarely suffered during his escape. In fact, on his first morning in Abbots Leigh, hunger pulled him to the buttery, where he ended up breakfasting alongside servants. Over bread and butter, one of them revealed he'd fought in the king's regiment at the Battle of Worcester, and 'William Jackson' responded with a perilous move; he asked him to describe the monarch. The man did so while staring him in the face.

Having ascertained what had been noted, Charles exited with speed, but was he getting a thrill from all the danger? If he thought his disguise foolproof, he was wrong. In the hall, accompanied by butler John Pope, he now doffed his hat to Ellen, and about half an hour later Lascelles came saying: 'I am afraid Pope knows you, for he says very positively to me that it is you'. Pope had worked for Charles's childhood groom of the bedchamber Thomas Jermyn[19] and reportedly recalled the Prince of Wales in Lichfield during the First Civil War.[20] Rather than 'leaving that suspicion upon him', Charles subsequently confided in Pope, but this proved beneficial as the butler became a colluder.[21]

As such, he dutifully cantered off enquiring about ships sailing from Bristol. It's just a pity he found none casting anchor for a month. Plans now needed hasty revision, particularly with Pope warning of untrustworthy household members. Just like in infancy, Charles quickly sought Wyndham care, resolving to head for Christabella's brother-in-law Francis Wyndham who had just moved to Trent,[22] four miles northeast of Yeovil.

But the king relied on Jane for the journey, just as tragedy struck. Bringing immense upset through the house, the baby was born dead, and Ellen fell gravely unwell. Charles did not act commendably. 'I thought the best way [to extricate Jane was] to counterfeit a letter from her father's house, old Mr Lane's, to tell her that her father was extremely ill', he informed Pepys in 1680, adding that, with Jane 'playing her part so dexterously, ... all believed old Mr Lane to be indeed in great danger, and [this] gave his daughter the excuse to go away with me'.[23]

In this era, women were often considered weak, gossipy creatures unable to keep secrets or control emotions, but the king was seeing plenty of contrary evidence, and Jane had impressed him in various ways. She'd not only successfully schemed and diverted threats (sometimes, for instance, taking Charles food herself to lessen his contact with others) but also helped keep composure when encircled by those Parliamentarians in Wootton. Having arrived at Francis's home Trent House on 17 September, Charles had parted from Jane, and he missed her already.

In Trent, he was also painfully aware of hostility when an unexpected scene developed, the thirteenth-century St Andrew's church next door ringing bells in jubilation and excitement exploding through the streets. Puzzled, he sent a maid to investigate, and she returned to say a soldier had arrived in the village, announcing he'd killed Charles Stuart. From a window, the said Charles watched resultant revelry.

Meanwhile Francis was on a quest to get Charles and Wilmot a ship. With a sailor he knew named William Ellesdon, he visited wine importer Stephen Limbry in Charmouth just along from Lyme Regis. Limbry had a ship bound for France and was told passage was wanted for two gentlemen seeking refuge following financial disputes. Without more ado, a plan was made whereby Limbry's ship was to embark from Lyme Regis before stopping for the fugitives at Charmouth. Charles consequently reached Charmouth on 22 September, with Wilmot, Francis, Francis's servant Henry Peters and Francis's cousin Juliana Coningsby, who's sometimes reported to have been masquerading as Charles's fiancée. The ship, however, made no appearance.

They hoped there had just been delay, but having waited up all night at Charmouth inn The Queen's Arms, Wilmot, with Peters, went seeking answers in Lyme Regis come morning. Meanwhile Charles kissed the lodgings' landlady Margaret Wade on the lips and took Francis and Juliana to the Crown-friendly Bridport, only to find it swarming with enemy soldiers en route to attack Jersey. The trio made for 'the best inn', but it seems the king's rage was so severe that he didn't care how much attention he attracted letting it out. Having dismounted to lead the horses through, Charles deliberately bumped himself into as many Roundheads as possible, nearly starting a brawl, and he'd recall: 'they were very angry with me for my rudeness'. His ire was set to peak though. That evening, Peters brought news that Limbry had pulled out of the arrangement.[24]

Chapter 17

So, from 24 September, Charles was at Trent House again. For a new scheme, he almost immediately sent Wilmot to resolute Royalist Colonel Robert Phillips in Salisbury, and within days Phillips secured passage. Unfortunately, however, the vessel was promptly commandeered by Parliament for the Jersey assault. Meanwhile, a proclamation was read aloud in public hotspots, calling for the apprehension of 'CHARLS STUART son to the late tyrant', and reports of his death were countered with reports he'd been spotted. Thanks to past Catholic occupants, Trent House included a priest-hole, but some of the household knew whom they were lodging, and the longer Charles stayed, the more vulnerable he felt.

While enquiries about ships discreetly continued, he departed on 6 October, with Juliana, Peters and Phillips, for Heale House near Salisbury. He posed as a friend of Phillips, but the hostess Katherine Hyde recognised the royal's distinctive features, just from one sighting back in the early 1640s, and stared during supper. Katherine was the widow of Lawrence Hyde, a cousin of Edward Hyde, and Charles admitted his identity to her, on the quiet, after the meal. He didn't regret it either, finding her devise a way to save him encounters. The following day, the staff would visit a Salisbury fair. She thus advised Charles to leave, as if permanently, in the morning, then return before they did. After this, a priest-hole could hide him. Where Charles went in the morning was Stonehenge, and this was a sight he needed to treasure; he realised he might never see England again.

If he ever left, that was. While Wilmot had gone to Sussex seeking maritime leads, Charles would be cooped up in a priest-hole in Wiltshire for nearly a week, his meals brought secretly and his thoughts often his sole companions, and this opportunity for reflection was becoming a theme. Both here and in Trent, days of inaction constituted roughly half his six weeks on the run.

From the early hours of 13 October, however, he was riding to Sussex's Shoreham, specifically to a coal boat named *Surprise*, courtesy of arrangements by Colonel George Gunter – a Cavalier who had just been fined for failing to contribute to Parliament's war efforts, his royalism firm. But the republic was closing in on the king. Charles's departure from Heale coincided with issuance of a document from the Council of State instructing customs officers to look for a man 'above two yards high, his hair a deep brown, near to black' and not to 'let any pass without a due and particular search'.[25]

What's more, there were eighty miles to negotiate before Shoreham. Gunter helped break the journey halfway by offering accommodation at the home of his brother-in-law Thomas Symonds, but this would make an interesting night. The king was still sporting short hair and that drab grey suit, and Symonds mistook him for a Roundhead. However, anyone under this illusion was unlikely to suspect the truth. So now Charles played it Puritan. His techniques included feigning disgust at swearing, and the performance earned him 'admirations' from fellow guests Gunter, Phillips and Wilmot, while the hospitality involved alcohol in ample measures. To keep his wits about him, the king passed his abettors his refills when Symonds wasn't looking.[26]

Twenty-four hours later, there would be less successful deception. By then, the king, alongside Wilmot and Gunter, was at a Brighton inn meeting Nicholas Tattersall, captain of *Surprise*. Gunter had spun a yarn stating the two men to be smuggled were fleeing to avoid punishment for duelling, and this seemed plausible until Tattersall set eyes on one of them. It transpired Tattersall had been victim to Charles's 1648 seizure of ships off the English coast. The royal's face was chiselled in his memory, and desire for revenge perhaps stirred. No longer fooled about the task requested, Tattersall demanded danger money. After an acrimonious scene, he acquired promise, from Gunter, of £200, but final agreement only came when Charles quelled fury.

According to Gunter, 'the King was cheerefull, not shewing the least signe of feare or apprehension of any danger … during the whole course of this busines'.[27] First-hand, the colonel could only vouch for two days of Charles's behaviour, but it's interesting to note that the king engaged in greater daring after his time in the oak tree. From between then and embarkation, there's also little evidence of despondency in Charles.

◆ ◆ ◆

Yet even once afloat with Wilmot on 15 October, he was still navigating problems. Despite France being the agreed destination, *Surprise* was actually bound for another English port, Poole, and changing course might look suspicious. Wanting exoneration, Tattersall was therefore avoiding

Chapter 17

giving necessary orders as Shoreham's coastline disappeared from his view. To attain the crew's cooperation, he turned to Charles.

Masquerading as a commoner, the king was devoid of authority, and although the crew totalled just one boy and four men, everything hinged on how he handled them. The duelling story was worryingly incriminating. Instead, Charles told these new faces that he and his companion had run into trouble regarding debt but were owed money in France. Receiving it would right the matter. Then he slipped them twenty shillings. In one fell swoop, he appealed to senses of pity, justice and gratification. The crew backed him in persuading Tattersall to take *Surprise* into French waters.

And so ended a month and a half dicing with death. From the Earl of Derby to Gunter and with Wilmot all along the way, help for Charles had never ceased. But, whether through acting a role or planning a strategy, much of his own contribution can be credited to his understanding of people, an understanding that experienced a tremendous growth spurt en route.

Chapter 18

Against the backdrop of the Franco-Spanish War, a vessel looking like a Spanish-controlled privateer filled *Surprise* with fears of plunder within two miles of the French coast. Tattersall hastened to make an England-bound retreat, and Charles and Wilmot were nearly back to square one. Thanks to a cockboat on *Surprise*, it was therefore by strenuous rowing that the pair landed at Normandy's Fécamp the morning after embarking from Shoreham. Nobody expected them, however, and nobody was likely to recognise them. When Charles entered Paris, his 'aspect' had him mistaken for a low-ranking servant and his attire seemed 'more calculated to move laughter than respect'.[1]

Joining Henrietta Maria and Minette as well as James at their Louvre home, Charles enthralled one and all with tales of his recent escapade,[2] yet within days his cheerfulness vanished. By November, he was allegedly 'very silent always'.[3] As the reason he'd returned to France sunk in, it was sobering, and of course it required explanation. 'He complains much against the Scotch for ... making him act directly against his own liking, and giving him no powers till almost the very end of all', came a report from Paris. 'This, he says, was partly the cause of his miscarriage. ... He says, at the battle of Worcester ... only 5,000 fought as they should.'[4]

He'd been foolish to expect many more. Leslie, already voicing concerns about invading, had warned that his men 'would not fight'.[5] In addition, Buckingham had spoken of English reluctance to support a Scottish-led force, putting his English self forward to replace Scotland's Leslie. Charles had laughed in Buckingham's face, then found barely a soul join up. He kept Leslie's advice quiet, however, and said English Presbyterians should have rallied; the defeated king sidestepped blame for his own ill-fated decisions, and discrediting the Scots became a main ambition of his. When informed of speculation he'd fled to Scotland after Worcester, Charles replied: 'I had rather have been hanged'.⁶ But although this may have been a quip, it seems to re-echo his poignant comments of the past twelve months. Once again, he had become 'very sad and sombre'.

His mother meanwhile appeared 'overjoyed' to see him safe beside her, yet she was 'grieved at his speaking so openly against the Scotch, still thinking that a force may be raised from the unconquered part of Scotland'. Despite previously pouring scorn on the concessions he'd made to the Kirk Party, she urged him not to 'show disregard' of the Covenanter oath.⁷ However, by pushing him towards the Reformed, she was banking on it sending him an opposite way, towards Catholicism. Her hopes of his conversion would be bolstered politically too, with Charles seeking financial help from Pope Innocent X.

Henrietta Maria's court was so destitute it deterred visitors, and her eldest son was forced to keep not only himself but also James, stacking up debts to feed and clothe them both. He hadn't a clue when he'd settle these debts. In France, money was elusive. While Charles had been in Worcester preparing for the battle that removed him as a ruler, Louis had turned 13, ending Anne's regency as the reins of power passed his way, and Louis was dealing in wars, one right on his doorstep. All during the Franco-Spanish hostilities, the Parliamentary Fronde of 1648–49 had seen the Prince of Condé help Anne and Mazarin quash attempts at constitutional reform, but in the newer Fronde of the Princes, Condé was the Gallic Crown's main adversary. This second Fronde conflict was a power struggle that pitched royalty against nobility, and both sides were channelling their cash into it.

How strange that Charles suddenly viewed Europe's richest heiress as a suitable bride after all. With his newly sharpened acting skills, what's more, he stood better chance of winning her heart. So it was that, after years in deliberately lacklustre mode around her, he utterly threw himself into a hopeful courtship with La Grande Mademoiselle over the cold months ahead. For most of this period, the 24-year-old duchess suffered poor health with a swollen face she hid from general company. Charles therefore visited her at the Tuileries, sometimes with Henrietta Maria, and he soon passed every alternate evening there, playing cards and dancing, the latter courtesy of a string orchestra at his request. Paris had little court entertainment just then, the Fronde having driven Louis away with Anne and Mazarin. The Tuileries consequently attracted fun-loving girls, but Charles remained attentive of the wealthy duchess. Acting towards her with deference, he sat on a mere stool and forever plied her with flattery, now conveniently speaking decent French. What he omitted from conversation, however, were plans for defeating Cromwell. When Charles thought Louis's consent to the marriage was coming, he told Mademoiselle that restoration would delight him all the more because she'd be his queen. He wasn't prepared for her reply. Caustically it came, asserting that he was unworthy of his crown unless he stopped hanging around dancing idly and instead went and endangered his life for it, i.e. for her crown too. Now, as Charles also implied he'd never convert to Rome, the couple exchanged more words, and he didn't go near her for three weeks. When he then did, he sat in a big chair. Having also heard Jermyn's intention of selling her estates once she'd become consort, Mademoiselle lost interest in Charles.

Yet both parties had shown increased interest. The duchess believed him pleasing to the eye, handsomer than in his teens and especially once he'd started wearing a wig till his post-Worcester haircut grew out. Meanwhile, on their first evening together that autumn, Charles had perhaps dropped hints – whining that in Scotland no women had been available, with boredom filling his days.[8] However, he may have thought bedding Mademoiselle could sway her into marriage; he wasn't necessarily lusting.

Despite talk, lust had no definite place in the equation with Jane Lane either. In December, Jane turned up in Paris. Her assistance in the royal escape had been reported to the Council of State in October, so in true fashion she'd donned a disguise and walked right over to Yarmouth and onto a ship. Charles immediately settled her into the exiled court, enjoying banter with her, but Jane wasn't considered a beauty,[9] and Charles placed immense value on looks when choosing lovers.

His taste was not unusual, as evidenced by his infatuation with Isabelle-Angélique. To gain her attention, Charles would be vying with virtually every man she passed (including French royalty), but she'd theoretically be more reciprocal now; Bablon, as this brunette was nicknamed, had been widowed in the Parliamentary Fronde. Meanwhile the 'very handsom'[10] Lucy won similar levels of wantonness. The father of her daughter Mary born in the 1650s may have been Irish viscount Theobald Taaffe, may have been James's unofficial secretary Henry Bennet or may have been almost any other admirer with status. However, by late 1651, Charles had ceased admiring Lucy and severed his relationship with her. Notably, this breakup coincided with his descent of mood in October. He had to consider Jemmy though, whose care was overseen by Henrietta Maria, and

Lucy's relationship with Taaffe would complicate matters. The viscount was a new attendant of Charles and, as a great merrymaker, a favourite. Awkwardly, Lucy hung on in Paris, probably at the Louvre in fact, and in April, Marchamont Nedham's new newsbook *Mercurius Politicus* would be feeding England gossip of an attempt to poison her at a royal banquet. The story celebrates English females as the culprits.[11]

Particularly given Lucy's behaviour over the coming years, Charles appears rather hypocritical for later joking that the mistresses James took were picked, by a confessor, as penance for the duke's sins. Sometimes, however, the *men* by James's side seemed far worse. Bampfield is remembered as a Cromwellian spy whom the Merry Monarch never forgave for arguably accusing him of taking insufficient action to save Charles I. There were also sirs Edward Herbert and George Radcliffe, who had wheedled their way into James's favour in Jersey. In 1650, they had used sheer rumours of Charles's death as excuse to begin representing James as if he'd ascended the throne. Now, in 1652, former Western Association officer Berkeley, chosen as James's governor in 1648, was urging James to pursue ideas of joining Louis's army. Aside from risking his brother's life, Charles would be siding against Spain and the Frondeurs if he officially allowed this, kissing goodbye to some significant possibilities of aid. But James clamoured 'daily',[12] saying it would prepare him for Cavalier service, and soldiering was his dream. Charles needed counsel.

Having already sent for Hyde, he'd been reunited with the chancellor since Christmas, but Brentford had died earlier in 1651, Cottington remained in Spain and Hopton was alienated by Charles's signing of the Covenants. Appointing replacements, the king announced Hyde, Wilmot, Ormond and Jermyn as members of his Council, whereupon Berkeley, disgruntled at his exclusion, claimed Charles I had promised to make him Master of the Wards. This traditionally meant admission to the Privy Council. Although unconvinced of the claim when Berkeley all but burst into the room, young Charles initially employed his usual placating tactic of avoiding point-blank refusal, swerving the issue, but Berkeley 'used so great importunity' that the king ended up giving him 'a positive denial and reprehension'.[13] His shunning of Berkeley irked Henrietta Maria too. Charles felt Jermyn's appointment should satisfy her enough though, as designed. If genuine in all his talk of birthright, Charles never suspected Jermyn to be his biological father, but the queen mother's affections for her favourite were certainly bothersome. According to James in 1650, Henrietta Maria 'loved and valued Lord Jermyn more then she did all her children'.[14]

Like Charles's, James's relationship with his mother had spiralled into habitual feuding, and in 1652 it gave the 18-year-old, who reputedly often spoke 'very childishly',[15] even more reason to run off to a battlefield. In the end, Hyde reasoned that, if the duke enlist as a volunteer and thus maintain Charles's neutrality, Charles shouldn't hold his brother back. Nevertheless, in April, when James departed for his new life, Charles accompanied him part-way, pretending they were going hunting. After three or four days at Saint-Germain, the teen then went off to war.

But Charles himself was sucked into the action from a diplomatic stance. After visits from Jermyn to Louis and Anne resulted in a French grant of 6,000 livres per month for Charles, Louis wrote from Melun in June, asking the new grantee to help facilitate mediation with the Duke of Lorraine, who had allied his troops (Lorrainers) with Condé's. Lorraine was no stranger to England's royals, and in July 1651 he'd signed an agreement with Irish Catholics hoping to extinguish the Cromwellian conquest of Ireland. Charles couldn't afford to lose Lorraine's support, but Louis's was vital too. Having sought and ignored Henrietta Maria's advice, Charles therefore made straight for Villeneuve-Saint-Georges and presented himself amiably to Lorraine, who was readying for battle. The duke had nevertheless become unnerved, meaning he himself wanted to prevent combat, but these were feelings to hide, and both armies were already in sight of each other, the clock ticking as they continued to advance while Charles entered the attempt for a treaty. The commander-in-chief of Louis's army was Henri de La Tour d'Auvergne, Viscount of Turenne, and propositions from this marshal of France were delivered by none other than James. However, because James said that Lorraine's failure to agree to Turenne's full terms meant 'it must then be decided by the sword', he maddened his brother, who was asking James to encourage compromise.[16] Charles went to speak to Turenne himself. On the surface at least, this was fruitless as Turenne issued his previous terms in writing, and Lorraine consequently ordered his cannoneers to fire. But they disobeyed. After this, Lorraine promptly signed the treaty, withdrawing his forces. Although Lorraine is thought to have arranged the disobeying, can Charles be cleared of suspicion here? Either way, Frondeur commander the Duke of Beaufort believed the Stuart king's presence was instrumental in Lorraine's decision to sign.[17] Inflamed by Lorraine's abandonment and Charles's meddling, Beaufort, with a trumpeter, now turned the Parisian populace against Charles, violently. They 'used all the insolent reproaches against the English court ... and loudly threatened to be revenged'.[18] It was more than enough to stir memories of the anti-Strafford mobs. Neither Charles nor Henrietta Maria dared venture from the Louvre for many days. After this, they took their chances during a tempest in July. Through the grey, Charles rode vigilantly beside his mother's coach, guarding it with his hand against the door, and Louis then provided cavalry to escort them to Saint-Germain by torchlight, where the pair remained for several weeks.

Keeping out of the Fronde was wise, but Charles would be tripping over himself to get involved in other hostilities, for the Commonwealth had just declared war on the United Provinces of the Netherlands. 'The Dutch have too much trade, and the English are resolved to take it from them', read words from George Monck, one of Cromwell's generals at sea[19] from November 1652. The First Anglo-Dutch War would be an ambitious naval conflict sparked partly by the Rump's Navigation Act 1651, which greatly restricted foreign exportation to England. Charles hardly disagreed with such policies of English monopolisation; in the 1660s he'd pass Acts to increase them. But in 1652 the fight against them seemed his best hope of reviving the level of Dutch support he'd enjoyed from his late brother-in-law. In this vein, he instantly contacted Willem Boreel, Dutch ambassador in France,[20] and expressed intention of offering Scottish and Irish lands to Holland to aggravate the Rump. Then Charles proposed to enable Dutch fishing rights by gifting the Orkneys to the United Provinces if Dutch assistance regained him the Scillies and the Channel Islands.[21] However, the States-General, risen in power since William's death, disliked Charles's Orangist leanings, not to mention his reverting to Anglican worship after leaving Scotland. To appeal to Reformed views in Holland, the king was therefore advised to attend the Huguenot church of Charenton, and Presbyterian Massey, miraculously surviving his wounds from Worcester, became one such advocate.[22] The idea was nothing new, Henrietta Maria having implored her eldest to attend Charenton to appease the Covenanters. Hyde, conversely, had set about dissuading Charles, and Charles remained unwilling. Monarch and chancellor disagreed in other departments though. By 1653, Charles was so desperate to ingratiate himself with the States-General that he pledged: 'if the States will assign me some ships ... I will ...

prevail with them [the Dutch], or perish in the attempt'²³ and instructed Hyde to communicate this to The Hague via Boreel. Discovering that, due to Hyde's reservations, no such communication had been made, Charles then fixed himself in the chancellor's room, immovable till the letter was dispatched. It nevertheless got him nowhere.²⁴

But what of Charles's own ships, those fallen into his lap in 1648? During their months penned in off Hellevoetsluis with Warwick poised to fire, Rupert had used strong-arm tactics to prevent full mutiny, with Charles subsequently handing him naval command. Since then, the Palatine prince had taken the fleet to Ireland, Portugal, Spain, Africa and the Caribbean, privateering for the Stuart cause. In the process, he'd survived an arrow in the chest off the African coast by removing the projectile with a knife²⁵ but lost his beloved brother Maurice in a hurricane near the Virgin Islands, also losing most of the flotilla there. Now, complete with aftermaths of fierce dysentery, Rupert arrived in Paris to disappoint England's Royalists. £14,000 worth of prizes was no vast success from a four-year expedition, and he promptly pressed Charles to pay expenses such as sailors' earnings, trying to deny the king much of the spoils' limited value.²⁶

The donations and loans Charles occasionally received were drops in the ocean, and because he refused to convert to Catholicism, hopes faded regarding Vatican funds. But as the Stuart monarch slumped ever lower, much of his financial disappointment revolved around France. Bad enough was the meagre remuneration entailed in French demands to buy the guns on surviving Royalist warship *Swallow*.²⁷ Far worse was France's failure to pay Charles his monthly allowance on time or in full.

Charles was again seriously discontented in the land of the Gauls. 'I longe to be gone from hence', he'd declared in November 1652.²⁸ His love of French culture is deceptive. He reportedly disgusted the French by living a debauched life. Yet doubt is cast on his reputation for debauchery in exile. Cromwellian-controlled reports must naturally be viewed with scepticism, and of course assessment depends on the definition of 'debauchery'. However, French courtier Motteville would recall: 'when he found that his struggles were doomed to failure, he sank into indifference, and bore the ills of poverty and exile with reckless nonchalance, snatching at whatever pleasures came in his way, even those of the most degraded kind'.²⁹ Hyde nevertheless asserted his confidence that Charles would 'outlive the

Chapter 18

scandals about him, and give the world evidence of another temper of mind',[30] and Hyde's main concern regarding his master's recreation was the fact it prevailed over paperwork. It kept on prevailing though. Climbing in admiration as a dancer and forever maintaining the charm he'd developed in childhood, Charles received invitations to masques and banquets and leapt at them. He considered them near-necessities though, and not just because they provided free food. The truth was he recognised a need for distractions. He advised Lord Beauchamp: 'take heed of melancholique, I keepe myselfe from it as well as I can'.[31]

Charles sometimes curbed the distractions anyway. He rarely got drunk. This is particularly remarkable as his courtiers imbibed to such excess that becoming 'pot-valiant' appeared essential for spies to blend in. 'I did as the wicked would have me', an agent therefore confessed in September 1653 but described Charles as 'goodly'.[32]

By avoiding inebriation, the king avoided hangovers, and he remained an early riser despite staying up late – except when in bed for activities that tired him further. A report from around his twenty-third birthday labels him 'whelmed in pleasures, specially women'.[33] It was perhaps through lovemaking that he found greatest solace.

As recorded by Pepys in 1667, a gentlewoman christened Eleanor Needham is branded Charles's 'seventeenth whore abroad'.[34] Her husband John, Baron Byron, whose peerage later passed to the Romantic poet Lord Byron, became superintendent of James's household in April 1651 but died in August 1652, making his wife, though only mid-twenties, a widow for the second time.[35] Whether Charles began relations with Eleanor before her second widowhood is unclear, but based on stories reported, most females who had thus far erotically interested him were unchaste, some with several years' experience as wives. Particularly if the bossy but maternal Christabella introduced him to sex of some form, Charles in youth seems to have preferred sharing his bed with women who could teach him something, not women he would wield dominance over.

The energetic king spent an awful lot of time in bed in August 1653, but awful was the operative word. Sick with 'a burning fever', he was bled at least five times,[36] concerns rising.

◈ ◈ ◈

It was with fever in the plague-ravaged Limerick area that Ireton had passed on in November 1651. Of all history's 'what if' questions, one deriving from this is frequently overlooked, but had Ireton survived, he would no doubt have shaped the period ahead, possibly with lasting consequences. According to Royalist historian James Heath in the Restoration era, Ireton was Cromwell's 'second self',[37] and few influenced Cromwell more than this son-in-law of his. But the two devout Puritans didn't see eye to eye entirely. Ireton, an instigator of Charles I's execution, found his zeal sometimes restrained by Cromwell, whose republicanism never reached the intensity of his son-in-law's. Ireton reportedly believed 'Presidents of Provinces were an unnecessary burthen to the state and country',[38] and chances are that Ireton would not have stood by while Cromwell took the route approached in 1653, a route ultimately leading to failure.

The failure was hard to envisage though. Reminiscent of Pride's Purge, military force appeared at Westminster on 20 April 1653, Cromwell arriving with musketeers and proceeding to 'put an end to' the Rump.[39] After this, replacement came in the form of the Nominated Assembly, a body comprising members chosen by the New Model Army's Council of Officers. The Commonwealth was undergoing incredible restructuring, and by December, England had a written constitution, the *Instrument of Government*. Drafted by Major General John Lambert, this aimed to restore the throne – and place Cromwell on it. Disliking the royal side of it, however, Cromwell substituted King with Lord Protector. It wasn't the first time England had seen a lord protector; some regents in centuries past had used the title while serving for their monarch, but this lord protector had no superior. On 16 December, creating the Protectorate, Cromwell was styled Olivarius Protector, an equivalent of Carolus Rex,[40] as he was installed, for life, as England's supreme power. Surely, thought Royalists, Charles would want Cromwell assassinated.

Chapter 19

Of all the relationships Charles formed in his life, the closest occasionally seem the coldest. In August 1651 Buckingham put on a ridiculous show of sulkily refusing to talk to the king for denying him Leslie's job, yet the duke himself deserved the silent treatment, or worse. His dealings with the Kirk Party were dubious, and in the wake of the regicide he'd made moves to befriend Parliament, hoping to regain the estates Parliament had sequestered from him. His efforts would continue as well. In the meantime, having fled to Holland post-Worcester, he not only tried wooing Charles's widowed sister but also began concocting restoration schemes with John Lilburne, a radical pamphleteer whose history in the Levellers implied he'd strive to make monarchy subservient to a vastly expanded electorate. At the French court for Christmas celebrations after this plotting, Buckingham fell ill, and Charles didn't even ask after him.

Hyde also seemed highly likely to slip from favour. He was constantly chiding the king for laziness. And in 1653, this irritating chancellor stood accused of operating as a Cromwellian spy. The story came from the old Western Association's vengeful Richard Grenville and was supported by Long, who himself was said to have fed the enemy intelligence, and in addition to this a whole trunk of papers Long left in Jersey had reportedly fallen into Parliament's possession. Nicholas wanted the job of Secretary of State and would soon get it because, after investigation by Hyde, Long's secretaryship had been terminated. Now the king was investigating Hyde, though turning the task into an investigation of others. During country retreat to Chantilly that October, Charles had been making relevant enquiries, and he'd 'examined other allegations' emanating from Grenville. 'His Majesty himself knew [some of them] to be false'.[1] Already a cynical character, the king then opened his ears to the devious Bampfield, Berkeley and Gerard, who was now Lord Gerard and captain of the royal guard. These men testified against Hyde's loyalty, and on 2 January 1654 Charles also probed his childhood tutor Massonnet, supposedly an author of some of the evidence. The next day, the royal verdict would be announced in council, where all eyes rested on the monarch even more than usual. Among them was a relatively new face too, Charles's 13-year-old sibling Henry, released from the Isle of Wight a year earlier after a decade's imprisonment under Parliament's care. Not since infancy had Henry seen his biggest brother, but now the boy could finally make him a role model, and that day the king was in exemplary mode. Having documents read aloud, Charles wanted it known that he'd taken pains to consider the attack on Hyde fairly and believed 'libel' and 'malice' were at play. With this, he declared the accusations 'groundless' and a 'calumny' for which he intended to punish the guilty, not the chancellor.[2]

Nevertheless, while Grenville was consequently banned from entering the sovereign's presence, Gerard got off lightly,[3] and courtiers weren't his only prey. When he brought his cousin John Gerard to the king, both Gerards proposed a plan of immense gravity, a plan to murder Oliver Cromwell. There was nothing unique about this; Cromwell's murder seemed to be all some Royalists thought about. But Charles knew it would require stringent orchestration, and little beyond zeal could be seen here. John Gerard was a small man in his early twenties who had already got heavily involved in Royalist conspiracies in England and narrowly escaped arrest upon discovery of one, the Ship Tavern plot, but by 13 May he was back on English soil, allegedly poised with thirty horsemen to kill the lord protector journeying to Hampton Court that morning. Unexpectedly travelling by water, however, Cromwell evaded his would-be assassins, and before they could try again at Whitehall's chapel the following Sunday, 21 May, they were rumbled. This isn't too surprising, as their groundwork included mustering for insurrection in the City and organising hundreds of men to overpower guards at Whitehall and St James's and divert attention with an attack on a regiment in Southwark.[4] But one man who perhaps didn't know these gambits were in progress was the king. A few weeks later, he'd write: 'ther was not the least derection from me'.[5] And signs of forgery are seen in what purports to be a proclamation from Charles,[6] dated in late April 1654, promising an annual £500 'for ever' to the family of anyone successful in 'cutting ... from the face of the earth' 'a certain mechanic fellow, by name Oliver Cromwell'.[7] In fact, unlike James, Charles would soon gain a reputation for refusing to back attempts at the protector's homicide.

Chapter 19

All told, it's unlikely Charles gave the Gerard plot the go-ahead. But if he did, he was double-dealing. By the spring of 1654, he'd established the Sealed Knot, a committee to which he promised to entrust plans for uprisings. As 1653's efforts to oust Hyde demonstrate, a toxic factionalism permeated the exiled court, and the Sealed Knot was closely linked to Hyde's clique the Old Royalists who lived at loggerheads with not only the Louvre group under Henrietta Maria but also the Swordsmen surrounding Rupert, a great friend of Lord Gerard.[8] The Gerard plot was quite independent of the Sealed Knot. In fact, the Knot should have stopped it. How well they would perform in future remained to be seen, but members of this hopeful new committee were clearly willing to die for their cause, just as John Gerard would after trial by the High Court of Justice. While guilty-pleader Somerset Fox was to be punished with transportation to Barbados, John Gerard claimed innocence and went to the block on Tower Hill where, upon the scaffold on 10 July 1654, he left no doubt about his loyalty to the king: 'had I ten thousand thousand lives I would glad[l]y lay them all down thus for his service'.[9] And something notable about the main members of the Sealed Knot is that each had at least one elder brother, meaning family estates were unlikely to be lost upon any imminent death of these six men. However, despite its martyrs' outlook, the Knot was designed to coordinate conspiracy carefully and replace the get-up-and-go approach manifest in many thoughts of the protector's elimination.

Cromwell nevertheless looked unstoppable. Numerous nations officially viewed him as England's rightful ruler, and his negotiations for an Anglo-Swedish alliance signed that April had been enhanced by a degree of romance between his married self and unmarried Swedish queen Christina. As part of this, a poem was written to Christina, as if by Cromwell. Translated from Latin, it ends:

> But soften'd, in thy sight, my looks appear,
> Not to all Queens or Kings alike severe.[10]

More seriously, meanwhile, the Cromwellian conquest of Ireland had wiped out a considerable proportion of the Irish population, and Cromwell's forces remained some of the most formidable in Europe.

As such, they had won the Anglo-Dutch war, which hadn't all been about trade – peace agreements placed restrictions on the House of Orange and in turn on Charles, barring him from Dutch refuge.[11] But France was no longer prepared to shelter him. Although the Fronde had concluded with victory for Louis, the Franco-Spanish War continued, and the French wanted support from the English government. Scarcely could there be such a blessing in disguise though. To lure him away in 1654, France promised the exiled king full and continuing payment of his grant if he left.[12] It lured him easily.

Charles wasn't the only beneficiary either. His poverty had knock-on effects for his entourage, but now the household he took would actually see their money, and to top it off they were accompanying their king on a joyous holiday with his sister Mary. This began in July in Spa, the siblings lovingly reuniting after four years. Then they concentrated on fun: 'all his embassadors and agents from all parts flock to him ... as merry as if they had the three kingdoms', enemy intelligence reported from Spa.[13] Charles also wrote to his aunt Elizabeth: 'there is such a noise that I never hope to end it', and he conveyed that his current concerns centred on how to acquire fiddlers and dance instructors.[14] Indeed Protectorate spy John Adams described the gang dancing daily and following supper with further jigs in the meadows. The king 'gaines the affection of all by his affable and free carriage amongst them', Adams continued.[15] So often could Cromwell's agents find nothing but praise to feed back regarding 'R. C.', as they often called Charles.

Charles's retinue, by contrast, weren't all so impressive. When a smallpox outbreak forced brother and sister to move to Aachen in August, disputes among the eighty or so 'gallant men' in the king's train were turning violent. Within just one twenty-four-hour period, Charles interposed to prevent a duel, Colepeper and another came together 'by the ears' and 'lord Wentworth and one major Boswel quarrell'd and knock'd one another ... in the next room to R. C's bed-chamber'. Wine was blamed.[16] However, Cæsar Bath offered a calming environment to immerse body and mind, and Charles was keeping a steady hand for hunting and hawking, again refraining from becoming paralytic.

This was particularly wise as he and Mary were often still on formal show. From Aachen's Catholic cathedral came a graceful invitation, and reception on 28 August offered them black velvet seating as well as an 'extraordinary' choral performance, though perhaps more memorable was Charles kissing Charlemagne's sword and comparing the length of it against his.[17] At the end of September, they then decamped to Cologne, where city magistrates presented wine and silverware while a 'curious house' provided 'decent rooms and pleasant gardens',[18] and on 19 October king and princess sailed along the Rhine to Düsseldorf, finding cannon volleys salute them before Palatinate-Neuburg palsgrave Philipp-Wilhelm entertained at his castle with a grand feast including music like none 'his majesty was accustomed to'.[19]

Charles was beginning new chances to absorb the diversity of Europe. As November neared, however, Mary had to return to Holland. A spy was struck by the sadness of the siblings' farewell in Xanten.

But as Charles settled back into his new home of Cologne, rage overtook all other emotions, for he learned his mother was attempting to have Henry convert to Catholicism. She'd promised to leave this young prince alone as regards religion. Now she was arranging his admission into a Jesuit college and had placed him under the charge of abbé Walter Montagu at the Catholic abbey Saint-Martin in Pontoise. She'd lost Charles's trust irrevocably.

However, as the king lunged into an irate letter-writing frenzy in a bid to maintain Henry's Anglicanism, the queen mother wasn't the only person building volcanicity within him. For a start, Jermyn had tried keeping him in the dark, writing Charles very recent letters without a single mention of Henry's situation. Having, with contempt, noted this in his reply, Charles continued: 'if you do not use all the means possible you can to prevent my brother from being seduced … this shall be the last time you shall ever hear from me'.[20] Another of the monarch's missives would direct James to intervene 'without any consideration' for anybody.[21] But a similar attitude from the potential convert could rebuff all such efforts.

At 14, Henry was hard to handle, his 'carriage to all persons' being 'unsupportable', and he'd shun almost every book put in front of him, ignoring or insulting his tutor Lovell.[22] Of course, the prince had experienced a huge transition, from Parliament-controlled captivity without excessive pampering to a royal court that suddenly made him feel important. Charles had tried to ease him into a princely role through a balance of study, grand entertainments and royal business such as meetings with advisers, and the siblings had formed a loving bond along the way. Henry's rude, uncooperative behaviour had really set in after Charles's departure. But now the teen was even disobeying Charles, who had told him to respect Lovell.

Already unhappy about this, the king began his message to Henry by pointing out the prince's failure to date his last letter and then referred to earlier guidelines emphasising adherence to the Church of England. Charles had implanted these in Henry's head before leaving France and now told him: 'I am confident you will observe them'. But this communication quickly turned into a giant warning: 'whatsoever mischief shall fall on me … [if you become Catholic], I must lay all upon you, as being the only cause of it'.[23]

Though he sent the Irish Protestant Ormond to dissuade in person, another tactic Charles employed in writing played on deeper emotion: 'remember the last wordes of my deade father', he hurled at Henrietta Maria and instructed Henry likewise, outlining how, the day before the regicide, the martyred sovereign had urged the little prince never to abandon the Anglican faith. Yet the most intense feelings of Charles II are reflected in another part of the text to his mother: 'I cannot expect [imagine] your Majesty does either believe or wish my return into England'.[24] From all four letters, it's clear that Charles's concerns focused not on the conversion itself but almost exclusively on how it would scupper restoration chances.

Charles often viewed religion as an impediment. However, although that doesn't mean he was an atheist, he calculated how much he would let it impede. Burnet's musings state that in 1673 Charles 'thought God would not damn a man for a little irregular pleasure',[25] and he'd seemingly believed that for at least twenty-five years by then. Within the tumultuous world he'd grown up in, what Charles feared more than the divine was the divide. This is the Charles who, aged 9, even before the Second Bishops' War, envisaged the Stuarts' loss of the kingdoms, and it worried him that his family either couldn't or wouldn't be guided by lessons learned, let alone by perception.

With guidance by God encouraged instead, Henry was now hearing the words of Catholics all around him while his mother persisted with her intentions to save his soul, love ultimately driving her. She nevertheless saw her efforts thrown back in her face. When in Paris again, the prince made it known that he'd come to a decision to remain Anglican. This wasn't impudence; it was his conscience speaking, yet Henrietta Maria disowned him, literally turfing Henry out never to plague her court again. He ran to

Chapter 19

his eldest sibling, and Charles's later admiration of him implies Henry's attitude problems then improved, when the brothers resided together again. However, the entire episode their mother triggered would soon become common knowledge, including the intervention from Charles – not exactly ideal as he set up home in Catholic Cologne. But while upset ripped through the family, the matriarch wanted to argue that Henry's conversion would have swayed the Pope into backing their quest for the crown. Realistically, however, only Charles's conversion could bring them effective papal assistance.

The crown itself was no more, Council of State instructions ensuring much of the ancient coronation regalia be melted down into coinage, and this followed a 1649 Act of Parliament ordering the sale of Charles I's, Henrietta Maria's and Charles II's belongings while Cromwell was established in royal palaces. His dreams weren't all coming true though.

On the third anniversary of the Battle of Worcester, the First Protectorate Parliament had assembled, and after well over a year without a Commons sitting, men elected during the summer included quite a few anti-Protectorate members – some radical republicans, some traditional monarchists. Representation was physically widespread too. Following Cromwell's conquests of Scotland and Ireland, these smaller realms had seats in Westminster for the first time ever, thirty each, and one was occupied by Cork MP Roger Boyle, Baron Broghill, who had helped Cromwell to victory in the Irish bloodshed. Yet while benefitting from direct access to the protector, Broghill also conducted secret communication with 'some persons' at the king's court.[26] He therefore detected a royal desperation. The Sealed Knot was reluctant to accept aid from nonconformists and foreign forces, and its resultant inertia riled Charles profusely, but while he turned to a more open-minded 'new council' for insurgence to bring down the Protectorate, he was also persuaded to pursue an incredibly friendly alternative. At Broghill's suggestion, the king now sought to marry a daughter of the lord protector.

The new parliament was voting against all the bills Cromwell wanted passed, and doubt hung over visions of a Cromwellian future, especially as Lord Protector was a non-hereditary title. In these circumstances, according to Broghill, Cromwell might be willing to restore the monarchy to his potential son-in-law and any grandchildren springing from the union proposed, even though Charles would probably wed Cromwell's youngest daughter Frances if the plan came to fruition. With myriad possibilities for the terms of a marriage treaty, constitutional scope existed, but could any of this really satisfy the House of Stuart? Broghill pictured an arrangement whereby Charles would be something of a figurehead leaving power in Cromwell's hands,[27] a forward-thinking arrangement perhaps but an arrangement quite abhorrent to the king. Nevertheless, where power already sat, this was a significant means of getting the Stuart foot in the door. Despite his inevitable need to be submissive in sealing the deal, Charles could attempt an agenda from there. In the meantime, Broghill had to focus on the submissiveness, as he was now to put the argument of a Stuart–Cromwell union to the lord protector.

Quite daringly, the Irishman tested the water with others first, not only Cromwell's daughter and wife but also the general populace of London, spreading rumour of these nuptials for all to hear. When then introducing the idea to the father of the bride-to-be, Broghill presented it 'in a jocular way' as gossip from around the city. 'And what do the fools think of it?' came the response from Cromwell with a corresponding 'merry countenance'. The matchmaker told him they thought it 'the wisest thing' the protector could do. Aware there could be something in this, Cromwell quickly turned serious, listening to how the scheme would maintain 'his greatness' forever through royalty. He did not seem to take issue with the concept of Charles as king. By raising another issue, however, the protector spoke a few rather insightful words: Charles, he said, would never forgive his father's execution. The account, penned by Broghill's chaplain Thomas Morrice, also describes Cromwell as experiencing guilt 'so heavy upon him, that he thought there could be no reconciliation'.[28] From inside Cromwell, what comes across here is a deep-seated fear of Charles. Scribblings from Burnet nevertheless claim Cromwell further reasoned against the marriage by declaring Charles 'so damnably debauched he would undo us all'.[29]

Debauchery could have uses though. Over the past two years, Wilmot had been deploying his well-tested drunken social skills to endearing effect on princes and aristocrats of the German states, and the result was thousands of pounds now rolling in for the Royalist cause. Tasked with this fundraising mission, he'd performed with aplomb, but he'd done well from it himself.

Chapter 19

To help Wilmot gain acceptance in high society, Charles had made him Earl of Rochester in December 1652.[30]

Basically, however, this was a thank you to Rochester for his assistance in the great escape of 1651. Nevertheless, more than ever now, the king failed to understand Rochester's aversion to disguise. It's said that, disappearing to seedy taverns for cheap meals, Charles took to prostitutes after his return to the Continent,[31] and the several years' gap between his second and third acknowledged child indeed implies he satisfied urges furtively in his mid-twenties. Condoms were costly. Moreover, made of animal innards such as a bladder, they were tied on[32] and slipped more easily than Charles would let his guard slip. With sex workers maybe unaware of his identity, the Merry Monarch probably fathered more children than *anyone* ever realised.

If he got what he wanted from Isabelle-Angélique, that was kept quiet too. In fact, frustration over its absence perhaps helped drive him into the taverns-cum-brothels, but he could combine business with pleasure when disguised among the lowly. He described his post-Worcester incognito status as opportunity 'to discover the humours of the people',[33] and he recognised the importance of this for political survival. Ultimately, Charles II preferred being a king to being treated like a king. For this reason, when Leveller Edward Sexby held potential for the Royalists in 1656, the egalitarian was to find no expectation placed on him to kneel or kiss the royal hand if, at his discretion, he met Charles secretly.

For the same reason meanwhile, in February 1655, Charles re-enacted something of his escape. He was again turning to disguise, again calling himself William Jackson and again hiding in a sympathiser's abode. This time sanctuary took the form of a snow-covered house in Middelburg, Zeeland, another Dutch zone closed to Charles officially, but he planned to leap across the sea from here and end up in London. Thanks to the 'new council', Royalist uprisings were scheduled to strike across England, and Charles had apologetically instructed the Sealed Knot to cooperate against their wishes as he committed all he could. Now he sat hoping for reports that the New Model Army was falling. Adding to the optimism, there had been talk of Fairfax joining the coup, but in this world of turncoats, Cromwell's intelligence network thrived. Under the super-efficient John Thurloe, Protectorate spies and double agents alike supplied a constant stream of information to Whitehall, and with men and arms seized, most risings were called off or stamped out in a flash. Just one remained. On the morning of 12 March, Colonel John Penruddock invaded Salisbury with around 400 Cavaliers, bursting into the bedchambers of officials and storming prisons to have inmates enlist, but as his forces then swept through the South West, skirmish in the streets of South Molton led to Penruddock's surrender and the end of the whole venture.

Charles had trusted too much in the inadequate, and his own disgruntled supporters spurned him. Having returned disheartened to Cologne, he wrote on 3 June: 'those … men … do me more hurt than my avowed enemies can'.[34]

But these enemies were causing hurt on an intercontinental scale. On Christmas Day, their fleet under general at sea William Penn had sailed for the Caribbean, hellbent on conquering islands of the Spanish Empire as Cromwell targeted Spanish trade. Of course, if Charles were restored to the British thrones, he could restore conquered lands to previous owners. In the meantime, he could do something about all the troops he had fighting with the French against the Spanish. And out of campaigning season, Spain had thousands of its own troops it could lend Charles. Alliance with the Spanish Empire seemed a dream. By his own admission, the exiled sovereign was 'building Castles in the Air',[35] yet the foundation stones were laid in solid ground.

Chapter 20

To find a chink in Cromwell's armour in 1655, a good place to look was the Protectorate navy. Here 'many principal Officers' would take 'any orders' that Charles might give.[1] At least that's what Charles wanted communicated to Spain's King Felipe IV. But feelings were more anti-Cromwellian than pro-Royalist, particularly as the protector was ruling without parliament again. Outrage at his rule had already generated a petition among the seamen, and it was secretly supported by their vice-admiral John Lawson, a Levellers abetter. Now Sexby was going to Madrid's Council of State to beg assistance, with the Levellers intent on 'a free Parliament' that would 'call the King, so that he be content to be an administrator, and not master, of the laws'.[2] Naturally Charles felt alarm at this, yet he had ample capability to mould the plan to his advantage. He turned Lawson into a promising contact.

Before long, the Cavaliers could have control of an English port, a route in for invasion. However, while Charles sought Spain's help to achieve victory in this invasion, France sought Cromwell's help to achieve victory in the Franco-Spanish War. The Spanish could ill afford to provoke the protector. They rather wanted him on their side instead, and they hoped to reach an agreement regarding his attempt to steal their trade. Encouragingly from the reports received so far, Spain's losses in the Caribbean seemed minimal.

Through the months ahead, Charles would thus be on tenterhooks in Cologne, monitoring the political story unfolding. Along the way, he ruminated over how to seduce Catholic Spain, but he'd rebuff recommendations from the nonetheless useful Peter Talbot, an Irish Jesuit closely linked to Madrid.

An even more useful man seemed to be new pope Alexander VII, initially. When Bishop Fabio Chigi, he'd wanted 'all Christian kings' to unite for the purposes of restoring Stuart monarchy,[3] and he and Charles had a mutual friend in Philipp-Wilhelm after Charles's visit to Düsseldorf. However, the monarch's 1650 surrender to Presbyterianism gave Alexander no reason to trust the monarch. When told, through Philipp-Wilhelm, that the Protectorate was fragile and susceptible to papal-funded attack, Rome knew better, withheld subsidies and practically called Charles a money-grabbing liar.

Charles was grabbing barely a penny though. Both the German and the French sources of income were drying up, rendering his existence somewhat hand-to-mouth in 1655. Despite pawning jewels,[4] he could pay neither rent nor butchers' bills, and he'd soon experience economic turmoil trying to feed twenty-eight hounds received as an unwanted present. By contrast, however, the spaniels Charles himself purchased[5] demonstrate his general policy, of simply letting debts mount. He struggled to accept unbecoming cutbacks. Therefore, while his Cologne dwelling was no castle or palace, his own person projected majesty through continual orders for suits, hats, footwear and accessories from France. Now very fashion-conscious, the king was discerning, turning his nose up at a sword accompanying new clothes in June and urging: 'go to the Shop where I bought mine, when I came out of *Paris*' as he sought a replacement. More instructions for a bespoke sword appear in his 1656 correspondence, as does a request for twelve pairs of shoes to add to those already received.[6]

He had little call for fine dress in Germany, however. Despite friendliness from citizens and city magistrates, powers such as Cologne's elector ignored him, though Charles ignored the snub. With 'marvellous contentedness' he spent hours shut away studying Italian.[7] Henry's arrival nonetheless saw Charles continue some family bonding, while dancing and games of cards brought interaction, and he entered the public eye for outdoor pastimes, no matter how ill-advised. As he swam in the cold, mucky Rhine, help stood by on a boat.[8] Rupert had almost drowned swimming in the Seine in 1653. Charles also habitually shrugged off the possibility of assassination around Cologne, like he would around London years later. Both cities saw him take walks, and his love of walking developed greatly in Cologne. Here, he perambulated through biting frosts and sometimes rode, straying into fields beyond the city walls.

Come autumn 1655, the penchant for leisure took Charles and Henry to Frankfurt, with Mary tagging along. Unfortunately though, news of this siblings' holiday reached Rupert's brother Charles Louis. Thanks to 1648's Peace of Westphalia concluding the Thirty Years' War, Charles Louis was officially Elector Palatine and thus a restored ruler, yet his Stuart cousins struggled to admire him. In England in the earlier 1640s, he'd supported Parliament, a potential route to usurping the English throne. Despite this, the elector had invited Charles II to Heidelberg in 1655 and didn't take no for an answer, consequently turning up at a comedy in Frankfurt – Charles and Mary were likely to attend a comedy. However, faced with their cousin's presence after the performance, the siblings uncharacteristically left so abruptly that he couldn't catch them. Then they ignored his offer to meet the next morning.

Religion brought Charles some contentment during the Frankfurt break. He'd gone to a Lutheran church one day 'and seemed much pleased with their ceremonies, coming somewhat near to the episcopal'.[9] And overall, with a fair, wine gifted and salutes from castles, Charles had enjoyed his few weeks' sojourn. Now in mid-October, he was back in Cologne, where he'd described some of the company as 'worse than none'.[10]

There was nonetheless Henry Manning, a genial 'proper' young man who had presented himself around New Year. Professing hatred of the Roundheads for killing his father in battle, Manning boasted connections to Royalist aristocracy, promised Charles £3,000 from the Earl of Pembroke and came bearing regular copies of a sought-after London news publication. Charles had admitted him right into the fold, unaware this new companion was also sending news *to* London – reams of it in cipher for Cromwell's spymaster. Manning provided intelligence from the king's court for almost a year before packets of post raised suspicions. But when Hyde and colleagues seized some of the correspondence prepared, they found it contained puzzling fabrication.[11] Interrogated, the Catholic Manning confessed his employment as a spy. He nevertheless claimed he was a spy who took the monthly pay of £100 and then fed Whitehall lies that could neither help the king's enemies nor harm the king. Not everything Manning reported was falsehood, however. He admitted to revealing Charles's presence in Zeeland, and he acknowledged guilt of treachery, with fright coursing through him when Nicholas and other counsellors put him through a makeshift trial. Angered and unnerved by being fooled, Charles oversaw the attempt to see justice done, describing his time as spent 'examining and discoursing one of the greatest Villains that ever was'.[12] But the powerless monarch was doing what the regicides are criticised for. The trial lacked legality; Manning's death sentence would have been considered murder if carried out in Cologne. Sadly for the now hysterical convict though, Philipp-Wilhelm permitted the execution in his domain. In a distant forest therefore, gunfire ended Manning's life on 5 December.

Of course, to try justifying this, Charles could explain how Royalist danger would rise if Protectorate espionage looked easy to get away with, but desire to counter the humiliation Manning caused is no fair justification, even though it was compounded; by now, Lucy was making a profession of humiliating Charles.

Shortly before Manning's arrival, Lucy had shown up in Cologne too, with proposed husband Henry de Vic – Charles's representative based in Brussels. Jemmy had also been with her. She'd then departed with a promise of 5,000 livres per annum from Charles,[13] married nobody and continued her high-profile life of promiscuity, currently around the Orange court. Though a Walter, Lucy sometimes called herself Mrs Barlow, but she was also known as the mother of Charles's son, and she was dragging Charles's name into the dirt. Then, after Charles sent gentleman of the bedchamber Daniel O'Neill to The Hague, this Irishman informed him in February 1656 that Lucy had been plotting to kill her maid who wanted to accuse her of two self-abortions by chemical means. The only reassuring news was the fact O'Neill bribed the maid to keep quiet, saving her life, but there was nothing reassuring about Lucy having charge of Jemmy. Though this intelligent child was safe from her malevolence, his mother couldn't really be bothered with bringing him up. Hence, even around his ninth birthday, in 1658, he'd still appear unable to count past nineteen.

In 1656, meanwhile, Charles was counting on Spain. Cromwell had snatched Jamaica from Felipe, France had secured alliance with the Protectorate and Sexby had proven uncooperative, and on 1 March the exiled king arrived for talks in the Spanish Netherlands. This was another covert episode. As Sexby seemed likely to upset the apple cart and emissaries of Cromwell were probable arrivals in disguise, Charles was hidden away, disconcerted by stares and enquiries. Added to this, his diplomatic skills were tested.

'The King is so confident of the good meaning of the Spanish Ministers that he will not, as they desire, take any of his Council ... only two attendants, and expects to arrive at the Sun inn in Louvain on Saturday', Hyde had informed De Vic.[14] Ormond and Rochester would be in Brussels, but Charles conducted most of the negotiations in Vilvoorde, armed with nothing beyond his charm and acumen. However, these qualities, at the very first meeting, had turned the Count of Fuensaldaña's 'dry' approach into one of speaking freely, and while Charles nicely referred religious matters to Ormond 'on account of the Irish treaties', the Spanish were quick to assure they expected 'nothing that was not thought reasonable' regarding religion.[15]

Charles nevertheless proposed not only to return English-held dominions to the Spanish Empire but also, for an extra-secret clause, to permit Catholicism in England. But to do either, he obviously needed to rule England. Proposing what they could themselves, Felipe's ministers responded accordingly – if the Cavaliers gained control of a port in Charles's homeland, Spain would provide arms, ammunition and 6,000 troops for Charles's invasion. Backed by anticipated insurgence in England, invasion with this golden support stood decent chances of success. And by 3 April, the propositions were concrete promises, together with others, forming the Treaty of Brussels.[16] To Charles, this was the greatest move of his career so far. Although it sucked the Royalists into the Franco-Spanish War, it appeared the key to the Royalist dream.

It left many points open to contention, however. Now it was signed, Charles wanted a home in Brussels. He had to settle for sleepy Bruges instead. There, an entire block of houses down to the canal started undergoing preparation to become his court's new base, and the iconic House of the Seven Towers was included.[17] Already consigned to Bruges in the meantime, Charles was, in his words, 'far from being in a good condition'.[18] He therefore appreciated temporary accommodation with the family of Anthony Preston, Viscount Tara.[19]

At every opportunity, Charles would be racing to the capital, but backing down regarding residence there seems to have knocked his confidence. His Spanish was limited, Spanish culture was foreign to him and, as he began a close alliance with Spain, frightful unease spilled all over a letter he wrote Hyde on 27 April. Because the chancellor failed to provide a book on customs such as forms of address, Charles told him: 'I would you were besh–t'.[20] Hyde, stricken with gout, was with his pregnant wife Frances in Breda, but this meant he 'played the truant' according to his king, who had allowed this for Frances's sake but was now panicked by it, peppering the communication with insults and deeming the chancellor's hasty return 'necessary'.[21]

Luckily, warmth was to radiate from Felipe's illegitimate son Juan-José, new governor of the Spanish Netherlands, and the main emissary was Alonso de Cárdenas, who had been ambassador in London but recently left the position, enraged by Cromwell. Also, of course, there were the people of Flanders. Though no master of Flemish either, Charles used 'familiarity with persons of so much inferior quality',[22] and the best way he could win hearts in Bruges was to meet and greet.

In June, he attended an event courtesy of the guild of Saint-George, a crossbowmen's guild, where he accurately fired at a (presumably stuffed) popinjay placed atop a tall pole. However, because wine merchant Pieter Pruyssenaere shot the bird down completely, the king cordially accepted defeat, then presented the prize, hanging the golden 'Bird of Honour' round Pruyssenaere's neck. Later that month, it was much the same story with gardener Michael Noé winning at archers' guild Saint-Sebastian, and by October Charles would be a proud member of both these guilds plus that of Saint-Barbara, which was dedicated to arquebusiers.

Henry participated too, having joined Charles in the spring. Their other brother, however, was conspicuous by his absence. Showered with praise for skill and gallantry, James had reached cloud nine in the French army and, when not on campaign, basked in admiration at the Parisian court. The Duke of York now felt real allegiance towards France. He had no desire to follow the numerous Irish Cavaliers abandoning French service. Providing excuses, he was lingering in Paris, hoping to join the next battle against Spain, and his big brother was fuming. Therefore, in July, Charles expressly commanded James to leave and come to Bruges. The duke took two months before obeying. Then he arrived harbouring a huge grudge against both Spain and Charles.

Towards the end of 1656, Mary journeyed to Bruges too and was siding with James, as was their mother in France. In addition, James surrounded himself with favourites Charles deplored. Berkeley was one. Another was Jermyn's nephew Harry Jermyn. Equally, however, men James deplored also attended him, at Charles's insistence, and prime example Bennet was accusing the duke of conducting dealings, with Royalists in England, behind the king's back.[23] Meanwhile Spanish-speaker Digby, 2nd Earl of

Bristol since January 1653, liaised with officials, butted into conversations and told the Spanish what they wanted to hear, vexing James.

In August, Charles had begun receiving a monthly 3,000 écus from the Spanish,[24] and more of the German funds were filtering in. But a miserable winter lay ahead, snow blanketing the landscape and hindering postal deliveries while tempers reached boiling point indoors. A company of French comedians seemed wasted on the dour James, who was certainly unamused when shut out of meetings. Berkeley consoled him, but this courtier also loudly vocalised views offensive to Spanish ears. By around New Year, Charles would tolerate Berkeley's presence no more. However, in appeasing Spain this way, he nearly lost James to France. Two days after Berkeley left, the 23-year-old duke ran away.[25] The weather forced him to Breda instead of Paris for the time being, but once tracked down, he stated he'd make no return to Bruges unless given control of his household. The truth was James felt belittled and vulnerable, and Charles was the reason. Reflective and desperate to keep James from France, Charles conceded.

While the duke therefore prepared to leave the United Provinces again, the king was escorting Mary back there, on what should have been an uneventful journey. However, in Damme, just northeast of Bruges, a volley of salute brought drama. Charles saw the sentry handle the musket with frightening ineptitude and shifted quickly, calling out a warning, but some of the 'many small bullets' ended up embedded 'farther ... than was convenient' in a man behind him.[26]

The military nevertheless represented Charles's main hopes now. At the expense of Spain and deployed in the Franco-Spanish conflicts, new Cavalier regiments were formed in 1656–57, seeing Englishmen, Irishmen and, in kilts causing comments, Scotsmen burst onto the scene in Bruges. Most of the regiments were infantry, limiting cavalry opportunities, but numbers stood in the thousands. However, in the summer of 1657, more than a year after completion of the Treaty of Brussels, there was still no English port at the king's disposal, nor was insurrection erupting. In England, Lawson had been dismissed from service, the Sealed Knot were gathering scant support and Sexby would soon be arrested and die. The Knot's usual policy of delay almost had excuse too. Spanish focus fell on French attack most of the time, and assault north of the Channel was pencilled in for winter. With the required assistance nonexistent in England for the first winter, Charles had little reason behind the confidence he expressed to Spain. In fact, inside, he was descending towards depression again. For Bristol's eyes, he wrote: 'if this winter pass without any attempt on my part, I shall take very little pleasure in living till the next'.[27]

Poverty yet again added to his woes. The Spanish, faking confidence themselves,[28] had pretended they could pay both his monthly grant and his soldiers, and desertions by unpaid soldiers showed the grant as a lower priority. Furthermore, creditors only cooperated up to a point. In 1657, Charles consequently had no guarantee of firewood or candles, and malnutrition risks loomed with one-course meals.[29] Yet what he now aimed for required physical fitness, unless it was to kill him. Unexpectedly, he was begging to fight on the frontline against France. This wouldn't even serve his own cause directly. However, when he finally won Spain's permission to lead his men into combat, he'd end up fighting Cromwell's force.

Mardyke, along the coast from Dunkirk, surrendered to France in September, but the Anglo-French agreement meant it was put into Protectorate hands. Now the following month, Juan-José took troops to Mardyke to destroy the fort, and Charles accompanied them. This was a night attack. The attackers, including Frondeurs, were compelled to light their way, whereupon their enemy saw them coming and lit up the fort, both sides preparing for siege, and Protectorate ships offshore primed their guns. Charles placed himself with his cavalry. It was the infantry, led by James, that advanced first, deadly shots raining down onto the squadrons behind. At this, however, Charles moved forward to join his infantry. With him was Ormond, whose horse was slain under him by cannon during this approach, and the Cavaliers spent much of the night slighting the outworks before retreating, guns still firing. Hyde sent words of concern, despairing at the king's unnecessary brush with death.

The king also had someone new to worry about him. This was Catherine Pegge, daughter of Derbyshire squire Thomas Pegge, and it seems her 'great beauty'[30] led Charles into a serious relationship in Flanders. She gave birth to perhaps three of his offspring – a boy 'Don Carlos' (a later nickname), christened Charles, and either one or two girls. Allegedly, an eighteenth-century nun was born to Catherine and the king in the late 1650s and named Catherine. Also allegedly, the couple had a daughter Catherine who suffered an early death. Confusion is cited, just one daughter thought to have existed, but the diversity of the stories does not imply confusion, and newborns often received the names of siblings of theirs who had passed away.

Whether or not therefore a bereaved father, Charles was certainly an anxious father in 1657, the year of Don Carlos's birth. Lucy kept Jemmy beside her throughout nerve-wracking experiences. One was incarceration at the Tower of London in 1656, and Jemmy emerged described publicly as Charles's heir.[31] The fact he was growing into a tall energetic slight Charles lookalike seemed gratifying for Lucy, yet she refused his father parental rights. He wanted a better life for Jemmy, away from Lucy, but the mother was treating the son as her own property, the pair residing together in Brussels. Charles also wanted a better situation for himself. As things stood, Jemmy was a potential bargaining chip at Lucy's disposal. Abduction had nearly worked in 1650. Now, on the night of 25 November 1657, Royalist colonel Arthur Slingsby made another attempt. But rather than deploy stealth, he turned to 'violence', trying to snatch Jemmy right in front of Lucy. Clutching the 8-year-old tightly, she yelled, 'the whole street' gathered and Slingsby, thwarted, revealed he was following orders from Charles II. In a flash, a letter from Cárdenas then landed in front of Charles, asking what he was playing at.[32] However, through Ormond, such reason and compassion were conveyed in response that the authorities quickly viewed the monarch as the one in the right, and despite Lucy's threats to publish letters he'd written her, Charles continued his quest. Sending one of his 'most confidential adherents' Scotsman Thomas Ross to visit the Welshwoman,[33] he'd ultimately succeed in the spring, Jemmy this time whisked off at a momentary turning of Lucy's back.[34]

While the child was destined for care in Paris, Charles was spending more time in Brussels, where he'd been bouncing around playing tennis when getting to know Juan-José. In Antwerp, however, more familiar faces awaited. Early in 1658, Charles's old governor Newcastle hosted a grand ball here, with Charles centre-stage. Music accompanied His Majesty's entrance, whereupon a poem penned by Newcastle was recited, rich in the 'highest hyperbole' complimenting the king. Then four hours' dancing began, a lady dressed in feathers sang and a sumptuous banquet proceeded. The climax was a speech prophesising Charles's restoration.[35]

This restoration was hard to believe though. In January, Ormond had adopted disguise and hopped over to England to assess insurgence probabilities, and he concluded the current plan was the wrong way round. Invasion first, he suggested. Insurgence seemed more likely if backed by thousands of Spanish troops already there, and weakness at Great Yarmouth implied they would get in.[36] The Spanish, however, were unconvinced. As they ignored pleas from Charles, a second winter ended without invasion.

The great alliance born through the Treaty of Brussels had turned into the stuff of nightmares. Now, to the Spanish, the Royalists were parasites sucking the last drops out of Spain's economy. And to Charles, 'Don Devil' appeared the most fitting name for a Spanish official.[37] They were all trapped too, Cromwell enforcing a blockade off the coast. Meanwhile disease swept through the barracks, conditions atrocious, and in February 1658, it killed Rochester, Charles's fun-loving faithful friend.

Then, the Spanish forbade the exiled sovereign to march into the field with them. His response was to move towards Holland, but not just physically. Current bickering between him and Mary improved his chances of befriending Mary's Dutch enemies, and he needed them; as more of Flanders fell into Protectorate control, Cromwell's strength was increasing. Politically speaking, that is.

From August to September, Charles was resident in the village of Hoogstraten, 'upon the skirts of' the United Provinces. Travelling the area, he visited places new to him,[38] and he set about stag-hunting and falconry,[39] barely sitting still for five minutes. He had no idea his nemesis was not so fit. When James dispatched an express telling Charles of reports that Cromwell was dead, such rumours had abounded for years; the king took little notice. But after this, 'every day brought confirmation of it'.[40] Indeed, in a grand bed at Whitehall, the mighty lord protector had departed this world on the anniversary of Dunbar and Worcester. The coincidence in dates certainly took some believing, but even once Cromwell's death sunk in, it was just the beginning of a slow process of realisation.

Chapter 21

Around the time of Cromwell's death, a birth occurred, and Charles may well have been responsible again. The son who emerged features nowhere on the average list of Charles's progeny. However, in the eighteenth century, one Hannah Robertson declared herself Charles's granddaughter through this son, her father. An autobiography by Mrs Robertson reports her father was born at Windsor Castle to a daughter of a 'noble and distinguished' family and grew up in Scotland, under a Mr Gibson, master of Edinburgh's Mint. It also specifies the king arranged this, and the boy – George – passed as Gibson's nephew.[1] Charles maybe respected discretion at the mother's request. In private he allegedly admitted: 'I did not dare to make a *deuke* [Scots for duck] of him, but I made a nobler bird'.[2] The child had his nurse's surname Swan.

Wife of a Windsor gunner, nurse Swan doesn't seem a surprising choice for little Swan's care, but Gibson does, particularly if Charles knew Gibson to be a Quaker. On the surface, the Quakers Act 1662 exemplifies anti-Quaker policies from Charles.

But anti-Quaker policies from another man appear more significant; they appear arguable catalysts in installing Charles on the throne. Sudden though the Restoration seemed, background influences brewed for years, and the Restoration's story is a long sequence of events that bursts with twists and turns. Even Royalist disasters contributed, indirectly.

One was Penruddock's uprising. In response to this show of violence, Cromwell in October 1655 introduced the Rule of the Major Generals, a military-controlled form of governance across England and Wales, and this brought severe taxation alongside strict enforcement of puritanical directives. Restrictions were applied to fairs and feasts, to swearing, drinking and socialising, to games such as billiards and to much more.[3] Citizen anger skyrocketed. That is until economic crisis called for the 1656–58 Second Protectorate Parliament, the major generals' tenure ended and in came 1657's *Humble Petition and Advice*, a new constitution MPs designed to stop Cromwell deviating too far from old-school government.

This quasi-monarchical constitution also placed expectation on the protector to nominate someone to succeed him, but his son Richard was an unlikely candidate, a low-profile civilian MP. Therefore, even following appointment to the Council of State, shock ensued when, just hours after his father's 3 pm death, fellow counsellors came telling Richard Cromwell that the late lord protector had declared him the next lord protector. For Royalists, the shock was unpleasant. The 31-year-old Richard Cromwell was docile and largely an unrecognised face, so according to Hyde received all Oliver's 'glory, without that public hate'. Insurrection unforthcoming, the king's prospects appeared record-breakingly hopeless.[4]

Such hopelessness took time to show, however. Consequently, despite settling back into Brussels and maintaining the Spanish alliance, Charles had decent chances of Orangist support. He naughtily paid Holland another flying visit. Cromwellian ambassador George Downing reported him for entering 'Amsterdam, and several other places',[5] but the king was making bolder moves. With excitement, he proposed himself as a husband for Henrietta Catherine, 21-year-old daughter of Orange dowager Amalia. In a letter to Amalia, Charles asks: 'how, with all possible secrecy, I may convey my mind in that particular to you' and acknowledges unconventionality about his approach but describes his 'value' for the hopeful bride as 'extraordinary'.[6] Nevertheless, although Henrietta Catherine was whispered to be in love with him, the only significant result of Charles's proposal was further upset from Mary, a fierce opponent of Amalia.

Charles meanwhile lost all opportunity of rekindling two of his earliest relationships. By December 1658, Lucy was dead, a victim of sexually transmitted disease according to James, and Christabella passed the same year. The king undoubtedly mourned Christabella's death more, yet it seems the ex-nurse entered his bad books around autumn 1653 when her husband Wyndham joined the gang accusing Hyde of Cromwellian espionage. Five years on, Charles received a visit in Brussels from the Wyndhams' daughter Elizabeth Elliot, wife to the groom of the bedchamber so influential on him in 1649. She begged money, but the monarch gave her no more than

Chapter 21

100 guilders, leaving this struggling mother to conclude he was 'unkind' and had 'not the least good nature left' for the Wyndham family.[7]

Till December 1658, Charles was unpaid by Spain for months. However, part of Mrs Elliot's upset stemmed from noting ostentation all around him. Spending was one area where Charles never fully understood the people. To make statements, he'd flaunt costly unnecessaries 'fit for a king' while mismanaging the economy over years ahead.

Oliver Cromwell had also mismanaged it though, rendering the Protectorate £2,000,000 in debt in 1658. And, partly because the Rule of the Major Generals had required more manforce than there was money, soldiers were owed almost £900,000 pay. Parliament being the only recourse again, a general election was called on 9 December. Charles was already prepared for this. In 1656, Royalists had been forbidden to stand, so in September 1658 he'd pushed for as many as possible to hide their loyalties and 'join other parties', having tactical instructions issued.[8] Several Trojan horses were subsequently voted in.

But they would soon be gone, as would Richard Cromwell. Never had this novice held the confidence of the army he'd inherited. Now, as MPs aimed to reduce the force, he caved under pressure from elite officers in 1659; before resigning in May, he dissolved the Third Protectorate Parliament on 22 April while the New Model Army took control. A fortnight later, the Rump returned, and it abolished the Protectorate.

Although the Commonwealth was promisingly fragile, 'Queen Dick' himself had actually represented some hushed Royalist hopes; in September, Richard Cromwell had been labelled 'too much a Cavalier',[9] and he appeared quite attached to his brother-in-law's uncle John, Baron Belasyse, a Sealed Knot leader. Through Belasyse in January 1659, the king had sought negotiations with Richard Cromwell.

Had these come to fruition, Belasyse would have proved more useful than the entire Sealed Knot put together. Due to its inactivity, the Knot was a bane of the Cavalier cause. Yet Charles viewed Knot members as shining examples of integrity. He'd lose almost all remaining traces of naivety after this. In the summer, certain letters were sent his way by Samuel Morland, secretary to spymaster Thurloe under Cromwell but now a convert to monarchism. These letters, addressed to Thurloe, divulged Royalist plots, and the distinctive handwriting was identified as that of the Knot's Richard Willys. Legend states that Morland even acted to divulge a Cromwellian plot to Charles and saved the monarch's life while Willys schemed to end it.[10]

Other tales conversely claimed the monarch failed to avoid nasty fates. In January 1659 his 'sickness, death, and assassination' had all been reported, and that May he'd been branded 'consumptive' with the Grim Reaper expected for him within two years. Dr Fraser was responsible for the consumption rumour, and for defamation of Charles's character,[11] but by terminating Fraser's employment in 1656 Charles had added insult to injury after blaming him for 'the Start', perhaps never forgiving this Scottish physician for advocating the alliance with the Covenanters.

Unlike Covenanters, some other Presbyterians nonetheless delighted Charles. Many of his supporters in the Third Protectorate Parliament were Presbyterians. These men wanted limitations on monarchy, but they wanted monarchy, and Charles was disinclined to look a gift horse in the mouth. Even Hyde saw worthy potential in John Mordaunt, a zealous Royalist plotter of Presbyterian background. Mordaunt appeared undeterred having been threatened with the axe for treason against the Protectorate in 1658, and in March 1659 Charles had appointed him to establish the Great Trust and Commission, a conspiracy ring to supersede the Sealed Knot.

Cocksure at the head of operations, Mordaunt inflamed nearly everyone under him, but by late July, he'd organised widespread anti-Commonwealth revolts, action in several English counties planned. Charles was determined to participate if the movement took hold, so he set sights on Kent and, with a 4 am departure from Brussels on 3 August, sneaked into Calais without permission. As in 1655 though, only one rising made progress, nowhere near Kent. Presbyterian ex-Roundhead Sir George Booth had thousands rallying in the North West and North Wales, and this left Charles contemplating sailing over the Celtic Sea instead. He moved towards Saint-Malo accordingly. En route in Boulogne, he gave James free rein to open 'all letters … directed to the King', then left him to make decisions for himself.[12] The brothers were dreaming of next meeting as ruling powers in England – if they survived. To Hyde, who remained with Nicholas in Brussels, Charles commented on 18 August: 'never people went so chearfully to venter [venture] their neckes as we doe'.[13] Chester, Liverpool and Wrexham were swallowed up in Booth's Uprising, and the king wanted to embark immediately. He'd procured a

Chapter 21

little galiot for the purpose. However, Jermyn at the Palais-Royal claimed a French frigate of thirty-six guns would be supplied. Charles waited with mounting impatience, but during the wait, news on 27 August announced the insurgence had ultimately been overpowered.

A French frigate for Charles though? This was now plausible. The Stuarts had only become opponents of France via the Franco-Spanish War, and that war was ending. Peace talks were still underway, however, in the Pyrenees, and Mazarin remained frosty towards Charles. Meanwhile, although ignored in Brussels, orders from Madrid tried to ensure Spanish assistance for the Stuart king. When Charles left Saint-Malo, he went missing. For a fortnight, he had no word sent till at La Rochelle on 12 September.[14] His anxious ministers in Brussels just hoped he'd gone to the Pyrenees conferences, but his best destination now was Spain.

With arrest threatening him in France, he travelled a less obvious route, in fact a leisurely route, with Ormond, Bristol, O'Neill and two or three lower servants, and it took him right over to Lyon. 'Wee wanderers haue the diuertisment of seeing new places to refresh the melancholy of our spirits', Ormond reported.[15] After Booth's defeat, efforts to generate laughter prevailed,[16] and the only problem the Merry Monarch encountered came from 'eating so much fruit, though hee would not acknowledge it'.[17]

At Aragon's metropolis Zaragoza from 4 October, Charles was an Englishman in a land he learned had not seen rain for four months, but he felt quite content, finding good mutton and comfortable beds at Spanish inns.[18] Even better experiences were coming though. Upon receipt of a letter from Charles, Spain's 'hypochondriac'[19] premier minister Don Luis de Haro invited him to Fuenterrabia on the Bidasoa river. While the Treaty of the Pyrenees was drawn up nearby, the Stuart king found himself hosted 'as if he were the King of Spain', accommodated in the minister's own quarters and 'much respected'.[20] His arrival had coincided with the death of Felipe's 10-month-old son, and Charles clearly reacted with sensitivity, winning 'the affection of all here'.[21]

Returning to Brussels in November, he still had to creep through France though. While snow fluttered down, he stayed in rural Colombes outside

Paris, but in doing so, he saw Henrietta Maria and Minette for the first time in five years. He'd be forever glad he did. Minette had matured with such sweetness that every minute of her company enchanted her eldest brother, and at 15 she hereafter became his very best pen-pal.

Charles the 'musing' toddler and sometimes reticent teenager[22] had reached 29 and loved to chat. He found 'immoderate delight in empty, effeminate, and vulgar conversations',[23] and he was an entertaining storyteller as well as a fine orator and an adept negotiator. Of course he kept secrets too, though sometimes physically. Thanks to his curly black periwig from the early 1660s onwards, few were to know that, around 30, he started going grey.[24]

Mazarin's bisexual niece Hortense Mancini would see the king minus wig in the 1670s, frequently and openly committing double adultery with him – an irony really, because in 1659 Charles tried to marry the 13-year-old Hortense to unite with France.

Meanwhile secret plans that October nearly had the king propose nuptials with a daughter of the Rule of the Major Generals mighty proponent John Lambert. Had marriage negotiations proceeded, Quakerism would have entered the equation more prominently. A number of Lambert's supporters subscribed to Quakerism, one of several dissenting sects founded in England during Charles's exile. Other sects had come *and* gone in that time, such was the pace of social activity, but the Quakers were growing, as evidenced earlier in 1659 by 7,746 signatures on a Quaker-led petition, a petition opposing church-funding tithes.[25] Now radical Quaker influence could have more impact as Lambert, with the Council of Officers, was winning a power struggle against the Rump. But not for long.

George Monck was a moderate Presbyterian from Devon who had been rewarded for taking Cromwell to victory in the Anglo-Dutch War. Consequently commander-in-chief of Scotland, he monitored Lambert's moves pensively, and he pointed his cannon at the Council of Officers. Thereby rescuing the Rump, Monck was then commissioned as England's commander-in-chief too.

The future now looked interesting. Monck had been a Cavalier and then a Roundhead. He'd supported the protectors, but he was defending the men who had axed both monarchy and protectorship. And in December 1659, he was also writing to the king: 'our ancient and accustomed wholesome laws, both of Church and State, are ... massacred ... ... I had never a better Opportunity of ... restoring the Crown to the right owner thereof'. Indeed Monck offered himself to Charles's cause, and Charles accepted with glee, 'for the Glory of God, and the manifest Good of me and my Subjects', he replied,[26] but the king received no letter back.[27]

Then, in January, the uncommunicative commander-in-chief marched on London, declaring for the republican Rump. Charles was crestfallen, and Monck meanwhile faced crisis. The capital Monck arrived in was turning riotous against the parliament created by Pride's Purge, rump steaks symbolically burned in streets filled with angry rants. Despite therefore 'disarming' London,[28] Monck wanted to hear the nation's voice, but through other means. His letter to the king had asked: 'will your Majesty consent to a Treaty to be had between your Majesty and a free Parliament which shall be lawfully elected'. Charles's answer read: 'there is not a thing that I can embrace with a greater Joy'.[29] The Rump would not agree to dissolve itself though. So, in February, Monck offered seats back to MPs ejected by Pride, and this majority complied with Monck's plan; Westminster thus ordered writs for a new parliament, a parliament to be elected with open Royalists as candidates.

Yet while enabling this, Monck claimed to oppose Stuart monarchy 'to the last drop of his blood'.[30] So how did he feel about non-Stuart monarchy? Monck monarchy, for instance? He was now the most powerful man of the British Isles and seemed likely to 'follow the example of Oliver'.[31] In secret, he'd also ordered the scrubbing of '*REGUM ULTIMUS*' from a statue of Charles I, it's said, but the general was not distraught by omnipresent yells of 'God save King Charles II'.

As news flooded into Brussels, a colossal fluctuation of emotion was sweeping over Charles. He wrote to Monck again: 'I know too well the power you have to do me good or harm', the king admitted but, promising 'kindness', decided his letter should recognise the Devonian's actions as efforts to restore the Stuarts.[32] This time, Monck responded. John Grenville, more cooperative than his uncle Richard, acted as messenger both ways, but the job proved taxing. Sir John had to memorise Monck's message before it was incinerated. Within it, Monck professed to be engineering Charles's restoration. He also asked the king to leave Spanish territory as Felipe was so intent on regaining Jamaica that the Spanish appeared liable to take Charles hostage. Moreover, however, Monck requested 'a conciliatory letter' in which Charles promise that Stuart restoration would bring the soldiers their arrears and offer pardon, religious toleration and 'confirmation of all sales of crown and church lands, and forfeited estates'.[33]

In 1657, Buckingham had decided the best way to recoup his York House estate was to marry the heir of its new owner. So having plunged into wooing this heir, the duke was now son-in-law to Fairfax. Understandably, Charles still considered Buckingham fiendish, but years of rumours about Fairfax were gaining credibility; to repel Lambert, Fairfax sided with Monck, and Monck's advice to the king appeared loyal, and sound.

Therefore, with Hyde, Nicholas and Ormond, Charles formulated the Declaration of Breda, an outline of his intentions in the event of restoring 'King, Peers, and People, to their just, ancient, and fundamental Rights',[34] and prepared to leave for Breda. Addressing the Marquis of Caracena, governor of the Spanish Netherlands since the previous spring, he claimed to expect beneficial 'propositions and information' in Holland and said his stay would not exceed three days. Caracena displayed apathy, but perhaps this Spanish general shared Charles's acting abilities. That night, Cárdenas's Irish page William Galloway came knocking on Hyde's door, trembling. Galloway had news he said 'concerned the King's life', and he revealed a written order he'd stolen as proof that Caracena was sending cavalry to detain Charles. Promptly woken, the king thus slipped away at 3 am, missing his jailers by six hours.[35]

It was a bitter end to four years' alliance with Spain, and if Charles achieved restoration, he would become Felipe's enemy, Spain still officially at war against England. Charles hoped both Spain and France would help him after the Franco-Spanish peace. However, Mazarin had deterred him from attending the Pyrenees talks and 'advised don Lewis ... that it was rather time for all Catholics to unite' to disempower Protestantism, not 'strengthen it by restoring the King'.[36] How pivotal this advice was is debatable, but in the end, practically all Stuart hopes rested in England.

And Charles seized upon them, finalising the Declaration of Breda. Essentially, this was everything Monck advised him to say, but with elaboration. Regarding religion, it stated 'Freedom of Conversation' could help individuals understand one another and 'no Man' under Charles's rule was to be censured for religious opinion unless jeopardising national peace. It further offered Monck's soldiers not only arrears but also employment in the king's service. But the most notable section centred on pardon. Subjects who within forty days returned to 'Loyalty and Obedience' would be forgiven, while lives, liberties, estates and even reputations should not be threatened for crimes 'committed against Us or Our Royal Father, before the Publication of this', Charles stipulated in the document, dated 4 April 1660. He also stipulated, however, that exceptions be determined by Parliament. In fact, the declaration repeatedly promised the monarch's cooperation with Westminster.[37] This was key. Nevertheless, judging by previous declarations of his, it was clear that reciprocal cooperation required Parliament to exclude the regicides from automatic pardon.

The Colombes visit had led Charles to elevate Henrietta Maria's favourite Jermyn to the earldom of St Albans, seemingly with respect, but the six-foot-two sovereign probably never respected anyone more than he respected the martyred sovereign, and signs countering gossip now existed; having developed further, Charles II's face shape and nose looked rather like Charles I's.[38]

To Royalists who spotted this, it fortified a feeling that justice loomed. In England, Stuart restoration was begged for and deemed 'unavoidable'. It was discussed in terms of how and when rather than whether.[39] While Charles resisted followers' suggestions of jumping straight on a ship, the new parliament was then presented with the Declaration of Breda on 1 May. However, when John Grenville's brother Bernard came to Breda carrying a letter from Monck a week later, Lambert had just attempted a republican takeover. Such scares meant bad news was hardly impossible.

Upon Bernard's arrival, the king leapt up, abandoning the supper table. He was about to learn whether the dream was coming true. And in suspense, he read the message. Then he flung his arms around the messenger. MPs and lords had voted unanimously. Without even one proviso, they wanted Charles to resume residence in London, for 'the exercise of his Regal Office'.[40]

❖ ❖ ❖

Now, in a flash, everything changed. Ex-Cromwellians such as Downing and England's general at sea Edward Montagu advertised Royalist allegiance, France and Spain panicked and the States-General went from banning Charles to gifting him £60,000 and allocating £30,000 to host him for an opulent sendoff. Overall, the king adopted a water-under-the-bridge attitude. Through the coming days, he'd converse amicably with the Spanish ambassador and Fairfax and maintain warmth for English Presbyterian clergymen while refusing their requests to abandon old Anglican practices. Meeting Kirk representative James Sharp, he even faked fondness for memories of Scotland.[41]

Memories of May 1660 would be a blur though. Charles declined both marriage to Amalia's 17-year-old daughter and the loan of Amalia's pinnace and chose a bigger yacht to travel to Delft. Sibling love returned, and on board he deferred dinner while Mary suffered seasickness. Mary, James and Henry then proceeded with him to The Hague, velvet-robed trumpeters leading a grand procession, and after John Grenville's arrival from London with a portmanteau packed with coins, the king dressed in elegant regal style. Musical masterpieces filled the air, fireworks illuminated the sky and fawning visitors streamed in. Between brief chances to play with Mary's 9-year-old son William of Orange, Charles effected a 'sober' aura,[42] especially important for conferring knighthoods and touching scrofula sufferers, and the climax was a magnificent banquet at what's now the Mauritshuis.

As scores of thousands lined the coast of Scheveningen,[43] the Stuart brothers upped anchor for England on 23 May, great guns of salute smoking. Now the king was under Edward Montagu's care on a full-rigged three-decker originally christened *Naseby* but renamed *Royal Charles* (by Charles himself that day), and this first-rate warship was luxuriously furnished to carry him in splendour on the final international journey he ever made. Pacing restlessly in 'glorious weather', the monarch nonetheless shook off majesty, pouring out tales of his 1651 escape, and he had jolly laughter surround him the following day. Then when shown the crew's breakfast, he unexpectedly tucked in, leaving finer fare up for grabs. He also left £500 for the sailors and £50 for Montagu's servants.[44]

Approaching Dover's shoreline on Friday, 25 May, the king transferred to a barge, and flocks of aristocrats, horsemen and citizens watched him steered towards them. It was the moment he'd been waiting for nearly half his life. So as he stepped onto English terra firma, he dramatically dropped onto his knees, sending thanks to Heaven before kissing Monck. Euphoria abounded, and the wind carried sounds of pealing bells amid cries of 'God save the king!' while Charles shot cold glances at the Duke of Buckingham. Still, ready to work his comical charm, Buckingham followed uninvited

Chapter 21

when the royal party continued to Canterbury. Charles was to pass the weekend there, deliberately delaying the journey, for he resolved to enter London on his thirtieth birthday, 29 May 1660.

Canterbury instantly had him distressed though. Besides calling on his Italian when Venetian representative Francesco Giavarina offered congratulations, the king found so many esteemed Royalists clamour for audience that he couldn't get to his chamber for hours, and some 'nauseated' him as they 'demanded' compensation for suffering during the troubles. After this, Monck thrust a list of at least seventy names into the king's hands, recommending unsuitable men for the Privy Council.[45] 'My head is so dreadfully stunned with the acclamations of the people, and the vast amount of business, that I know not whether I am writing sense', Charles remarked in a note for Minette the next day.[46]

Morris dancers nevertheless made him feel at home in Rochester, where he spent the final night of his thirtieth year. Then, with an early-morning start, he departed for Whitehall.

In a dark suit, he rode on horseback, exuberant faces crowded in such multitudes that the route 'seemed one continued street', and at Blackheath senior army officers kissed his hand as if their history in the New Model never existed.[47] Via Deptford, with flowers strewn in his path, the birthday boy then proceeded, flanked by his brothers around 2 pm as he crossed London Bridge. He hadn't seen the capital for eighteen years. Now, for this monumental day, it was adorned with tapestries and flags, silvers and golds shone and wine flowed from fountains, all to mark an occasion accomplished without the flowing of blood. Swords were brandished, but only in celebration, music played magnificently and a seven-hour pageant made its triumphant way through the din of a revelling city preparing to set alight effigies of Cromwell. During a stopoff at St Paul's, the noise rendered Charles inaudible three feet away, but by the evening, he hardly spoke, utterly dazed when he reached Banqueting House and Parliament's speakers 'commended to his Princely care his three Kingdomes'.[48]

Charles II was restored. As such, he enjoyed a personal restoration too. Of course, he'd received the Crown of Scotland in 1651, but during the lead-up to his 1661 coronation with the brand-new St Edward's Crown, he was highly unlikely to mutter those words, 'I think I must repent … that ever I was born'.

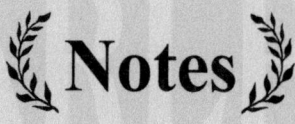

Notes

Introduction

1. Burnet, *Burnet's History of My Own Time*, Part One, Volume I, p. 166
2. Historical Manuscripts Commission, *The Manuscripts of the Earl Cowper*, Volume II, pp. 18, 26
3. Duppa, *Prince Charles His Gracious Resolution Concerning the Present Affaires of this Kingdome*, p. 6
4. This son seems to have been Charles's firstborn. He became Duke of Monmouth, of 1685 rebellion fame, and sired a legitimate family, raising questions about the succession.
5. Welwood, *Memoirs of the Most Material Transactions in England*, pp. 129–30
6. Hughes, *The Boscobel Tracts*, p. 147
7. The poem known as *A Satyr on Charles II* refers to Charles as a merry monarch. He'd be displeased to find us remembering him by the resultant sobriquet, though. The poet responsible was one of Charles's most incorrigible courtiers John Wilmot, 2nd Earl of Rochester, and the verse attacked the king to such a shocking degree that he banished Rochester from court.

Prologue

1. Weir, *Mary, Queen of Scots and the Murder of Lord Darnley*, pp. 1, 250, 405–6
2. Like Darnley, and a certain descendant, Mary was incredibly tall too, around six feet. Ibid., p. 56
3. Herries, *Historical Memoirs of the Reign of Mary Queen of Scots*, p. 82
4. Weir, *Mary, Queen of Scots and the Murder of Lord Darnley*, p. 413
5. Stewart, *The Cradle King*, p. 168
6. Walter, *James I*, pp. 38–39
7. Nichols, *The Progresses, &c. of King James the First*, p. 113
8. Taylor, *The Works of the Judicious and Learned Divine Thomas Taylor*, p. 222
9. Turnbull, *Charles I's Private Life*, Chapter 6
10. *CSPV*, Volume XV, pp. 405–22
11. Ibid.
12. *A Miscellany*, pp. 112, 127

13. Hacket, *Scrinia Reserata*, pp. 120–21
14. *ODNB*, 'Villiers, George, first duke of Buckingham (1592–1628), royal favourite' by Roger Lockyer
15. *CSPV*, Volume XV, pp. 108–26
16. Stewart, *The Cradle King*, pp. 280–81, 299
17. Weldon, *The Court and Character of King James*, p. 47
18. de Lisle, *The White King*, pp. 38, 54
19. Porter, *Royal Renegades*, pp. 14–16
20. Oman, *Henrietta Maria*, p. 44
21. *ODNB*, 'Villiers, George, first duke of Buckingham (1592–1628), royal favourite' by Roger Lockyer
22. Ibid., 'Felton, John (d. 1628), assassin' by Alastair Bellany
23. *The Parliamentary or Constitutional History of England*, Volume VIII, pp. 239–40
24. Ibid., p. 390
25. Turnbull, *Charles I's Private Life*, Chapter 8
26. Pearce, *Henrietta Maria*, p. 99
27. Oman, *Henrietta Maria*, pp. 65–66
28. Ibid., p. 67
29. Adolph, *The King's Henchman*, Chapter 4
30. Knowler, *The Earl of Strafforde's Letters and Dispatches*, Volume I, p. 51
31. Michel, *Rubens*, p. 125

Chapter 1

1. *CSPV*, Volume XXII, pp. 279–93
2. Oman, *Henrietta Maria*, pp. 68–69
3. Strickland, *Lives of the Queens of England*, Volume IV, p. 185
4. Fraser, *Cromwell*, pp. 8–9, 44–45
5. *CSPV*, Volume XXII, pp. 65–72
6. Ibid., pp. 313–29
7. Ibid.
8. Oman, *Henrietta Maria*, p. 69
9. Keay, *The Magnificent Monarch*, pp. 9–10, 236
10. *CSPV*, Volume XXII, pp. 345–64
11. Soria, Balestrieri and Ohtsuka, 'On Cas A, Cassini, Comets, and King Charles', p. e028
12. Ibid.
13. *CSPV*, Volume XXII, pp. 345–64
14. Aikin, *Memoirs of the Court of King Charles the First*, Volume I, p. 295
15. *CSPV*, Volume XXII, pp. 345–64
16. Jackson, *Charles II*, Chapter 2
17. *CCSP*, Volume I, p. 33
18. Noble, 'Description of a Gold Medal Struck upon the Birth of King Charles II', pp. 20–22
19. *CSPD*, 1629–1631, p. 283
20. Ibid.

21. Keay, *The Magnificent Monarch*, pp. 15–16
22. Noble, 'Description of a Gold Medal Struck upon the Birth of King Charles II', p. 22
23. *CSPD*, 1629–1631, p. 291
24. 'Royal Christenings', p. 262
25. *CSPD*, 1629–1631, pp. 331, 439
26. Keay, *The Magnificent Monarch*, p. 19
27. *CSPD*, 1629–1631, pp. 548, 551
28. Ibid., p. 331
29. Abbott, *History of King Charles the Second*, p. 19
30. *CSPD*, 1629–1631, pp. 329, 334
31. Green, *Letters of Queen Henrietta Maria*, pp. 16–17
32. Fraser, *King Charles II*, p. 13
33. Ibid.
34. *CSPD*, 1629–1631, pp. 336, 346, 397, 477
35. Wyndham, *A Family History 1410–1688*, pp. 177–78

Chapter 2

1. Green, *Letters of Queen Henrietta Maria*, pp. 18–19
2. Chapman, *The Tragedy of Charles II*, pp. 27–28
3. Jesse, *Memoirs of the Court of England during the Reign of the Stuarts*, Volume II, pp. 399–400
4. Pepys, *The Diary of Samuel Pepys*, 3 December 1665
5. Historical Manuscripts Commission, *The Manuscripts of the Earl Cowper*, Volume II, pp. 11–12
6. Appleby, 'Nutrition and Disease: The Case of London, 1550–1750', p. 20
7. Historical Manuscripts Commission, *The Manuscripts of the Earl Cowper*, Volume II, pp. 12, 17, 26
8. Having been at Richmond, Charles and Mary were moved to Whitehall a few days before the birth. *CSPD*, 1633–1634, pp. 229, 242
9. Chapman, *The Tragedy of Charles II*, p. 28
10. *CSPD*, 1633–1634, p. 375
11. Hutton, *Charles the Second*, p. 124
12. Bryant, *The Letters of King Charles II*, pp. 45–46
13. Loth, *Royal Charles*, p. 160
14. Keay, *The Magnificent Monarch*, p. 25
15. Pett, *The Autobiography of Phineas Pett*, p. 156; Turnbull, *Charles I's Private Life*, Chapter 17
16. Wyndham, *A Family History 1410–1688*, p. 178
17. Keay, *The Magnificent Monarch*, p. 21
18. Appleby, 'Nutrition and Disease: The Case of London, 1550–1750', p. 20
19. Rideal, *1666*, p. 26
20. Bradwell, *Physick for the Sicknesse, Commonly called the Plagve*, p. 3
21. Creighton, *A History of Epidemics in Britain*, p. 526
22. Newman, 'Shutt Up: Bubonic Plague and Quarantine in Early Modern England'
23. Appleby, 'Nutrition and Disease: The Case of London, 1550–1750', p. 20

Notes

Chapter 3

1. Historical Manuscripts Commission, *The Manuscripts of the Earl Cowper*, Volume II, p. 18
2. Dunois, *Memoirs of the Court of England*, pp. 398–40. The prince is termed 'the King' in this post-1660 source.
3. Spencer, *Prince Rupert*, pp. 23, 28, 30
4. Astington, 'The King and Queenes Entertainement at Richmond', p. 12
5. Chapman, *The Tragedy of Charles II*, p. 35
6. Crystal, *The Cambridge Encyclopedia of the English Language*, second edition, p. 69
7. Ibid.
8. de Lisle, *The White King*, p. 9
9. Fraser, *King Charles II*, p. 240
10. *CSPV*, Volume XXIV, pp. 118–35
11. *King Charls His Speech Made upon the Scaffold at Whitehall-Gate, Immediately Before His Execution*, p. 6
12. Twain, *The Prince and the Pauper*, p. 291
13. Donne, *The Works of John Donne*, Volume II, pp. 449, 475
14. *ODNB*, 'Duppa, Brian (1588–1662), bishop of Winchester' by Ian Green
15. These words were written by Charles's governor the Earl of Newcastle, who knew Duppa well. Newcastle, *The Life of William Cavendish Duke of Newcastle*, pp. 326–27
16. Kippis, *Biographia Britannica*, Volume V, p. 515
17. Koot, *A Biography of a Map in Motion*, p. 168
18. *CSPD*, 1638–1639, p. 182. Massonnet was one of many the Crown failed to pay properly. He ended up in debt as a result and in the early 1660s petitioned Charles II to confirm an annual £170 13s. 4d. for attending him in years past. Gallagher, *Learning Languages in Early Modern England*, p. 24
19. *CSPD*, 1635, pp. 456–57
20. Keay, *The Magnificent Monarch*, p. 21
21. Daniels and Morrill, *Charles I*, p. 70
22. *Historical Collections of Private Passages of State*, Volume I, Appendix pp. 1–11
23. *The National Covenant of the Kirk of Scotland, and the Solemn League and Covenant of the Three Kingdoms*
24. *CSPV*, Volume XXIV, pp. 285–90
25. Ashmole, *The Institution, Laws & Ceremonies of the most Noble Order of the Garter*, p. 297
26. Knowler, *The Earl of Strafforde's Letters and Dispatches*, Volume II, pp. 57, 167

Chapter 4

1. *CSPD*, 1637–1638, p. 361
2. Worsley, *If Walls Could Talk*, p. 157
3. Porter, *Royal Renegades*, p. 27
4. Knowler, *The Earl of Strafforde's Letters and Dispatches*, Volume II, pp. 166–67
5. Whitaker, *A Royal Passion*, p. 120
6. *CSPV*, Volume XXIV, pp. 175–93

7. Groom, *Discover the Gardens*, p. 8
8. Sturgis, *Hampton Court Palace*, pp. 13, 95
9. Strickland, *Lives of the Last Four Princesses of the Royal House of Stuart*, p. 2
10. Fraser, *King Charles II*, p. 16
11. Porter, *Royal Renegades*, p. 26
12. Sorbière, *A Voyage to England*, p. 16
13. Coote, *Royal Survivor*, p. 9
14. Lysons, *The Environs of London*, Volume I, pp. 441–42
15. Keay, *The Magnificent Monarch*, p. 32
16. 'A Royal Tutor's Advice', p. 61
17. Keay, *The Magnificent Monarch*, pp. 21, 32
18. Historical Manuscripts Commission, *The Manuscripts of the Earl Cowper*, Volume II, p. 176
19. John, *King Charles I*, p. 5
20. *ODNB*, 'Cavendish, William, first duke of Newcastle upon Tyne (bap. 1593, d. 1676), writer, patron, and royalist army officer' by Lynn Hulse
21. Newcastle, *The Life of William Cavendish Duke of Newcastle*, pp. 120–21
22. Ibid., pp. 194, 326–27
23. *History*, Volume I, p. 104
24. Newcastle, *The Life of William Cavendish Duke of Newcastle*, pp. 328–29
25. Pepys, *The Diary of Samuel Pepys*, 30 May 1667
26. 'A Royal Tutor's Advice', p. 61
27. Smuts, *Court Culture and the Origins of a Royalist Tradition in Early Stuart England*, p. 191
28. Newcastle, *The Life of William Cavendish Duke of Newcastle*, p. 245
29. *ODNB*, 'Cavendish, William, first duke of Newcastle upon Tyne (bap. 1593, d. 1676), writer, patron, and royalist army officer' by Lynn Hulse
30. Strickland, *Lives of the Queens of England*, Volume IV, pp. 197–98
31. Keay, *The Magnificent Monarch*, p. 30

Chapter 5

1. Keay, *The Magnificent Monarch*, p. 27
2. *CSPV*, Volume XXIII, pp. 356–73
3. Burnet, *Burnet's History of My Own Time*, Part One, Volume I, p. 90
4. Smith, *The Poems of Andrew Marvell*, p. 11
5. *ODNB*, 'Sackville [née Curzon], Mary, countess of Dorset (bap. 1586, d. 1645), royal governess' by David L. Smith
6. Ferrar and Jebb, *Nicholas Ferrar*, pp. 128, 133–38
7. *CSPD*, 1639, pp. 508–9
8. Wyndham, *A Family History 1410–1688*, p. 193
9. *CSPD*, 1639, pp. 508–9
10. Wade, *John Pym*, pp. 177–78
11. *The Parliamentary or Constitutional History of England*, Volume VIII, p. 432
12. Wade, *John Pym*, p. 180
13. These certificates had to bear the signatures of a clergyman, a churchwarden and a justice of the peace. Hibbert, *Charles I*, p. 250

14. Newcastle, *The Life of William Cavendish Duke of Newcastle*, p. 330
15. Since the fourteenth century, sovereigns on the throne of England had claimed to sit on the French throne too, meaning Stuart monarchs from 1603 considered their kingdoms to be not only England, Scotland and Ireland but, in name, also France.
16. *CSPD*, 1640, pp. 192–93
17. Hester W. Chapman states that members of the prince's household told the prince of revolutionary possibilities. Chapman, *The Tragedy of Charles II*, p. 45. I see no evidence of this in primary sources, but I agree Parliament supporters in his household are likely to have scared Charles this way.
18. Evelyn, *The Diary of John Evelyn*, pp. 22–23
19. *CSPV*, Volume XXIII, pp. 426–57
20. Gardiner, *History of England: From the Accession of James I. to the Outbreak of the Civil War 1603–1642*, Volume IX, p. 122
21. *ODNB*, 'Wentworth, Thomas, first earl of Strafford (1593–1641), lord lieutenant of Ireland' by Ronald G. Asch
22. Clark, *The English Civil War*, p. 24
23. Ibid., pp. 22–23, 27
24. Chapman, *The Tragedy of Charles II*, p. 48
25. From a report written by Mayerne following his postmortem on the princess. Green, *Lives of the Princesses of England*, Volume VI, p. 394
26. Ibid.
27. Zuvich, *Sex and Sexuality in Stuart Britain*, p. 157
28. de Lisle, *The White King*, p. 38

Chapter 6

1. Wade, *John Pym*, p. 188
2. *History*, Volume I, pp. 222–27
3. Rushworth, *The Tryal of Thomas Earl of Strafford*, p. 39
4. Gardiner, *History of England*, Volume IX, pp. 120–22
5. *History*, Volume III, p. 323
6. *CSPV*, Volume XXV, pp. 141–58
7. Pearce, *Henrietta Maria*, p. 177
8. Strickland, *Lives of the Tudor and Stuart Princesses*, pp. 252–53, 258–59
9. Porter, *London*, p. 209
10. de Lisle, *The White King*, p. 132. I also wish to express wider gratitude to Leanda de Lisle, as her *White King* helped me make sense of 1641 and much more.
11. *CSPV*, Volume XXV, pp. 141–58
12. de Lisle, *The White King*, p. 133
13. Halliwell, *Letters of the Kings of England*, Volume II, pp. 328–29
14. *CSPV*, Volume XXV, pp. 141–58
15. *ODNB*, 'Grimston, Sir Harbottle, second baronet (1603–1685), barrister and politician' by Christopher W. Brooks
16. Pearce, *Henrietta Maria*, p. 225
17. *CSPD*, 1641–1643, p. 11
18. *CSPV*, Volume XXV, pp. 158–70
19. *Ten Propositions*

20. *History*, Volume I, p. 564
21. Ibid., Volume II, p. 529
22. Ibid., Volume I, p. 564
23. *CSPV*, Volume XXV, pp. 158–70
24. D'Ewes, *The Journal of Sir Simonds D'Ewes*, p. 37
25. *CSPV*, Volume XXV, pp. 231–42
26. Ibid.
27. Adolph, *The King's Henchman*, Chapter 4. I thank Anthony Adolph for relating rumours surrounding Jermyn and Henrietta Maria and bringing some focus to the question over Charles II's parentage. Although I think Charles I was Charles II's biological father, the accusations make for intriguing consideration.
28. *CSPD*, 1660–1661, p. 179
29. Gardiner, *History of England*, p. 136
30. *CSPD*, 1641–1643, p. 241
31. Hibbert, *Cavaliers & Roundheads*, p. 32
32. de Lisle, *The White King*, pp. 149–50

Chapter 7

1. *CSPV*, Volume XXV, pp. 286–98
2. Green, *Lives of the Princesses of England*, Volume VI, p. 130
3. *CSPV*, Volume XXVI, pp. 13–28
4. Cooper, *Annals of Cambridge*, Volume III, p. 321
5. Ibid., pp. 321–23
6. Clarendon, *The Life of Edward Earl of Clarendon*, Volume I, p. 48
7. Ibid.
8. Ferrar and Jebb, *Nicholas Ferrar*, pp. 150–55
9. Griffin, *Blood Sport*, p. 98
10. *CSPD*, 1641–1643, p. 336
11. *Nineteen Propositions Made by Both Houses of Parliament*, pp. 3, 14
12. Duppa, *Prince Charles His Gracious Resolution Concerning the Present Affaires of this Kingdome*, pp. 3, 5
13. 'Civil War Proceedings in Yorkshire', p. 393
14. *Acts and Ordinances of the Interregnum, 1642–1660*, pp. 14–16
15. Porter, *Royal Renegades*, p. 81
16. Phillips, *Memoirs of the Civil War in Wales and the Marches*, Volume I, pp. 123, 145–46
17. *ODNB*, 'Devereux, Robert, third earl of Essex (1591–1646), parliamentarian army officer' by John Morrill
18. Turnbull, *Charles I's Private Life*, Chapter 21
19. Phillips, *Memoirs of the Civil War in Wales and the Marches*, Volume II, pp. 26–29
20. Baxter, *Reliquiæ Baxterianæ*, p. 34
21. Scott, *A Collection of Scarce and Valuable Tracts*, Volume IV, pp. 478–79
22. Ibid., p. 478
23. Clark, *Aubrey's 'Brief Lives'*, Volume I, p. 297
24. Hinton, *Memoires*, pp. 11–12

25. *CSPV*, Volume XXVI, pp. 204–21
26. Duppa, *Prince Charles His Gracious Resolution Concerning the Present Affaires of this Kingdome*, pp. 6–7
27. Ibid.

Chapter 8

1. Turnbull, *Charles I's Private Life*, Chapters 23–25
2. My thinking is swayed partly by Lady Antonia Fraser, who cites 1642–45 as the crucial period in the forming of the love Charles II felt for his father. Fraser, *King Charles II*, pp. 27–28. Specifically, though, I believe the pair were closest in 1644, when the king was playing a direct parental role. At that point, the prince preferred to stay with him than to take command in the west.
3. Lake, *Diary of Dr. Edward Lake*, p. 26
4. Carlton, *Going to the Wars*, p. 93
5. Hibbert, *Cavaliers & Roundheads*, p. 99
6. Ibid., p. 96
7. Fanshawe, *The Memoirs of Ann Lady Fanshawe*, pp. 24–25
8. Warburton, *Memoirs of Prince Rupert, and the Cavaliers*, Volume II, p. 46
9. Fairfax, *A Catalogue of the Curious Collection of Pictures of George Villiers, Duke of Buckingham*, pp. 25–26
10. Hibbert, *Cavaliers & Roundheads*, p. 98
11. *CSPD*, 1641–1643, p. 493
12. de Lisle, *The White King*, p. 177
13. Pearce, *Henrietta Maria*, pp. 224, 226
14. Ibid., p. 219; Green, *Letters of Queen Henrietta Maria*, pp. 59–61, 128
15. Wraxall, *Historical Memoirs of My Own Time*, Volume II, p. 181
16. Hibbert, *Cavaliers & Roundheads*, p. 133
17. *History*, Volume III, pp. 187–89
18. Lewis, *Lives of the Friends and Contemporaries of Lord Chancellor Clarendon*, Volume I, pp. 162–64
19. Carlton, *Going to the Wars*, pp. 77, 79
20. Peacey, 'The Struggle for Mercurius Britanicus: Factional Politics and the Parliamentarian Press, 1643–1646', pp. 519, 525
21. Ibid., pp. 526–27
22. Washbourn, *Bibliotheca Gloucestrensis*, p. clxvii
23. Carte, *A Collection of Original Letters and Papers*, Volume I, p. 26
24. Pearce, *Henrietta Maria*, p. 228
25. Wade, *John Pym*, p. 308
26. Fraser, *Cromwell*, pp. 104–5
27. Warburton, *Memoirs of Prince Rupert, and the Cavaliers*, Volume II, pp. 363–64
28. Carlton, *Going to the Wars*, p. 92
29. Pearce, *Henrietta Maria*, p. 229
30. Porter, *Royal Renegades*, pp. 109–10
31. *History*, Volume III, p. 146
32. Warburton, *Memoirs of Prince Rupert, and the Cavaliers*, Volume II, p. 328
33. *History*, Volume III, p. 258

34. Ibid., p. 259
35. For this purpose, Henrietta Maria requested Charles's measurements. Oman, *Henrietta Maria*, p. 164
36. *History*, Volume III, p. 449
37. *CSPV*, Volume XXVII, pp. 104–11
38. Gregg, *King Charles I*, p. 384
39. Chapman, *The Tragedy of Charles II*, p. 69
40. Lake, *Diary of Dr. Edward Lake*, p. 27
41. Wallington, *Historical Notices of Events Occurring Chiefly in the Reign of Charles I.*, Volume II, pp. 217–18
42. Scott, *The Battles of Newbury*, pp. 92, 151
43. Longueville, *The First Duke and Duchess of Newcastle-upon-Tyne*, p. 172
44. *History*, Volume III, p. 524

Chapter 9

1. de Lisle, *The White King*, p. 200
2. Halliwell, *Letters of the Kings of England*, Volume II, pp. 417–18
3. *CSPD*, 1644–1645, pp. 260–62
4. Fraser, *Cromwell*, pp. 147, 156
5. *History*, Volume III, p. 502
6. Longueville, *The First Duke and Duchess of Newcastle-upon-Tyne*, p. 172
7. Chapman, *The Tragedy of Charles II*, p. 69
8. *History*, Volume III, p. 503
9. Ibid.
10. Ibid., Volume IV, p. 13
11. Pepys, *The Diary of Samuel Pepys*, 3 December 1664
12. *ODNB*, 'Grenville, Sir Richard, baronet (bap. 1600, d. 1659), royalist army officer' by Ian Roy
13. *History*, Volume IV, p. 8
14. Ibid., p. 13
15. Carte, *A Collection of Original Letters and Papers*, Volume I, pp. 76–77
16. Gardiner, *History of the Great Civil War 1642–1649*, Volume II, pp. 199–200
17. *ODNB*, 'Grenville, Sir Richard, baronet (bap. 1600, d. 1659), royalist army officer' by Ian Roy
18. *History*, Volume IV, p. 21
19. This one constituted twenty yards of tissue for a gown.
20. Wyndham, *A Family History 1410–1688*, pp. 178, 204
21. *History*, Volume IV, p. 23
22. *ODNB*, 'La Cloche, Jacques de (1644/1647?–1669), pretended son of Charles II' by Giovanni Tarantino
23. *History*, Volume IV, p. 23
24. Pepys, *The Diary of Samuel Pepys*, 3 December 1665
25. *History*, Volume IV, pp. 22, 29
26. Like Andrea Zuvich highlights, the comment implies Charles II believed people under around mid-teens should not have sex. Zuvich, *Sex and Sexuality in Stuart Britain*, p. 167
27. *The Kings Cabinet Opened*, pp. 10–11

28. Bulstrode, *Memoirs and Reflections upon the Reign and Government of King Charles the I$^{st.}$ and K. Charles the II$^{nd.}$*, p. 134
29. de Lisle, *The White King*, p. 206
30. *History*, Volume IV, pp. 54–55
31. Ibid., pp. 57–58
32. Ibid., pp. 168–69
33. *The Kings Cabinet Opened*, pp. 7, 43
34. Instead, Joana would be remembered as the first Princess of Beira, a Portuguese title akin to the English Princess Royal. The Princess Royal title was created for Charles's sister Mary in 1642, to equate with France's Madame Royale.

Chapter 10

1. Spencer, *To Catch a King*, p. 6
2. *ODNB*, 'Grenville, Sir Richard, baronet (bap. 1600, d. 1659), royalist army officer' by Ian Roy
3. Hutton, *Charles the Second*, p. 11
4. *History*, Volume IV, pp. 78, 81–82
5. Ibid., Volume III, p. 449
6. Ibid., Volume IV, p. 22
7. Hutton, *Charles the Second*, p. 8
8. Lady Antonia Fraser's *King Charles II* helped guide me in composing parts of this chapter and makes several relevant points about Hyde's character. Fraser, *King Charles II*, pp. 35–36
9. *History*, Volume IV, p. 21
10. Hoskins, *Charles the Second in the Channel Islands*, Volume I, p. 372
11. Warner, *The Nicholas Papers*, Volume II, p. 279
12. *History*, Volume IV, p. 87
13. Duppa, *Prince Charles His Gracious Resolution Concerning the Present Affaires of this Kingdome*, pp. 3, 5, 8
14. Halliwell, *Letters of the Kings of England*, p. 394
15. *The Parliamentary or Constitutional History of England*, Volume XII, p. 423
16. *History*, Volume IV, p. 110
17. Ibid., p. 109
18. Green, *Letters of Queen Henrietta Maria*, p. 312
19. *History*, Volume IV, p. 138
20. *ODNB*, 'Hyde, Edward, first earl of Clarendon (1609–1674), politician and historian' by Paul Seaward. Charles I endorsed Hyde's efforts on *History of the Rebellion*, and information made its way to Hyde so events beyond the chancellor's initial knowledge could be included. Turnbull, *Charles I's Private Life*, Chapter 30
21. Fanshawe, *The Memoirs of Ann Lady Fanshawe*, pp. 40–41
22. Green, *Letters of Queen Henrietta Maria*, p. 314
23. Harris, *An Historical and Critical Account of the Lives and Writings of James I. and Charles I. and of the Lives of Oliver Cromwell and Charles II.*, Volume IV, p. 23
24. *History*, Volume IV, pp. 168–69
25. Harris, *An Historical and Critical Account of the Lives and Writings of James I. and Charles I. and of the Lives of Oliver Cromwell and Charles II.*, Volume IV, pp. 24–25

26. Hoskins, *Charles the Second in the Channel Islands*, Volume I, p. 351
27. Ibid., pp. 151–52
28. *ODNB*, 'La Cloche, Jacques de (1644/1647?–1669), pretended son of Charles II' by Giovanni Tarantino
29. Fraser, *King Charles II*, p. 43
30. Hardy, *Report to the Master of the Rolls on Documents in the Archives of Venice*, pp. 87–90
31. Ibid.

Chapter 11

1. *History*, Volume IV, p. 169
2. Hoskins, *Charles the Second in the Channel Islands*, Volume I, pp. 354, 356
3. Ibid., pp. 361–63
4. Ibid., p. 106
5. Ibid., pp. 364–65
6. Ibid., p. 365
7. Pepys, *The Diary of Samuel Pepys*, 14 August 1665
8. *CSPD*, 1660–1661, p. 585
9. Fanshawe, *The Memoirs of Ann Lady Fanshawe*, p. 42
10. Hoskins, *Charles the Second in the Channel Islands*, Volume I, pp. 372–73
11. Ibid., pp. 366–67
12. Clarendon, *State Papers Collected by Edward, Earl of Clarendon*, Volume II, p. 287
13. Hoskins, *Charles the Second in the Channel Islands*, Volume I, pp. 376–78
14. de Lisle, *The White King*, p. 211
15. Ibid., pp. 212–13
16. Clarendon, *State Papers Collected by Edward, Earl of Clarendon*, Volume II, pp. 231–36
17. *History*, Volume IV, p. 169
18. Green, *Letters of Queen Henrietta Maria*, p. 316
19. Halliwell, *Letters of the Kings of England*, Volume II, pp. 401–2
20. Fanshawe, *The Memoirs of Ann Lady Fanshawe*, p. 42
21. Hoskins, *Charles the Second in the Channel Islands*, Volume I, pp. 402, 413–14
22. *CSPV*, Volume XV, pp. 343–48
23. *History*, Volume IV, pp. 174, 179, 207
24. Hoskins, *Charles the Second in the Channel Islands*, Volume I, p. 430
25. *History*, Volume IV, pp. 198–99

Chapter 12

1. Halliwell, *Letters of the Kings of England*, Volume II, p. 410
2. Barine, *La Grande Mademoiselle*
3. Hutton, *Charles the Second*, p. 20
4. Ibid., p. 21
5. Green, *Letters of Queen Henrietta Maria*, pp. 248, 250
6. Porter, *Royal Renegades*, p. 111

7. Spencer, *Prince Rupert*, p. 180
8. Chapman, *The Tragedy of Charles II*, pp. 95–96
9. Motteville, *Memoirs of Madame de Motteville*, Volume I, pp. 211–12
10. Breeching was a boy's transition from wearing dresses to wearing breeches. Zuvich, *Sex and Sexuality in Stuart Britain*, p. 9
11. *CSPV*, Volume XXVII, pp. 266–81
12. Clarendon, *State Papers Collected by Edward, Earl of Clarendon*, Volume II, pp. 277, 319
13. Burnet, *Burnet's History of My Own Time*, Volume I, p. 138
14. Bobbio, *Thomas Hobbes and the Natural Law Tradition*, p. 104
15. Burnet, *Burnet's History of My Own Time*, Volume I, p. 138
16. Savile, *A Character of King Charles the Second*, p. 40
17. Halliwell, *Letters of the Kings of England*, Volume II, p. 417
18. Barine, *La Grande Mademoiselle*
19. Halliwell, *Letters of the Kings of England*, Volume II, p. 463
20. Barine, *La Grande Mademoiselle*
21. Pitts, *La Grande Mademoiselle at the Court of France*, p. 38
22. *CSPV*, Volume XXVII, pp. 304–8
23. de Lisle, *The White King*, pp. 210, 217–18
24. Berkley, *Memoirs of Sir John Berkley*, p. 27
25. Hutton, *Charles the Second*, p. 19
26. *CSPV*, Volume XXVII, pp. 313–17
27. Gardiner, *The Hamilton Papers*, p. 178
28. Gardiner, *History of the Great Civil War 1642–1649*, Volume IV, pp. 56–57

Chapter 13

1. Hutton, *Charles the Second*, pp. 22–23
2. *CSPV*, Volume XXVIII, pp. 45–51
3. Ibid., pp. 40–45
4. Turnbull, *Charles I's Private Life*, Chapter 30
5. *ODNB*, 'Mary, princess royal (1631–1660), princess of Orange, consort of William II' by Marika Keblusek
6. Fraser, *King Charles II*, p. 57
7. Hutton, *Charles the Second*, p. 24
8. Fairfax, *A Catalogue of the Curious Collection of Pictures of George Villiers, Duke of Buckingham*, p. 27
9. Hutton, *Charles the Second*, p. 24
10. Laing, *The Letters and Journals of Robert Baillie*, Volume III, p. 88
11. James had become so difficult in captivity that, having been admonished for spouting spiteful language upon hearing of his father's recapture in November 1647, he grabbed a longbow to shoot the admonisher and required physical restraint. Turner, *James II*, p. 15
12. *History*, Volume IV, p. 339
13. Ibid., p. 338
14. Callow, *The Making of King James II*, p. 54
15. Evelyn, *The Diary of John Evelyn*, p. 201

16. Clarke, *The Life of James the Second*, Volume I, p. 492
17. Dunois, *Memoirs of the Court of England*, p. 3
18. Ibid.
19. *CSPD*, 1648–1649, p. 216
20. *ODNB*, 'Batten, Sir William (1600/01–1667), naval officer' by C. S. Knighton
21. Hutton, *Charles the Second*, p. 27
22. Gardiner, *The Hamilton Papers*, pp. 239–43
23. Ibid., p. 244
24. Fraser, *King Charles II*, p. 59
25. Hinton, *Memoires*, pp. 19–22
26. *CCSP*, Volume I, pp. 438–39
27. Hinton, *Memoires*, pp. 23–24
28. Ibid., pp. 24–25
29. *CSPV*, Volume XXVIII, pp. 79–81
30. *CSPV*, Volume XXVIII, pp. 81–83
31. Gardiner, *History of the Great Civil War 1642–1649*, Volume IV, pp. 235–36
32. *CSPV*, Volume XXVIII, pp. 84–86
33. *CSPD*, 1648–1649, pp. 345–47
34. *CSPD*, 1649–1650, p. 5
35. Gardiner, *History of the Commonwealth and Protectorate 1649–1660*, Volume I, p. 20
36. Ellis, *Original Letters, Illustrative of English History*, p. 347
37. *History*, Volume IV, p. 454

Chapter 14

1. Blencowe, *Sydney Papers*, p. 56
2. Ibid., p. 237
3. *History*, Volume V, p. 1
4. *CCSP*, Volume II, p. 2
5. Charles finally issued a declaration in October 1649 while in Jersey again, further explaining: 'we have thought fit rather from hence ... than from any foreign country where we have been hitherto necessitated to reside'. Then he continued by declaring himself lawful successor 'without any condition or limitation' and describing himself as 'a severe avenger' of the spilling of Charles I's 'innocent blood'. Penn, *Memorials of the Professional Life and Times of Sir William Penn*, Volume II, pp. 3–7
6. *CSPV*, Volume XXVIII, pp. 86–88
7. Ibid.
8. Ibid., pp. 88–93
9. de Lisle, *The White King*, pp. 260, 276. Charles wasn't getting the 'George' anytime soon. Instead, it was confiscated from Juxon and sold for £70 following a 1649 parliamentary Act ordering the sale of Charles I's belongings, for Commonwealth profit. Nevertheless, these belongings could then work their way into others' hands. By 7 February 1650, Colonel Thomlinson, a sympathetic companion of the convicted king, had promised it to Charles II, and the young king accordingly made arrangements to receive it, offering recompense. Liljegren, *Studies in Milton*, pp. 75–76

10. *Acts and Ordinances of the Interregnum, 1642–1660*, pp. 1263–64
11. Penn, *Memorials of the Professional Life and Times of Sir William Penn*, Volume II, p. 3
12. *History*, Volume V, p. 2
13. Hutton, *Charles the Second*, p. 34
14. *CCSP*, Volume II, p. 4
15. Laing, *The Letters and Journals of Robert Baillie*, Volume III, p. 88
16. Fraser, *King Charles II*, p. 73
17. Heath, *A Brief Chronicle of the Late Intestine War in the Three Kingdoms of England, Scotland and Ireland*, pp. 435–36
18. *CCSP*, Volume II, pp. 13–14
19. *CSPV*, Volume XXVIII, pp. 109–11
20. *History*, Volume V, p. 49
21. Yarrow and Brooks, *Mademoiselle de Montpensier Memoirs*, p. 34
22. Barine, *La Grande Mademoiselle*
23. *History*, Volume V, p. 50
24. Ibid., pp. 51–52
25. Ibid., pp. 54–55
26. Hutton, *Charles the Second*, p. 40
27. *CSPV*, Volume XXVIII, pp. 116–20
28. Bryant, *The Letters of King Charles II*, p. 14
29. Fraser, *King Charles II*, p. 84
30. Hutton, *Charles the Second*, pp. 42–43
31. Laing, *The Letters and Journals of Robert Baillie*, Volume III, p. 523
32. Gardiner, *Letters and Papers Illustrating the Relations between Charles the Second and Scotland in 1650*, p. 25
33. Ibid., pp. 24, 29–30
34. Fraser, *King Charles II*, p. 89
35. Hutton, *Charles the Second*, p. 47
36. Gardiner, *Letters and Papers Illustrating the Relations between Charles the Second and Scotland in 1650*, p. 74

Chapter 15

1. Napier, *The Life and Times of Montrose*, p. 537
2. Coote, *Royal Survivor*, p. 83
3. Hutton, *Charles the Second*, p. 48
4. Jaffray, *Diary of Alexander Jaffray*, pp. 32–33
5. Hutton, *Charles the Second*, p. 49
6. Lyon, *Personal History of King Charles the Second*, pp. 34–35
7. Ibid., pp. 40–41
8. Hutton, *Charles the Second*, p. 49
9. Lyon, *Personal History of King Charles the Second*, p. 34
10. Ibid., p. 42
11. *History*, Volume V, p. 135
12. Ibid., p. 134
13. *Memoirs of Sir Ewen Cameron of Locheill*, pp. 91–92

14. Whitelock, *Memorials of the English Affairs from the Beginning of the Reign of Charles the First to the Happy Restoration of King Charles the Second*, Volume III, pp. 209, 211
15. Hutton, *Charles the Second*, pp. 51–52
16. Bryant, *The Letters of King Charles II*, p. 17
17. Douglas, *Cromwell's Scotch Campaigns*, p. 130
18. Gardiner, *History of the Commonwealth and Protectorate 1649–1660*, Volume I, p. 368
19. *Correspondence of Sir Robert Kerr, First Earl of Ancram and His Son William, Third Earl of Lothian*, Volume II, pp. 497–98
20. Warner, *The Nicholas Papers*, Volume I, p. 174
21. Porter, *Royal Renegades*, pp. 221–25
22. *CCSP*, Volume II, p. 71
23. Keay, *The Last Royal Rebel*, pp. 17–19
24. Lyon, *Personal History of King Charles the Second*, p. 102
25. Hutton, *Charles the Second*, pp. 56–57
26. Scott, *The King in Exile*, pp. 189–90
27. Hutton, *Charles the Second*, p. 57
28. Scott, *The King in Exile*, pp. 191–93
29. Lyon, *Personal History of King Charles the Second*, pp. 148–54
30. Ibid., pp. 154–56
31. Fraser, *King Charles II*, p. 99
32. Scott, *The King in Exile*, p. 195

Chapter 16

1. Nicoll, *A Diary of Public Transactions and Other Occurrences, Chiefly in Scotland, from January 1650 to June 1667*, p. 48
2. Lyon, *Personal History of King Charles the Second*, p. 163
3. Hutton, *Charles the Second*, p. 61. Although I hope my referencing acknowledges sources fairly, I'd here like to give further credit to Professor Ronald Hutton. Some of his work really helped my understanding of matters in Charles's early adulthood, and I feel Hutton's *Charles the Second* biography guided me with the Scottish affairs particularly.
4. Carte, *A Collection of Original Letters and Papers*, Volume II, p. 15
5. Hutton, *Charles the Second*, pp. 61, 63
6. Carlson, 'A History of the Presbyterian Party from Pride's Purge to the Dissolution of the Long Parliament', p. 118
7. Atkin, *Cromwell's Crowning Mercy*, pp. 21, 36, 182
8. Ibid., p. 37
9. Ibid., pp. 49, 51–52
10. Ibid., p. 49
11. Ibid., pp. 42, 45, 48
12. Gardiner, *History of the Commonwealth and Protectorate 1649–1660*, Volume I, p. 385
13. Ackroyd, *Civil War*, p. 320
14. Ralph, 'Boscobel and the Royal Oak', p. 104

15. Hughes, *The Boscobel Tracts*, p. 40
16. Carlyle, *Oliver Cromwell's Letters and Speeches*, Volume III, p. 46
17. Spencer, *To Catch a King*, pp. 91, 101
18. Massey, *The Declaration of Major General Massey upon his Death Bed in the Newark at Leicester*, p. 3
19. Hughes, *The Boscobel Tracts*, p. 148
20. Matthews, *Charles II's Escape from Worcester*, p. 9
21. Spencer, *To Catch a King*, pp. 103–5
22. Charles reported this. Hughes, *The Boscobel Tracts*, pp. 147–48
23. Matthews, *Charles II's Escape from Worcester*, p. 160
24. Spencer, *To Catch a King*, p. 109
25. Via Humphrey, news of this prize reached Charles a few hours after his time in the oak tree on 6 September. The king was visibly alarmed, realising all and sundry had incentive to hunt him, and this followed hopelessness from him on 4–5 September. However, his subsequent moods and behaviours indicate that near-misses in the oak tree gave him confidence in his ability to outwit the Roundheads after all. To me, this seems the reason Charles made such a big story of hiding in the oak tree. He perhaps saw his experience as an epiphany.

Chapter 17

1. Hughes, *The Boscobel Tracts*, p. 152
2. Ibid., p. 153
3. *History*, Volume V, p. 190
4. Scott, *The King in Exile*, p. 225
5. Hughes, *The Boscobel Tracts*, pp. 154–57
6. Fea, *The Flight of the King*, p. 192
7. Spencer, *To Catch a King*, p. 114
8. *History*, Volume V, pp. 197–98
9. Spencer, *To Catch a King*, p. 146
10. Fea, *The Flight of the King*, p. 194
11. This sheep belonged to a sheepcote owned by a William Staunton on Boscobel land. William Penderel later offered Staunton reimbursement.
12. These were Whitgreave's nephews Thomas Paylin (a relative of Monty Python's Michael Palin) and Francis Reynolds as well as John Preston, son of a Lancashire knight of the same name.
13. Hughes, *The Boscobel Tracts*, p. 296
14. Ibid., pp. 297–99
15. Spencer, *To Catch a King*, pp. 69, 134–35
16. Hughes, *The Boscobel Tracts*, p. 262
17. Ibid., pp. 162–63
18. *History*, Volume V, p. 204
19. Hughes, *The Boscobel Tracts*, pp. 164, 166
20. Matthews, *Charles II's Escape from Worcester*, p. 81
21. Hughes, *The Boscobel Tracts*, pp. 166–67
22. Spencer, *To Catch a King*, p. 171
23. Hughes, *The Boscobel Tracts*, p. 168

24. Ibid., pp. 171–73
25. Spencer, *To Catch a King*, pp. 209–10, 217–18
26. Matthews, *Charles II's Escape from Worcester*, pp. 156–57
27. Ibid., pp. 159–60

Chapter 18

1. *CSPV*, Volume XXVIII, pp. 202–6
2. Unless confusion can be attributed to some listeners' reports, Charles lied about certain details, for instance seemingly claiming he'd gone through London and disguised himself as a woman with a bag of laundry on his head. Till the Restoration, he had a duty to withhold some of the truth, to protect those who had helped him.
3. *CSPD*, 1651–1652, p. 3
4. Ibid., p. 2
5. *History*, Volume V, p. 179
6. *CSPD*, 1651–1652, p. 3
7. Ibid.
8. Yarrow and Brooks, *Mademoiselle de Montpensier Memoirs*, pp. 39–42
9. *ODNB*, 'Lane, Jane, Lady Fisher (d. 1689), royalist heroine' by John Sutton
10. Clarke, *The Life of James the Second*, Volume I, p. 492
11. Keay, *The Last Royal Rebel*, p. 20
12. Clarke, *The Life of James the Second*, Volume I, p. 54
13. *History*, Volume V, pp. 227–29
14. Warner, *The Nicholas Papers*, Volume I, pp. 195–96
15. *CSPD*, 1651–1652, p. 3
16. Clarke, *The Life of James the Second*, Volume I, pp. 84–87
17. Scott, *The King in Exile*, p. 353
18. *History*, Volume V, pp. 244–45
19. Spencer, *Killers of the King*, p. 86
20. Mijers and Onnekink, *Redefining William III*, pp. 237–38
21. Sadly for Charles, the Roundheads he'd nearly exchanged punches with in Bridport had gone on to victory in their Jersey attack.
22. Scott, *The King in Exile*, p. 379
23. Clarendon, *State Papers Collected by Edward, Earl of Clarendon*, Volume III, p. 141
24. Scott, *The King in Exile*, p. 380
25. Spencer, *Prince Rupert*, p. 231
26. Ibid., pp. 241–43
27. Ibid., p. 243
28. Firth, *Publications of the Scottish History Society*, Volume XVIII, pp. 60–61
29. Cartwright, *Madame*, p. 43
30. *CCSP*, Volume II, p. 228
31. Briscoe, *A Stuart Benefactress*, p. 91. Lord Beauchamp was a son of Charles's old governor Hertford and was dying when the king wrote him these words.
32. *CSPT*, Volume I, pp. 470–81
33. *CCSP*, Volume II, p. 220
34. Pepys, *The Diary of Samuel Pepys*, 26 April 1667

35. *ODNB*, 'Byron, John, first Baron Byron (1598/9–1652), royalist army officer' by Ronald Hutton
36. *CCSP*, Volume II, p. 240
37. Heath, *Flagellum*, p. 120
38. Ludlow, *The Memoirs of Edmund Ludlow*, Volume I, p. 497
39. Ackroyd, *Civil War*, p. 325
40. Ibid., p. 333

Chapter 19

1. *CSPD,* 1653–1654, p. 359
2. Ibid.
3. It's worth noting that Charles, Lord Gerard opposed the king's ill-fated move to Scotland in 1650, as did Hyde. Long and Buckingham helped talk the king into it.
4. Underdown, *Royalist Conspiracy in England 1649–1660*, p. 101
5. Ibid., p. 104
6. Hutton mentions style as one reason to suspect forgery here. Hutton, *Charles the Second*, p. 82. Indeed, I note that some of the sharp wording in this proclamation does not align with documents such as an open letter from Charles written to gather support for uprisings in 1659.
7. *CSPT*, Volume II, pp. 244–58
8. Hutton, *Charles the Second*, pp. 40, 82
9. *England's Black Tribunal*, pp. 142, 145
10. Cowper, *The Works of William Cowper*, Volume V, p. 353
11. Hutton, *Charles the Second*, p. 84
12. Ibid.
13. *CSPT*, Volume II, pp. 476–90
14. Green, *Lives of the Princesses of England*, Volume VI, p. 213
15. Scott, *The Travels of the King*, p. 8
16. *CSPT*, Volume II, pp. 563–90
17. Ibid., pp. 563–80
18. Fraser, *King Charles II*, p. 138
19. *History*, Volume V, pp. 358–60
20. Bryant, *The Letters of King Charles II*, p. 32
21. *CCSP,* Volume II, pp. 420–21
22. Warner, *The Nicholas Papers*, Volume II, pp. 90–91
23. Strickland, *Lives of the Queens of England*, Volume V, p. 414
24. Scott, *The Travels of the King*, pp. 37–38
25. Burnet, *Bishop Burnet's History of His Own Time*, Volume I, p. 499
26. Morrice, *A Collection of the State Letters of the Right Honourable Roger Boyle*, p. 21
27. Jordan and Walsh, *The King's Bed*, pp. 61–62
28. Morrice, *A Collection of the State Letters of the Right Honourable Roger Boyle*, pp. 21–22
29. Burnet, *Bishop Burnet's History of His Own Time*, Volume I, pp. 95–96
30. *ODNB*, 'Wilmot, Henry, first earl of Rochester (bap. 1613, d. 1658), royalist army officer' by Ronald Hutton
31. Chapman, *The Tragedy of Charles II*, pp. 267–68

32. Zuvich, *Sex and Sexuality in Stuart Britain*, p. 76
33. *CSPT*, Volume I, pp. 733–44
34. Charles II, *An Account of the Preservation of King Charles II. After the Battle of Worcester*, pp. 106–8
35. Brown, *Miscellanea Aulica*, p. 113

Chapter 20

1. Carte, *A Collection of Original Letters and Papers*, Volume II, p. 54
2. *CCSP*, Volume III, p. 40
3. *History*, Volume V, pp. 364–65
4. Chapman, *The Tragedy of Charles II*, p. 292
5. Hutton, *Charles the Second*, p. 89
6. Brown, *Miscellanea Aulica*, pp. 115–16, 126–27
7. *History*, Volume V, p. 360
8. Hutton, *Charles the Second*, p. 89
9. *CSPT*, Volume IV, pp. 79–96
10. Charles II, *An Account of the Preservation of King Charles II. After the Battle of Worcester*, pp. 146–47
11. *History*, Volume V, pp. 383–88
12. Brown, *Miscellanea Aulica*, p. 124
13. Keay, *The Last Royal Rebel*, p. 22
14. *CCSP*, Volume III, pp. 99–102
15. Ibid., pp. 100–1
16. Ibid., pp. 109–10
17. Soden, *Royal Exiles*, p. 113
18. Dasent, *The Private Life of Charles the Second*, p. 66
19. For services in Ireland during the wars, Charles created this Irish title in 1650 for the man's father Thomas Preston.
20. Clarendon, *State Papers Collected by Edward, Earl of Clarendon*, Volume III, pp. 298–99
21. Ibid.
22. Soden, *Royal Exiles*, p. 117
23. Miller, *James II*, Chapter 2
24. Hutton, *Charles the Second*, p. 102
25. Miller, *James II*, Chapter 2
26. *CCSP*, Volume III, p. 252
27. Clarendon, *State Papers Collected by Edward, Earl of Clarendon*, Volume III, p. 351
28. One of Hutton's many great observations highlights how Charles and the Spanish worked to deceive each other. Hutton, *Charles the Second*, pp. 106–7
29. Fraser, *King Charles II*, p. 145
30. Jesse, *Memoirs of the Court of England during the Reign of the Stuarts*, Volume III, p. 168
31. Keay, *The Last Royal Rebel*, pp. 26–28
32. *CCSP*, Volume III, pp. 392–93
33. *CSPD*, 1657–1658, p. xlvii

34. Keay, *The Last Royal Rebel*, p. 33
35. *CSPD*, 1657–1658, p. 311
36. Underdown, *Royalist Conspiracy in England 1649–1660*, p. 219
37. Clarendon, *State Papers Collected by Edward, Earl of Clarendon*, Volume III, pp. 403–4
38. *History*, Volume VI, p. 86
39. Scott, *The Travels of the King*, p. 367
40. *History*, Volume VI, p. 88

Chapter 21

1. Robertson, *The Life of Mrs. Robertson, Grand-Daughter of Charles II*, pp. 1–2
2. Anderson, *The Scottish Nation*, Volume III, p. 727
3. Durston, *Cromwell's Major-Generals*, pp. 154–55, 174–75
4. *History*, Volume VI, p. 98
5. *CSPT*, Volume VII, pp. 417–29
6. Carte, *A Collection of Original Letters and Papers*, Volume II, p. 157
7. Smith, *The Cavaliers in Exile, 1640–1660*, p. 107
8. *CCSP*, Volume IV, p. 87
9. Ibid., p. 82
10. The story reports that around New Year 1657 Willys, Thurloe and the protector concocted a ploy to invite all three Stuart brothers to England as if for talks, then shoot them dead upon their landing at Sussex. Supposedly, Morland eavesdropped and ensured Charles was warned, resulting in the king sending 'frivolous' excuses showing no seriousness for such a momentous opportunity and Cromwell deducing Charles knew not to take the invitation at face value. *CSPT*, Volume I, pp. xi–xx
11. *CCSP*, Volume IV, pp. 130, 199
12. Clarke, *The Life of James the Second*, Volume I, p. 373
13. Scott, *The Travels of the King*, pp. 402–3
14. Warner, *The Nicholas Papers*, Volume IV, p. 181
15. Ibid., p. 182
16. Hutton, *Charles the Second*, p. 117. Given Booth's defeat, the upbeat mood is interesting, and it sits in contrast to the period after Penruddock's defeat.
17. Warner, *The Nicholas Papers*, Volume IV, p. 182
18. Bryant, *The Letters of King Charles II*, pp. 76–77
19. *History*, Volume VI, p. 132
20. *CCSP*, Volume IV, p. 418
21. Warner, *The Nicholas Papers*, Volume IV, p. 188
22. Alongside the quietness and shyness noted in Charles during his first stay in France, the observation that Charles 'speaks not much' was made by the Covenanters' Baillie when conferring with him in 1649. Laing, *The Letters and Journals of Robert Baillie*, Volume III, p. 88
23. Words from Ormond. Pope, *The Works of Alexander Pope*, Volume VI, p. 215
24. By 33, he was 'mighty gray'. Pepys, *The Diary of Samuel Pepys*, 2 November 1663
25. Kent, '"Hand-Maids and Daughters of the Lord": Quaker Women, Quaker Families, and Somerset's Anti-Tithe Petition in 1659', p. 32
26. *A Second Collection of Scarce and Valuable Tracts*, Volume III, pp. 1–5

27. In March 1660, Charles wondered whether his reply had even reached Monck.
28. *History*, Volume VI, p. 177
29. *A Second Collection of Scarce and Valuable Tracts*, Volume III, pp. 1–5
30. Lister, *Life and Administration of Edward, First Earl of Clarendon*, Volume I, p. 494
31. *CCSP*, Volume IV, p. 558
32. Bryant, *The Letters of King Charles II*, p. 83
33. Lister, *Life and Administration of Edward, First Earl of Clarendon*, Volume I, p. 497
34. *Journal of the House of Lords*, 11, pp. 6–9
35. *History*, Volume VI, pp. 200–1
36. Ibid., p. 136
37. *Journal of the House of Lords*, 11, pp. 6–9
38. On Restoration Day 1660, the slenderness of Charles II's face was noted to resemble Charles I's.
39. Lister, *Life and Administration of Edward, First Earl of Clarendon*, Volume I, pp. 493–94
40. Walker, *The Compleat History of Independencie upon the Parliament begun 1640*, p. 101. The new parliament, later dubbed the 1660 Convention Parliament, had first assembled on 25 April, whereupon it reversed the 1649 abolition of the House of Lords.
41. Hutton, *Charles the Second*, pp. 131–32
42. Pepys, *The Diary of Samuel Pepys*, 17 May 1660
43. Hutton, *Charles the Second*, p. 132
44. Pepys, *The Diary of Samuel Pepys*, 23, 24, 25 May 1660
45. Clarendon, *The Life of Edward Earl of Clarendon*, Volume I, pp. 274–76
46. Green, *Lives of the Princesses of England*, Volume VI, p. 427
47. Clarendon, *The Life of Edward Earl of Clarendon*, Volume I, pp. 278–79
48. Walker, *The Compleat History of Independencie upon the Parliament begun 1640*, p. 107

Selected Bibliography

A Miscellany (George Routledge & Sons, London, 1888)
'A Royal Tutor's Advice'. *Titan*, Volume XXIII (1856), pp. 60–63
A Second Collection of Scarce and Valuable Tracts, Volume III (F. Cogan, London, 1750)
Abbott, Jacob, *History of King Charles the Second* (Harper & Brothers, New York, 1849)
Ackroyd, Peter, *Civil War* (Macmillan, London, 2014)
Acts and Ordinances of the Interregnum, 1642–1660 (His Majesty's Stationery Office, London, 1911) www.british-history.ac.uk/no-series/acts-ordinances-interregnum
Adolph, Anthony, *The King's Henchman*, Kindle edition (Gibson Square Books, 2012)
Aikin, Lucy, *Memoirs of the Court of King Charles the First*, Volume I (Longman, Rees, Orme, Brown, Green & Longman, London, 1833)
Anderson, William, *The Scottish Nation*, Volume III (A. Fullarton & Co., Edinburgh, 1867)
Appleby, Andrew B., 'Nutrition and Disease: The Case of London, 1550–1750'. *The Journal of Interdisciplinary History*, 6(1) (1975), pp. 1–22 www.jstor.org/stable/202822
Ashmole, Elias (ed.), *The Institution, Laws & Ceremonies of the most Noble Order of the Garter* (Nathanael Brooke, London, 1672)
Astington, John H., 'The King and Queenes Entertainement at Richmond'. *Records of Early English Drama*, 12(1) (1987), pp. 12–18 www.jstor.org/stable/43505531
Atkin, Malcolm, *Cromwell's Crowning Mercy: The Battle of Worcester 1651* (Sutton Publishing, Stroud, 1998)
Barine, Arvède, *La Grande Mademoiselle*, trans. Helen Meyer www.gutenberg.org/files/50717/50717-h/50717-h
Baxter, Richard, *Reliquiæ Baxterianæ* (T. Parkhurst, J. Robinson, J. Lawrence & J. Dunton, London, 1696)
Berkley, John, *Memoirs of Sir John Berkley* (A. Baldwin, London, 1699)
Blencowe, R. W. (ed.), *Sydney Papers* (John Murray, London, 1825)
Bobbio, Norberto, *Thomas Hobbes and the Natural Law Tradition*, trans. Daniela Gobetti (University of Chicago Press, Chicago, 1993)
Bradwell, Stephen, *Physick for the Sicknesse, Commonly Called the Plagve* (Benjamin Fisher, London, 1636)
Briscoe, A. Daly, *A Stuart Benefactress: Sarah, Duchess of Somerset* (Terence Dalton, Lavenham, 1973)

Brown, T. (ed.), *Miscellanea Aulica* (J. Hartley, Robert Gibson & Thomas Hodgson, London, 1702)

Bryant, Arthur (ed.), *The Letters of King Charles II* (Cassell & Company, London, 1935)

Bulstrode, Richard, *Memoirs and Reflections upon the Reign and Government of King Charles the I$^{st.}$ and K. Charles the II$^{d.}$* (Charles Rivington, London, 1721)

Burnet, Gilbert, *Bishop Burnet's History of His Own Time*, Volume I, ed. Thomas Burnet (A. Millar, London, 1753)

Burnet, Gilbert, *Burnet's History of My Own Time*, Part One, Volume I, ed. Osmund Airy (Clarendon Press, Oxford, 1897)

Callow, John, *The Making of King James II: The Formative Years of a Fallen King* (Sutton Publishing, Stroud, 2000)

Carlson, Leland H., 'A History of the Presbyterian Party from Pride's Purge to the Dissolution of the Long Parliament'. *Church History*, 11(2) (1942), pp. 83–122 www.jstor.org/stable/3160290

Carlton, Charles, *Going to the Wars: The Experience of the British Civil Wars 1638–1651* (Routledge, London, 1992)

Carlyle, Thomas (ed.), *Oliver Cromwell's Letters and Speeches*, Volume III (Chapman & Hall, London, 1845)

Carte, Thomas (ed.), *A Collection of Original Letters and Papers, Concerning the Affairs of England, from the Year 1641 to 1660*, 2 volumes (Society for the Encouragement of Learning, London, 1739)

Cartwright, Julia, *Madame: A Life of Henrietta, Daughter of Charles I. and Duchess of Orleans* (Seeley & Co., London, 1894)

CCSP: Calendar of the Clarendon State Papers, Volume I, ed. O. Ogle and W. H. Bliss (Clarendon Press, Oxford, 1872)

CCSP, Volume II, ed. W. Dunn Macray (Clarendon Press, Oxford, 1869)

CCSP, Volume III, ed. W. Dunn Macray (Clarendon Press, Oxford, 1876)

CCSP, Volume IV, ed. F. J. Routledge (Clarendon Press, Oxford, 1932)

Chapman, Hester W., *The Tragedy of Charles II in the years 1630–1660* (Little, Brown & Company, Boston, 1964)

Charles II, *An Account of the Preservation of King Charles II. After the Battle of Worcester* (Robert & Andrew Foulis, Edinburgh, 1766)

'Civil War Proceedings in Yorkshire'. *The Yorkshire Archæological and Topographical Journal*, Volume VII (1882), pp. 369–400

Clarendon, Edward, Earl of, *The Life of Edward Earl of Clarendon*, Volume I (Oxford University Press, Oxford, 1857)

Clarendon, Edward, Earl of (ed.), *State Papers Collected by Edward, Earl of Clarendon*, Volume II (Clarendon Printing-House, Oxford, 1773)

Clarendon, Edward, Earl of (ed.), *State Papers Collected by Edward, Earl of Clarendon*, Volume III (Clarendon Printing-House, Oxford, 1786)

Clark, Andrew (ed.), *Aubrey's 'Brief Lives'*, Volume I (Clarendon Press, Oxford, 1898)

Clark, David, *The English Civil War* (Pocket Essentials, Harpenden, 2008)

Clarke, J. S. (ed.), *The Life of James the Second*, Volume I (Longman, Hurst, Rees, Orme & Brown, London, 1816)

Cooper, Charles Henry, *Annals of Cambridge*, Volume III (Warwick & Co., Cambridge, 1845)

Coote, Stephen, *Royal Survivor* (St Martin's Press, New York, 2000)

Selected Bibliography

Correspondence of Sir Robert Kerr, First Earl of Ancram and His Son William, Third Earl of Lothian, Volume II (R. & R. Clark, Edinburgh, 1875)

Cowper, William, *The Works of William Cowper*, Volume V (H. G. Bohn, London, 1854)

Creighton, Charles, *A History of Epidemics in Britain from A.D. 664 to the Extinction of Plague* (Cambridge University Press, Cambridge, 1891)

Crystal, David, *The Cambridge Encyclopedia of the English Language*, second edition (Cambridge University Press, Cambridge, 2003)

CSPD: Calendar of State Papers, Domestic Series, 1629–1631, ed. John Bruce (Longman, Green, Longman & Roberts, London, 1860)

CSPD, 1633–1634, ed. John Bruce (Longman, Green, Longman, Roberts & Green, London, 1863)

CSPD, 1635, ed. John Bruce (Longman, Green, Longman, Roberts & Green, London, 1865)

CSPD, 1637–1638, ed. John Bruce (Longmans, Green & Co., London, 1869)

CSPD, 1638–1639, ed. John Bruce and William Douglas Hamilton (Longman & Co. et al., London, 1871)

CSPD, 1639, ed. William Douglas Hamilton (Longman & Co. et al., London, 1873)

CSPD, 1640, ed. William Douglas Hamilton (Longmans & Co. et al., London, 1880)

CSPD, 1641–1643, ed. William Douglas Hamilton (Her Majesty's Stationery Office, London, 1887)

CSPD, 1644–1645, ed. William Douglas Hamilton (Her Majesty's Stationery Office, London, 1890)

CSPD, 1648–1649, ed. William Douglas Hamilton (Her Majesty's Stationery Office, London, 1893)

CSPD, 1649–1650, ed. Mary Anne Everett Green (Longman & Co. et al., London, 1875)

CSPD, 1651–1652, ed. Mary Anne Everett Green (Longman & Co. et al., London, 1877)

CSPD, 1653–1654, ed. Mary Anne Everett Green (Longman & Co. et al., London, 1879)

CSPD, 1657–1658, ed. Mary Anne Everett Green (Longman & Co. et al., London, 1884)

CSPD, 1660–1661, ed. Mary Anne Everett Green (Longman, Green, Longman & Roberts, London, 1860)

CSPT: A Collection of the State Papers of John Thurloe www.british-history.ac.uk/series/thurloe-state-papers

CSPV: Calendar of State Papers, Venice www.british-history.ac.uk/series/calendar-state-papers-venice

D'Ewes, Simonds, *The Journal of Sir Simonds D'Ewes*, ed. Willson Havelock Coates (Archon Books, 1970)

Daniels, Christopher W. and Morrill, John, *Charles I* (Cambridge University Press, Cambridge, 1988)

Dasent, Arthur Irwin, *The Private Life of Charles the Second* (Cassell & Company, London, 1927)

de Lisle, Leanda, *The White King: Charles I, Traitor, Murderer, Martyr* (PublicAffairs, New York, 2017)

Donne, John, *The Works of John Donne*, Volume II (John W. Parker, London, 1839)

Douglas, W. S., *Cromwell's Scotch Campaigns: 1650–51* (Elliot Stock, London, 1898)

Dunois, Countess of, *Memoirs of the Court of England* (B. Bragg, London, 1707)

Duppa, Brian, *Prince Charles His Gracious Resolution Concerning the Present Affaires of this Kingdome* (Leonard Lichfield, Oxford, 1642) https://quod.lib.umich.edu/e/eebo2/A79222.0001.001?rgn=main;view=fulltext

Durston, Christopher, *Cromwell's Major-Generals: Godly Government during the English Revolution* (Manchester University Press, Manchester, 2001)

Ellis, Henry (ed.), *Original Letters, Illustrative of English History*, Second Series, Volume III (Harding & Lepard, London, 1827)

England's Black Tribunal, third edition (J. Playford, London, 1680)

Evelyn, John, *The Diary of John Evelyn*, ed. William Bray (Frederick Warne & Co., London)

Fairfax, Brian, *A Catalogue of the Curious Collection of Pictures of George Villiers, Duke of Buckingham* (W. Bathoe, London, 1758)

Fanshawe, Ann, *The Memoirs of Ann Lady Fanshawe* (John Lane The Bodley Head, London, 1907)

Fea, Allan, *The Flight of the King*, second edition (Methuen & Co., London, 1908)

Ferrar, John and Jebb, Doctor, *Nicholas Ferrar: Two Lives* (Cambridge University Press, Cambridge, 1855)

Firth, C. H. (ed.), *Scotland and the Commonwealth* (Edinburgh University Press, Edinburgh, 1895)

Fraser, Antonia, *Cromwell: Our Chief of Men* (Phoenix, London, 2002)

Fraser, Antonia, *King Charles II* (Macdonald Futura Publishers, 1980)

Gallagher, John, *Learning Languages in Early Modern England* (Oxford University Press, Oxford, 2019)

Gardiner, Samuel R., *History of England: From the Accession of James I. to the Outbreak of the Civil War 1603–1642*, Volume IX (Longmans, Green & Co., London, 1894)

Gardiner, Samuel R., *History of the Great Civil War 1642–1649*, Volume II (Longmans, Green & Co., London, 1905)

Gardiner, Samuel R., *History of the Great Civil War 1642–1649*, Volume IV (Longmans, Green & Co., London, 1905)

Gardiner, Samuel Rawson (ed.), *The Hamilton Papers* (Camden Society, Westminster, 1880)

Gardiner, Samuel Rawson, *History of the Commonwealth and Protectorate 1649–1660*, Volume I (Longmans, Green & Co., London, 1894)

Gardiner, Samuel Rawson (ed.), *Letters and Papers Illustrating the Relations between Charles the Second and Scotland in 1650* (Edinburgh University Press, Edinburgh, 1894)

Green, Mary Anne Everett (ed.), *Letters of Queen Henrietta Maria* (Richard Bentley, London, 1857)

Green, Mary Anne Everett, *Lives of the Princesses of England, from the Norman Conquest*, Volume VI (Longman, Brown, Green, Longman & Roberts, London, 1857)

Gregg, Pauline, *King Charles I* (University of California Press, Berkeley, 1984)

Griffin, Emma, *Blood Sport: Hunting in Britain Since 1066* (Yale University Press, New Haven, 2008)

Groom, Susanne, *Discover the Gardens* (Historic Royal Palaces, Surrey, 2008)

Hacket, John, *Scrinia Reserata* (Samuel Lowndes, 1693)

Halliwell, James Orchard (ed.), *Letters of the Kings of England*, Volume II (Henry Colburn, London, 1848)

Hardy, Thomas Duffus, *Report to the Master of the Rolls on Documents in the Archives of Venice* (Longmans, Green, Reader & Dyer, London, 1866) www.british-history.ac.uk/no-series/master-of-rolls-report

Harris, William (ed.), *An Historical and Critical Account of the Lives and Writings of James I. and Charles I. and of the Lives of Oliver Cromwell and Charles II.*, Volume IV (F. C. & J. Rivington et al., London, 1814)

Heath, James (ed.), *A Brief Chronicle of the Late Intestine VVarr in the Three Kingdoms of England, Scotland and Ireland* (W. Lee, London, 1663)

Heath, James, *Flagellum* (Randal Taylor, London, 1672)

Herries, Lord, *Historical Memoirs of the Reign of Mary Queen of Scots, and a Portion of the Reign of King James the Sixth* (Edinburgh Printing Company, Edinburgh, 1836)

Hibbert, Christopher, *Cavaliers & Roundheads: The English Civil War, 1642–1649* (Charles Scribner's Sons, New York, 1993)

Hibbert, Christopher, *Charles I* (Harper & Row, New York, 1968)

Hinton, John, *Memoires* (1679)

Historical Collections of Private Passages of State, Volume I (D. Browne, London, 1721) www.british-history.ac.uk/rushworth-papers/vol1

Historical Manuscripts Commission, *The Manuscripts of the Earl Cowper*, Volume II (Her Majesty's Stationery Office, London, 1888)

History: Clarendon, Edward, Earl of, *The History of the Rebellion and Civil Wars in England Begun in the Year 1641*, ed. W. Dunn Macray, 6 volumes (Clarendon Press, Oxford, 1888)

Hoskins, S. Elliott, *Charles the Second in the Channel Islands*, Volume I (Richard Bentley, London, 1854)

Hughes, J. (ed.), *The Boscobel Tracts*, second edition (William Blackwood & Sons, Edinburgh, 1857)

Hutton, Ronald, *Charles the Second: King of England, Scotland, and Ireland* (Clarendon Press, Oxford, 1989)

Jackson, Clare, *Charles II: The Star King*, Kindle edition (Allen Lane, 2016)

Jaffray, Alexander, *Diary of Alexander Jaffray*, ed. John Barclay (Harvey & Darton, London, 1833)

Jesse, John Heneage, *Memoirs of the Court of England during the Reign of the Stuarts*, 3 volumes (Richard Bentley, London, 1855)

John, Evan, *King Charles I* (Arthur Barker, London, 1933)

Jordan, Don and Walsh, Michael, *The King's Bed: Sex, Power and the Court of Charles II* (Little, Brown, 2015)

Journal of the House of Lords, 11, pp. 6–9 www.british-history.ac.uk/lords-jrnl/vol11/pp6-9

Keay, Anna, *The Last Royal Rebel: The Life and Death of James, Duke of Monmouth* (Bloomsbury, London, 2016)

Keay, Anna, *The Magnificent Monarch: Charles II and the Ceremonies of Power* (Bloomsbury, London, 2008)

Kent, Stephen A., '"Hand-Maids and Daughters of the Lord": Quaker Women, Quaker Families, and Somerset's Anti-Tithe Petition in 1659'. *Quaker History*, 97(1) (2008), pp. 32–61 www.jstor.org/stable/41947618

King Charls His Speech Made upon the Scaffold at Whitehall-Gate, Immediately Before His Execution (Peter Cole, Francis Tyton & Iohn Playford, London, 1649)

Kippis, Andrew (ed.), *Biographia Britannica*, second edition, Volume V (T. Longman et al., London, 1793)

Knowler, William (ed.), *The Earl of Strafforde's Letters and Dispatches*, 2 volumes (William Knowler, London, 1739)

Koot, Christian J., *A Biography of a Map in Motion* (New York University Press, New York, 2018)

Laing, David (ed.), *The Letters and Journals of Robert Baillie*, Volume III (Robert Ogle, Edinburgh, 1842)

Lake, Edward, *Diary of Dr. Edward Lake*, ed. George Percy Elliott (Camden Society, 1846)

Lewis, Lady Theresa, *Lives of the Friends and Contemporaries of Lord Chancellor Clarendon*, Volume I (John Murray, London, 1852)

Liljegren, S. B., *Studies in Milton* (C. W. K. Gleerup, Lund, 1918)

Lister, T. H., *Life and Administration of Edward, First Earl of Clarendon*, Volume I (Longman, Orme, Brown, Green & Longmans, London, 1838)

Longueville, Thomas, *The First Duke and Duchess of Newcastle-upon-Tyne* (Longmans, Green & Co., London, 1910)

Loth, David, *Royal Charles: Ruler and Rake* (George Routledge & Sons, London, 1931)

Ludlow, Edmund, *The Memoirs of Edmund Ludlow*, Volume I, ed. C. H. Firth (Clarendon Press, Oxford, 1894)

Lyon, C. J., *Personal History of King Charles the Second* (Thomas George Stevenson, Edinburgh, 1851)

Lysons, Daniel, *The Environs of London*, Volume I (T. Cadell, London, 1792)

Massey, Edward, *The Declaration of Major General Massey upon his Death Bed in the Newark at Leicester* (George Wharton, London, 1651) https://quod.lib.umich.edu/e/eebo2/A88907.0001.001/1:2?rgn=div1;view=fulltext

Matthews, William (ed.), *Charles II's Escape from Worcester* (University of California Press, Berkeley, 1966)

Memoirs of Sir Ewen Cameron of Locheill (Edinburgh Printing Company, Edinburgh, 1842)

Michel, Émile, *Rubens: His Life, His Work, and His Time*, Volume II, trans. Elizabeth Lee (William Heinemann, London, 1899)

Mijers, Esther and Onnekink, David (eds), *Redefining William III: The Impact of the King-Stadholder in International Context* (Ashgate, Aldershot, 2007)

Miller, John, *James II*, Kindle edition (Yale University Press, New Haven, 2000)

Morrice, Thomas (ed.), *A Collection of the State Letters of the Right Honourable Roger Boyle* (James Bettenham, London, 1742)

Motteville, Madame de, *Memoirs of Madame de Motteville*, Volume I (Hardy, Pratt & Company, 1899)

Napier, Mark, *The Life and Times of Montrose* (Oliver & Boyd, Edinburgh, 1840)

Newcastle, Margaret, Duchess of, *The Life of William Cavendish Duke of Newcastle*, ed. C. H. Firth (John C. Nimmo, London, 1886)

Newman, Kira L. S., 'Shutt Up: Bubonic Plague and Quarantine in Early Modern England'. *Journal of Social History*, 45(3) (2012), pp. 809–34 https://academic.oup.com/jsh/article/45/3/809/1746067

Nichols, John (ed.), *The Progresses, &c. of King James the First*, Volume I (J. B. Nichols, London, 1828)

Nicoll, John, *A Diary of Public Transactions and Other Occurrences, Chiefly in Scotland, from January 1650 to June 1667* (T. Constable, Edinburgh, 1836)

Selected Bibliography

Nineteen Propositions Made by Both Houses of Parliament, to the Kings Most Excellent Majestie: With His Majesties Answer Thereunto (Roger Daniel, Cambridge, 1642)

Noble, Mark, 'Description of a Gold Medal Struck upon the Birth of King Charles II'. *Archaeologia*, 13 (1800), pp. 20–22

ODNB: Oxford Dictionary of National Biography www.oxforddnb.com/

Oman, Carola, *Henrietta Maria* (Hodder & Stoughton, London, 1936)

Peacey, Jason, 'The Struggle for *Mercurius Britanicus*: Factional Politics and the Parliamentarian Press, 1643–1646'. *Huntington Library Quarterly*, 68(3) (2005), pp. 517–43 www.jstor.org/stable/10.1525/hlq.2005.68.3.517

Pearce, Dominic, *Henrietta Maria: The Betrayed Queen* (Amberley Publishing, Stroud, 2015)

Penn, Granville, *Memorials of the Professional Life and Times of Sir William Penn*, Volume II (James Duncan, London, 1833)

Pepys, Samuel, *The Diary of Samuel Pepys*, ed. Henry B. Wheatley (George Bell & Sons, London, 1893) www.pepysdiary.com/

Pett, Phineas, *The Autobiography of Phineas Pett*, ed. W. G. Perrin (Navy Records Society, 1918)

Phillips, John Roland, *Memoirs of the Civil War in Wales and the Marches*, 2 volumes (Longmans, Green & Co., London, 1874)

Pitts, Vincent J., *La Grande Mademoiselle at the Court of France* (Johns Hopkins University Press, Baltimore, 2000)

Pope, Alexander, *The Works of Alexander Pope*, Volume VI (C. & J. Rivington et al., London, 1824)

Porter, Linda, *Royal Renegades: The Children of Charles I and the English Civil Wars* (Macmillan, London, 2016)

Porter, Roy, *London: A Social History* (Penguin Books, London, 2000)

Ralph, Rowland W., 'Boscobel and the Royal Oak'. *The Reliquary*, 15, pp. 102–8

Rideal, Rebecca, *1666: Plague, War and Hellfire* (John Murray, London, 2016)

Robertson, Hannah, *The Life of Mrs. Robertson, Grand-Daughter of Charles II* (J. Robertson, Edinburgh, 1792)

'Royal Christenings'. *The St. James's Magazine*, Number I (1842), pp. 256–64

Rushworth, John (ed.), *The Tryal of Thomas Earl of Strafford*, second edition (Richard Chiswell et al., London, 1700)

Savile, George, *A Character of King Charles the Second* (J. & R. Tonson & S. Draper, London, 1750)

Scott, Christopher L., *The Battles of Newbury: Crossroads of the Civil War* (Pen & Sword Military, Barnsley, 2008)

Scott, Eva, *The King in Exile: The Wanderings of Charles II. from June 1646 to July 1654* (Archibald Constable & Company, London, 1905)

Scott, Eva, *The Travels of the King: Charles II. in Germany and Flanders 1654–1660* (Archibald Constable & Company, London, 1907)

Scott, Walter (ed.), *A Collection of Scarce and Valuable Tracts*, second edition, Volume IV (T. Cadell & W. Davies et al., London, 1810)

Smith, Geoffrey, *The Cavaliers in Exile, 1640–1660* (Palgrave Macmillan, Basingstoke, 2003)

Smith, Nigel (ed.), *The Poems of Andrew Marvell* (Pearson Education, Harlow, 2007)

Smuts, R. Malcolm, *Court Culture and the Origins of a Royalist Tradition in Early Stuart England* (University of Pennsylvania Press, Philadelphia, 1987)

Soden, Iain, *Royal Exiles: From Richard the Lionheart to Charles II* (Amberley Publishing, Stroud, 2013)

Sorbière, Samuel, *A Voyage to England* (J. Woodward, London, 1709)

Soria, Roberto, Balestrieri, Riccardo and Ohtsuka, Yasuyo, 'On Cas A, Cassini, Comets, and King Charles'. *Publications of the Astronomical Society of Australia*, 30 (2013), p. e028 www.cambridge.org/core/journals/publications-of-the-astronomical-society-of-australia/article/on-cas-a-cassini-comets-and-king-charles/B46896EC2800AED6EDFD2BE9AA6902D1

Spencer, Charles, *Killers of the King: The Men Who Dared to Execute Charles I* (Bloomsbury, London, 2014)

Spencer, Charles, *Prince Rupert: The Last Cavalier* (Weidenfeld & Nicolson, London, 2007)

Spencer, Charles, *To Catch a King: Charles II's Great Escape* (William Collins, London, 2017)

Stewart, Alan, *The Cradle King: The Life of James VI & I, the First Monarch of a United Great Britain* (St. Martin's Press, New York, 2003)

Strickland, Agnes, *Lives of the Last Four Princesses of the Royal House of Stuart* (Bell & Daldy, London, 1872)

Strickland, Agnes, *Lives of the Queens of England, from the Norman Conquest*, Volume IV (Bell & Daldy, London, 1865)

Strickland, Agnes, *Lives of the Queens of England, from the Norman Conquest*, Volume V (George Bell & Sons, London, 1885)

Strickland, Agnes, *Lives of the Tudor and Stuart Princesses* (George Bell & Sons, London, 1907)

Sturgis, Matthew, *Hampton Court Palace* (Channel 4 Books, London, 1998)

Taylor, Thomas, *The Works of the Judicious and Learned Divine Thomas Taylor* (John Bartlet, London, 1659)

Ten Propositions (London, 1641)

The Kings Cabinet Opened (Robert Bostock, London, 1645)

The National Covenant of the Kirk of Scotland, and the Solemn League and Covenant of the Three Kingdoms (Society of Stationers, Edinburgh, 1660)

The Parliamentary or Constitutional History of England, Volume VIII (Thomas Osborne & William Sandby, London, 1751)

The Parliamentary or Constitutional History of England, Volume XII, second edition (William Sandby, London, 1762)

Turnbull, Mark, *Charles I's Private Life*, Kindle edition (Pen & Sword History, Barnsley, 2023)

Turner, F. C., *James II* (Eyre & Spottiswoode, London, 1948)

Twain, Mark, *The Prince and the Pauper* (Harper & Row, New York, 1817)

Underdown, David, *Royalist Conspiracy in England 1649–1660* (Archon Books, 1971)

Wade, C. E., *John Pym* (Sir Isaac Pitman & Sons, London, 1912)

Walker, Clement, *The Compleat History of Independencie upon the Parliament begun 1640* (Iohn Wiliams, London, 1661) https://quod.lib.umich.edu/e/eebo2/A71223.0001.001/1:62?rgn=div1;view=fulltext

Wallington, Nehemiah, *Historical Notices of Events Occurring Chiefly in the Reign of Charles I.*, Volume II (Richard Bentley, London, 1869)

Walter, David, *James I* (Wayland, Hove, 1975)

Warburton, Eliot, *Memoirs of Prince Rupert, and the Cavaliers*, Volume II (Richard Bentley, London, 1849)

Warner, George F. (ed.), *The Nicholas Papers*, Volume I (Camden Society, Westminster, 1886)

Warner, George F. (ed.), *The Nicholas Papers*, Volume II (Camden Society, Westminster, 1892)

Warner, George F. (ed.), *The Nicholas Papers*, Volume IV (Offices of the Society, London, 1920)

Washbourn, John (ed.), *Bibliotheca Gloucestrensis: A Collection of Scarce and Curious Tracts, Relating to the County and City of Gloucester* (John Washbourn, Gloucester, 1825)

Watkins, Sarah-Beth, *Charles II's Illegitimate Children: Royal Bastards*, Kindle edition (Pen & Sword History, Barnsley, 2023)

Weir, Alison, *Mary, Queen of Scots and the Murder of Lord Darnley* (Vintage, London, 2008)

Weldon, Anthony, *The Court and Character of King James* (R. J., London, 1650)

Welwood, James, *Memoirs of the Most Material Transactions in England, for the Last Hundred Years, Preceding the Revolution in 1688* (Society of Stationers, London, 1710)

Whitaker, Katie, *A Royal Passion: The Turbulent Marriage of King Charles I of England and Henrietta Maria of France* (W. W. Norton & Company, New York, 2010)

Whitelock, Bulstrode, *Memorials of the English Affairs from the Beginning of the Reign of Charles the First to the Happy Restoration of King Charles the Second*, Volume III (Oxford University Press, Oxford, 1853)

Worsley, Lucy, *If Walls Could Talk: An Intimate History of the Home* (Walker & Company, New York, 2011)

Wraxall, N. William, *Historical Memoirs of My Own Time*, Volume II (T. Cadell & W. Davies, London, 1815)

Wyndham, H. A., *A Family History 1410–1688: The Wyndhams of Norfolk and Somerset* (Oxford University Press, London, 1939)

Yarrow, P. J. (trans.) and Brooks, William (ed.), *Mademoiselle de Montpensier Memoirs* (The Modern Humanities Research Association, London, 2010)

Zuvich, Andrea, *Sex and Sexuality in Stuart Britain* (Pen & Sword History, Barnsley, 2020)

Index

Aachen 152–53
Abbots Leigh 134–35
abdication/exclusion/usurpation xiii, 60, 74, 75, 77, 90, 94, 98, 105, 161
Amalia, Princess of Orange 96, 170, 178
Anglicanism/Church of England/Anglicans xiv, xvi, xviii, 3, 4, 5, 19, 20, 47, 62, 73, 78, 91, 112, 145, 154, 174–75, 177–78
Anglo-Dutch War, First 145–46, 152, 174
Anna of Denmark xiv, xv, 7
Anne of Austria xvi, 85, 88, 108, 141, 144
Anne, Princess 23, 36
architecture of royal residences 23–26
Argyll, Archibald Campbell, Marquis of 106, 114, 115, 116, 117, 118, 120, 121, 122
Army Plot, First 39, 40

Baillie, Robert 107, 199
Bampfield, Joseph 95–96, 97, 104, 143, 149–50
Barnstaple 68–69
Basilikon Doron xv
Batten, William 99
Belasyse, John, Baron 171
Bennet, Henry 142, 164
Bentley Hall 134
Berkeley, John 64, 143, 149–50, 164, 165
Berkenhead, John 58
Berkshire, Thomas Howard, Earl of 59, 65–66, 67, 69, 72, 73, 77, 86
Bishops' Wars 29, 33, 35–36, 37, 74

Blair, Robert 115
Booth, George 172 *see also* uprisings/insurgence
Boscobel 126, 128, 131, 132, 133, 195
Bothwell, James Hepburn, Earl of xiii
Boyle, Elizabeth 110
Breda 108, 111, 113, 163, 165, 176, 177
Breda, Declaration of 176–77
Breda, Treaty of 112, 113, 114
Brentford, Patrick Ruthven, Earl of 65, 86, 96, 105, 115, 143
Bridgwater 66–67, 68, 71
Bridport 136, 196
Bristol 57, 63, 64, 66, 67, 73, 134
Bristol, Earl of *see* Digby, George
Broghill, Roger Boyle, Baron 155–56
Bruges 163–65
Brussels 2, 108, 162, 163, 167, 170, 172, 173, 175
Brussels, Treaty of 163, 168
Buckingham, 1st Duke of *see* Villiers, George
Buckingham, George Villiers, 2nd Duke of 10, 15, 16, 30–31, 36, 46, 55–56, 90, 91, 92, 95, 100, 112, 118, 119, 125, 126, 140, 149, 176, 178–79, 197
Burnet, Gilbert 18, 30, 90, 154, 156
Byron, Eleanor 147
Byron, John, Baron 59, 147

Cambridge 46, 58
Cambridge University 26, 46, 55, 58
Capell, Arthur, Baron 63, 65, 72, 86, 105
Caracena, Marquis of 176

Cárdenas, Alonso de 164, 167
Careless, William 131, 132
Caribbean 146, 158, 159
   Jamaica 162, 175
Carisbrooke Castle 95, 104, 117–18
Carteret, George 81, 82, 84, 110, 111
Carteret, Marguerite 78, 98
Catherine of Braganza 12, 70
Catholicism/Church of Rome/Catholics xiii, xiv, xvi, 3, 4, 5, 15, 17, 19, 37, 38, 41–42, 44, 45, 49, 50, 54, 62, 69–70, 78, 84, 88, 89, 91, 93, 95, 108, 111, 114, 116, 128, 131, 133, 134, 141, 142, 144, 146, 153, 154–55, 159–60, 161, 163, 176
Chambers, James 6, 9
Charles I, King xiii, xiv, xv–xvi, xvii, 3–4, 5, 7, 9, 14, 15, 17, 19, 26, 33, 37, 38, 39, 40, 41, 42–43, 44, 45, 46, 48, 54, 58, 62, 82, 83, 85, 88, 92–93, 95, 115, 122, 143, 175, 177, 200 *see also* execution of Charles I
   character/aura xv, xvi, 4, 30, 35, 36, 73
   stutter xv, 30, 92
   as a husband xvi, xvii, xviii, 1, 2, 17, 43, 68, 69
   Personal Rule xvii, 9, 29, 33
   relationship with Westminster xvii, 20, 33, 39, 40, 41, 42, 44, 47, 48, 59, 69, 90, 94
   as a father/kingship trainer 6, 9, 11, 12, 17–18, 19, 20, 24, 29, 34, 35, 36, 46, 47, 52, 53, 54–55, 56, 57, 59–60, 61, 62, 63, 68, 69, 72, 73, 74, 84, 87, 91, 93–94, 103, 187
   attitude to kingship and monarchy 8, 18, 20, 23, 29, 33, 47, 54, 60, 69, 73, 74, 77, 114
   relationship with Scotland 9, 19–20, 28–29, 33, 42, 54, 83, 88, 92, 94
   military role 48, 50–51, 53, 55, 57, 61, 68, 73
   trial 101–2, 104, 162
Charles II, King
   conception xviii, 43, 143–44, 177
   birth 2–4
   predictions for his future 3, 4, 8
   natural appearance 3, 6, 7, 8, 21, 23, 61, 87, 97, 128, 137, 138, 174, 177, 199, 200
   physical health 3, 6, 9–10, 35, 52, 101, 119, 130, 131, 133, 147
   baptism 4–5
   attire and hairstyles 6, 12–13, 21, 61, 62, 104, 110–11, 119, 120, 128–29, 130, 133, 134, 138, 140, 142, 160, 174, 178, 179
   family role and interaction 8, 10, 28, 31–32, 41, 45, 86, 99, 105, 109, 110, 111, 114, 117, 125, 141, 143, 144, 145, 150, 153–55, 160, 164–65, 167, 168, 173–74, 178
   intellect and perception/imperception 8, 28, 32, 34, 65, 93, 104, 123, 139, 140, 149–50, 154, 161–62, 163
   sense of humour 10, 27, 58, 125, 131, 133, 140–41, 143, 161, 168
   education/tuition 11, 12, 13, 18–19, 26–27, 46, 90–91
   languages 11–12, 17, 19, 30, 46, 91–92, 108, 142, 160, 163, 179
   maritime passion 12, 25, 77, 83, 84–85, 96, 110
   speech and accents 17, 92, 129, 130, 134, 174, 199
   charm and geniality 25, 32, 46, 50, 60, 80, 82, 90, 92, 100, 101, 105, 107, 109, 110, 112, 117, 147, 152, 163, 164
   feelings regarding his mother 28, 35, 105, 109, 110, 111, 112, 153, 154
   people skills 28, 65, 107, 119, 125, 138, 139, 142, 143, 157, 173, 175, 177–78 *see also* charm and geniality
   stance on religion 28, 99–100, 114, 116, 133, 142, 145, 146, 153, 154, 160, 177–78
   feelings regarding his father 30, 35, 54, 60, 69, 80, 109, 112, 177, 187, 192

mental health and despondency 34–35, 48, 52–53, 57–58, 72, 105, 118–19, 125–27, 131–32, 138, 140–41, 142, 146–47, 158, 166, 179, 195
  sex and sexual attraction 36, 54, 66–67, 68–69, 77, 78, 92, 97–99, 107, 109, 110, 116, 142, 147, 157, 166, 169, 174, 188
  mooted attempts at his murder 36, 122, 123, 160, 171–72, 199
  mooted marriages 45, 62–63, 91, 92, 98–99, 108, 120, 141–42, 155–56, 170, 174, 178
  kindness and callousness 47, 52, 53, 60–61, 80, 109, 113, 117, 122, 131, 162, 169, 172, 178
  military/naval role 48, 53, 60, 61, 63, 64, 65, 66, 68, 72, 75, 82, 95, 97, 99–101, 122, 123–26, 140, 146, 166
  bravery and boldness 51–52, 93–94, 100–1, 105, 117, 122, 125, 126, 134, 135, 136, 138, 145–46, 166, 170, 172–73
  finances and poverty 63, 64, 102, 105, 107, 111, 114, 123, 141, 144, 146, 147, 152, 156, 160, 162, 165, 166, 170–71, 177, 178
  conscientiousness and self-restraint 64, 66, 73, 82, 122, 147, 152
  debauchery, arguable and non-sexual 90, 111, 146–47, 152, 156
  bereavement 103, 104–5, 109, 110, 118
  political moves 106, 108, 111, 112, 113–14, 120, 122, 141, 144, 145–46, 155–56, 159–60, 162–63, 168, 170, 171, 173, 174, 175, 176–77
  deviousness and deceit 108, 114, 117, 119, 120–21, 135, 137, 138, 140, 144, 157, 159, 165–66, 167, 171, 176, 178, 196, 198
Charles Louis, Elector Palatine 3, 16, 161
Charmouth 136

Châtillon, Isabelle-Angélique, Duchess of 92, 98, 142, 157
Church of Scotland and its General Assembly xiii–xiv, 19–20, 28–29, 106–7, 114, 115, 117, 178
Colepeper, John, Baron 65, 72, 85–86, 96, 105, 118, 152
Cologne 153, 155, 158, 159, 160, 161, 162
Condé, Prince of 141
Coningsby, Juliana 136, 137
Cornwall 60, 64, 72, 75
coronations 9, 81, 120–21, 179
Cottington, Francis 105, 109, 112, 143
Council of Officers 148, 174
council of Prince Charles 63, 65–66, 67, 68–69, 72, 73, 74–75, 76, 77, 84, 86, 105
Council of State, English 117, 137–38, 142, 155, 170
Covenanters/Kirk Party 20, 28, 29, 33, 35, 58, 83, 88, 92–93, 94, 96, 106–7, 111, 112, 113–17, 118–19, 120, 121, 122, 123, 124, 125, 141, 145, 149, 172, 199
Covenants 20, 28, 58, 83, 92, 94, 106, 107, 111, 114, 115, 116, 120, 123, 143
Cromwell, Frances 155–56
Cromwell, Oliver 1–2, 42, 58–59, 64, 93, 94, 100, 102, 106, 110, 111, 116–17, 119, 122, 123, 124, 125, 126, 148, 150, 151, 155–56, 158, 159, 162, 164, 168, 169–70, 171, 174, 179, 199
Cromwell, Richard 170, 171, 174
Cropredy Bridge, Battle of 60
crown jewels 45, 120–21, 155, 179

Darnley, Henry Stuart, Lord xiii, 180
De Haro, Luis 173, 176
De Vic, Henry 162, 163
Derby, James Stanley, Earl of 126, 128, 139
Digby, George (subsequently Earl of Bristol) 83, 85–86, 94, 164–65, 166, 173
divine right xv, 33, 69

Index

dogs and other animals 7, 25–26, 47, 55, 56, 110, 160
Dorislaus, Isaac 107–8
Dorset, Mary Sackville, Countess of 5, 6, 7, 21, 31
Douglas, Robert 117, 120
Dover 45, 178
duelling 55, 94, 138, 152
Dunbar, Battle of 117, 124, 168
Duppa, Brian 18, 19, 32, 46, 48, 52, 68–69, 74, 91, 183

Earle, John 46, 91
Edgehill, Battle of 50–52
Edinburgh xiii, 9, 20, 106, 113
Elizabeth Castle 79–81, 86, 110, 111
Elizabeth I, Queen xiv, 79
Elizabeth of Bohemia xiv, xvi, xvii, 3, 16, 108, 152
Elizabeth, Princess 13, 56, 90, 93, 95, 117–18
Elliot, Elizabeth 170–71
Elliot, Thomas 109, 118
Engagement 94, 95
Engagers 94, 95, 96, 99–100, 105, 106, 112, 115, 117, 118, 119, 122–23
episcopacy xiii–xiv, 28–29, 37, 39, 54, 83, 112, 114, 161
Essex, Robert Devereux, Earl of 49, 59, 60, 68
Evelyn, John 34, 98
execution of Charles I 93, 102–3, 104–5, 106, 108–9, 114, 118, 148, 154, 156, 177, 192
Exeter 59, 73, 75, 98, 100

Fairfax, Thomas 66, 68, 71, 74, 75, 102, 105, 116, 157, 176, 177–78
Falkland, Lucius Cary, Viscount 57–58
Fanshawe, Ann 76, 81
Feilding, Richard 53
Felipe IV, King 108, 112, 159, 162, 175
Felton, John xvii
Fitzroy, Charlotte 110
Franco-Spanish War 88, 140, 141, 143, 152, 158, 159, 162, 163, 164, 165, 166, 173, 176

Frankfurt 161
Fraser 118, 119, 172
Fronde/Frondeurs 96, 141, 142, 143, 144–45, 152, 166
Fuenterrabia 173

Garter, Order of the 20, 23, 105, 192
Gerard, Charles (subsequently Lord Gerard) 55, 56, 149–50, 151, 197
Gerard, John 150, 151
Giffard, Charles 126, 128
Gloucester, Siege of 57
Goffe, Stephen 102–3
Goring, George, Baron 64, 65, 68, 71, 72, 75
Grand Remonstrance 42
Greenwich 23–24
Grenville, Bernard 177
Grenville, John 68, 79, 175, 178
Grenville, Richard 64–65, 66, 68, 72, 75, 79, 149, 150, 175
Gunpowder Plot xiv, 41–42
Gunter, George 137, 138, 139

Hague, The 38, 95–96, 101, 106, 107, 162, 178
Hamilton, James Hamilton, 1st Duke of 43, 100, 105
Hamilton, William Hamilton, 2nd Duke of 106, 112, 115, 125, 126
Hampton Court 24, 42, 44, 95, 150
Harvey, William 51
Heale House 137
Hellevoetsluis 96, 101, 146
Henrietta Catherine of Orange 170
Henrietta Maria, Queen xvi, 3, 24, 37, 39, 41–44, 45, 54, 56–57, 59, 87, 88, 94, 105, 116, 140, 142, 143–44, 145, 151, 173–74
  character xvi, xvii, 16, 28, 56–57, 87
  as a wife/advice-giver to Charles I xvi, xvii, xviii, 1, 17, 57, 92, 68, 69, 87, 92
  pregnancies/childbearing xvii, xviii, 1, 2, 10, 29, 30, 36, 59, 87

as a mother/advice-giver to her offspring 6, 8, 10, 16, 17, 28, 35, 60, 76, 83–84, 85–86, 87–88, 91, 92, 94, 108–9, 111, 117, 120, 141, 144, 145, 153, 154, 155, 164, 188

Henriette Anne, Princess 87–88, 100, 140, 173–74, 179

Henry, Duke of Gloucester 36, 56, 90, 93, 95, 117–18, 150, 153–55, 160, 161, 164, 178–79, 199

Henry, Prince of Wales xiv, xv, 26, 49

Herbert, Edward Somerset, Lord 49

Hertford, William Seymour, Marquis of 40–41, 42, 49, 59, 66, 196

Hinton, John 51–52, 100

History of the Rebellion 76, 189

Hobbes, Thomas 27, 90–91

Holland, Henry Rich, Earl of 33, 105–6

Hollar, Wenceslaus 18–19

Hopton, Ralph, Baron 63, 65, 72, 75, 76, 86, 96, 105, 143

Huddleston, John 133

Humble Petition and Advice 170

Hyde, Edward 42, 46, 57, 59, 65, 66, 67, 69, 72, 73, 76, 83, 86, 96, 102, 104–5, 106, 112, 143, 144, 145–47, 149–50, 151, 161, 163–64, 166, 170, 172, 176, 189, 197

Hyde, Katherine 137

Instrument of Government 148

Ireton, Henry 93, 101–2, 147–48

Irish affairs 35, 37, 44, 47, 69–70, 72, 83, 93, 95, 107, 110, 111, 112, 114, 126, 144, 151, 155, 163, 198

James I & VI, King xiii–xiv, xv, xvi, xvii, 18, 19, 20, 28–29, 53, 120

James, Duke of York 10, 17, 31–32, 38, 39, 41–42, 44, 49, 51, 53, 55, 56, 57, 58, 82, 86, 90, 93, 95–96, 97, 98, 101, 102, 110, 111, 127, 140, 141, 143, 144, 150, 153, 164–65, 166, 168, 170, 172, 178–79, 191, 199

Jemmy *see* Monmouth, James, Duke of

Jermyn, Henry (subsequently Earl of St Albans) xviii, 43, 59–60, 85–86, 111, 142, 143–44, 153, 173, 177

Jersey 77, 78, 79–82, 84, 85, 86, 110–11, 136, 143, 145, 149, 192, 196

Joana, Princess of Beira 62, 70, 99, 189

Juan-José 164, 166, 167

Junto 41, 42, 44

Kings Cabinet Opened 69–70

Kirk *see* Church of Scotland

La Cloche, Jacques de 66, 77–78

Lambert, John 148, 174, 176, 177

Lane, Jane 134–36, 142

Langport, Battle of 71

Lascelles, Henry 134, 135

Laud, William 4, 5, 19, 39–40, 62

Lauderdale, John Maitland, Earl of 100, 106, 112, 115

Lawson, John 159, 165

Le Grys, Robert 11

Lennox, Duchess of *see* Villiers, Lady Mary

Leslie, David 116–17, 123, 126, 140

Levellers 93, 116, 149, 157, 159

Lilburne, John 149

Limbry, Stephen 136

London 3, 5, 10, 13, 14, 16, 24, 34, 39, 44, 54, 100, 127–28, 156, 160, 175, 177, 179

Long, Robert 66, 109, 115, 149, 197

Lorraine, Duke of 144

Louis XIII, King 5, 30

Louis XIV, King 85, 88–89, 91, 108, 141, 142, 144, 145, 152

Louise Henriëtte of Orange 45, 62

Louvre 93, 140, 143, 145

Mademoiselle, La Grande *see* Montpensier, Anne-Marie-Louise d'Orléans, Duchess of

Madrid xvi, 4, 112, 159, 173

Mall *see* Villiers, Lady Mary

Mancini, Hortense 174

Manning, Henry 161–62

Mardyke, Seige of 166

Index

Maria de' Medici, Queen xvi, 1, 2, 5, 8, 30, 45
Marston Moor, Battle of 60, 63, 116–17
Mary, Princess of Orange 8, 10, 23, 31, 37, 38–39, 44, 45, 56, 96, 97, 105, 108, 149, 152–53, 161, 164, 165, 168, 170, 178, 182, 189
Mary, Queen of Scots xiii, 93, 180
Massey, Edward 126, 127, 145
Massonnet, Peter 18, 150, 183
Mayerne, Theodore de 1, 2, 9, 58, 185
Mazarin, Jules 85, 88, 93, 94, 95, 96, 141, 173, 176
Militia Bill and Militia Ordinance 47–48
Minette *see* Henriette Anne, Princess
mobs and rioters 20, 34, 39, 44, 50, 144–45, 175
Monck, George 145, 174–77, 178, 179, 200
Monmouth, James, Duke of 67, 98, 107, 118, 142, 162, 167, 180
Montagu, Edward 177, 178
Montpensier, Anne-Marie-Louise d'Orléans, Duchess of 91, 92, 108, 141–42
Montrose, James Graham, Marquis of 106, 107, 111, 113
Mordaunt, John 172
Morland, Samuel 171–72, 199
Moseley Hall 133–34
Motteville, Mme de 89, 92, 146

Naseby, Battle of 68, 70, 83
National Covenant *see* Covenants
naval affairs 71, 76–77, 96, 97, 99, 100–1, 108, 145–46, 158, 159, 166, 168, 178
Nedham, Marchamont 58, 143
New Model Army, founding of 61, 68
Newbury, First Battle of 57
Newbury, Second Battle of 61
Newcastle, Margaret Cavendish, Marchioness (subsequently Duchess) of 27, 90
Newcastle, William Cavendish, Earl (subsequently Duke) of 21, 22, 23, 25, 26–28, 31, 34, 36, 40, 61, 63, 90, 112, 167, 183
news publications 58, 94, 143, 161
Nicholas, Edward 112, 149, 161–62, 172, 176
Nineteen Propositions 48
Norton, Ellen 134, 135

O'Neill, Daniel 162, 173
Oatlands xviii, 24, 41
Ormond, James Butler, Marquis of 11, 93, 107, 110, 143, 154, 163, 166, 167, 173, 176, 199
Oxford 52, 53, 54–56, 58, 59, 60, 61, 62, 82, 86
Oxford University 18, 56

Palais-Royal 92, 173
Paris 83, 89, 91, 96, 140, 142, 143, 144–45, 146, 154, 160, 164, 167
Parliament of Scotland and Committee of Estates 106–7, 111, 112, 114, 116, 117, 119, 122
parliaments, English
  pre-1640 Stuart parliaments xiv, xvii, 2, 9, 20
  Short Parliament 33, 35
  Long Parliament pre-Rump 36, 37, 38, 39–40, 41, 42, 44, 45, 46, 47–48, 49, 52, 53, 54, 56, 58–59, 60, 61, 62, 63, 66, 69, 70, 71, 74, 75, 76–77, 80, 82–83, 84, 85, 86, 88, 89–90, 92–93, 94, 96, 100, 101–2, 161
  Rump Parliament 36, 102, 104, 105–6, 110, 117–18, 123, 126, 130, 131, 137, 145, 148, 149, 155, 171, 174, 175, 192
  Oxford Parliament 59, 123
  Protectorate parliaments 155, 159, 170, 171, 172
  Convention Parliament (1660) 175, 177, 179, 200
peace efforts xv, 29, 54, 59, 60, 74, 75, 83, 90, 107, 144, 161, 173, 176
Pegge, Catherine 166
Pendennis Castle 75–76

Penderel, George 128, 129
Penderel, Humphrey 129, 133, 195
Penderel, Joan 131, 132
Penderel, John 129, 133
Penderel, Richard 129, 130–31
Penderel, William 128, 132, 195
Penruddock, John 158 *see also* uprisings/ insurgence
Pepys, Samuel 9, 64, 67, 81, 127, 147
Peronne, Mme 2
Peters, Henry 136, 137
Philipp-Wilhelm, Palsgrave 153, 159–60, 162
Phillips, Robert 137, 138
plague 13–14, 41, 66, 68, 147
Pope, John 135
Powick Bridge 124, 126
Presbyterianism/Presbyterians, English 58, 83, 93, 94, 99, 114, 123, 140, 145, 172, 174, 177–78
Preston, Battle of 100
Pride's Purge 102, 175
privy councils xv, 4, 14, 35, 56, 81, 104–5, 111, 112, 143, 150, 163, 179
Puritanism/Puritans 3, 4, 16, 19, 42, 47, 50, 89, 93, 138, 169–70
Pym, John 33, 37, 38, 40, 41, 42, 47–48, 50, 58
Pyne, Hugh 7, 9

Quakerism/Quakers 169, 174

Raglan Castle 50
raising of royal standard 49
Reading 52, 53
Reformation xiii, 2, 30, 128
Richmond 13, 25–26, 35, 36, 42, 182
Ripon, Treaty of 35, 37
Robertson, Hannah 169
Rochester, Earl of *see* Wilmot, Henry
royal ceremony 5, 12, 20, 23, 36, 80, 81, 108, 120–21, 123 *see also* coronations
  touching for the king's evil 34, 178, 184
royal court entertainments xv, xvii, 10, 16, 89, 92, 93, 165

royal image and extravagance 2, 5, 22–24, 27, 56, 62, 79, 81–82, 115, 129, 153, 160, 167, 171, 177, 178, 179
Royal Oak 127, 132, 138, 195
Rule of the Major Generals 169–70, 171, 174
Rupert, Prince 16, 51, 53, 55, 56, 59, 63, 65, 73, 83, 88, 94, 96, 97, 99, 146, 151, 160

Saint-Germain-en-Laye 83, 84, 87, 90, 91, 93, 95, 102, 108, 144, 145
Saint-Malo 87, 172, 173
Scheveningen 178
Scilly Isles 76–77, 145
Scone 120–21
Sealed Knot and other conspiracy rings 151, 155, 157, 165, 171, 172
seventeenth-century life 12–13, 47, 50, 55, 56, 89, 169–70, 191
Sexby, Edward 157, 159, 162, 165
Shoreham 137, 138–39
Solemn League and Covenant *see* Covenants
Sophia, Princess 107
Spa 152
spies and espionage 61, 95, 112, 143, 147, 149, 152–53, 157–58, 161–62, 171–72
sports/games and toys 8, 10–11, 12, 14, 24, 26, 36, 47, 56, 93, 94, 95, 108, 110–11, 116, 141, 152, 160, 164, 167, 168, 170
St Albans, Earl of *see* Jermyn, Henry
St James's xvi, 2, 5, 10, 11, 12, 24, 30, 56, 90, 95, 150
Star Castle 76
Start, the 118–19, 120, 122, 125, 172
States-General, United Provinces 101, 102, 108, 145–46, 177
Steenie *see* Villiers, George
Stonehenge 137
Strafford, Earl of *see* Wentworth, Thomas
Surprise 137, 138–39, 140
Swan, George 169
Symonds, Thomas 138

Taaffe, Theobald, Viscount 142–43
Tattersall, Nicholas 138–39, 140

taxation 33, 169
   tonnage and poundage xvii
   ship money 33, 41, 112
Ten Propositions 40
Thirty Years' War xvi, 16, 161
Thurloe, John 157, 161, 171, 199
Tower of London 5, 39, 41, 105, 167
Trent 135, 136, 137
Tuileries 91, 92, 141–42
Turenne, Henri de La Tour d'Auvergne, Viscount of 144

uprisings/insurgence 47, 94, 99, 118–19, 123, 151, 155, 157–58, 163, 167, 169, 172–73, 177, 197, 199

Van Dyck, Anthony 12, 20, 31, 89
Villiers, George (subsequently 1st Duke of Buckingham) xv–xvii, 4, 10, 15, 43
Villiers, Lady Mary (subsequently Duchess of Lennox) 10, 15–16
Villiers, Lord Francis 10, 15, 16, 31, 46, 55–56, 90, 95, 96
Vilvoorde 163

Wake, Baldwin 77, 81
Waller, William 60, 64
Walter, Lucy 98–99, 107, 110, 118, 142–43, 162, 167, 170
Warwick, Robert Rich, Earl of 41, 80, 100–1
Wentworth, Thomas (subsequently Earl of Strafford) 31, 35
   trial and execution 37–38, 39–40, 41

Wentworth, Thomas, Baron 75, 152
Western Association 63, 64–66, 68, 71, 72, 75, 76, 87
Wheeler 68–69
Whitehall 12, 24, 29, 39, 105, 150, 157, 168, 179, 182
Whiteladies 128, 129, 130
Whitgreave, Thomas 133
William II, Prince of Orange 38–39, 45, 96, 101, 104, 112, 113, 120, 145
Willys, Richard 171–72, 199
Wilmot, Henry (subsequently Earl of Rochester) 60, 65, 126, 127–28, 129, 132–33, 134, 136, 137, 138, 139, 140, 143, 156–57, 163, 168
Windsor 20, 25, 169
Woolf, Francis 131
Worcester 123–26
Worcester, Battle of 123–26, 135, 140, 141, 149, 155, 168
Wren, Christopher 25
Wyndham, Christabella 7, 8–9, 12, 13, 17, 32, 66–67, 71, 109, 147, 170
Wyndham, Edmund 9, 12, 32, 66, 109, 170
Wyndham, Francis 135, 136
Wyndham, Hugh 66, 69

York 36, 47, 49, 56

Zaragoza 173